The Complete
HOME CARPENTER

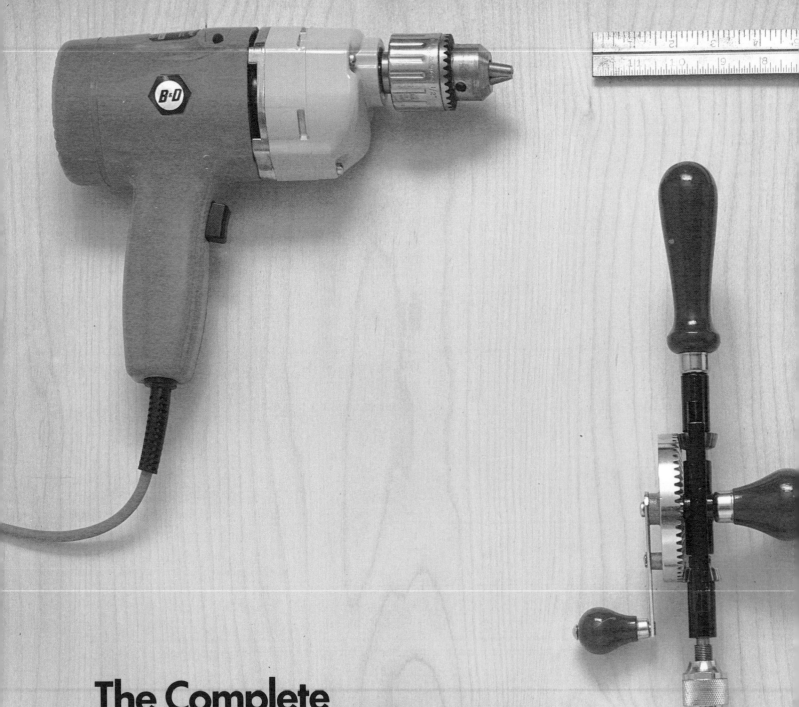

The Complete
HOME CARPENTER:

Techniques,
Projects and Materials

Edited by Mike Lawrence

ORBIS · LONDON

Acknowledgements
Photographers: Jon Bouchier, Simon Butcher, Paul Forrester,
Simon Gear, Jem Grischotti, Barry Jell, Keith Morris,
Karen Norquay, Roger Tuff.

Artists: Roger Courthold Associates, Bernard Fallon,
Nick Farmer, Trevor Lawrence, Linden Artists, David Pope,
Mike Saunders, Ed Stuart, Craig Warwick, Brian Watson.

Printed in Yugoslavia
ISBN: 1-85155-002-X

CONTENTS

1 Carpentry materials   7
Softwood and hardwoods   8
Man-made boards   14
Finishes for furniture   17
Nails and screws   18
Hinges   20

2 Basic techniques   23
A guide to woodwork joints   24
Butt joints   27
Halving and mitre joints   32
Dowel joints   36
Housing joints   40

3 Basic projects   44
Hanging a door   45
Fitting front door furniture   48
Shelving: the basics   52
Panelling walls with timber   56
Building basic box furniture   60

4 Advanced Techniques   64
Mortise-and-tenon joints   65
Using a router: 1   70
Using a router: 2   75
Using a router: 3   80
Using circular saws safely   85
Veneering   90
Making dovetail joints   95
Laminating wood   99

5 Handyman projects   104
Building cupboards in alcoves   105
Adding doors to basic boxes   110
Building beds: the basics   114
Building bunks: the basics   118
Installing sliding doors   123
Building shelving units   128
Fitting drawers to cabinets   132
Making kitchen base units   136
Fitting a kitchen: 1   141
Making kitchen wall units   145
Fitting a kitchen: 2   150

6 Advanced projects   154
Built-in wardrobes   155
Repairing handrails and balusters   160
Making frames in timber   165
Fitting doors and frames   171
Laying a new timber floor   175
Building chairs: 1   180
Building chairs: 2   185

Index   190

INTRODUCTION

Wood and allied products are probably the do-it-yourselfer's favourite materials. With them he can fit his house out with all manner of furniture and fittings, and expect to achieve very satisfying results, whether he's an absolute beginner or an experienced craftsman. This is because wood is such an adaptable — and forgiving — material, easy to obtain, to work and to finish. Furthermore, the development of man-made boards and the growth in the range and capacity of modern power tools have opened up whole new areas to the home carpenter, enabling him to carry out wood-working jobs and projects that a professional would be proud of.

The Complete Home Carpenter aims to provide the keen woodworker with both essential background information on the raw material and a range of projects he can carry out. To begin with, there are comprehensive articles on softwoods, hardwoods and man-made boards, followed by detailed sections on screws and nails, hinges and furniture finishes. Next comes a chapter on basic techniques — how to choose the right joint for the job you want to do, and step-by-step instructions to help you cut and assemble butt joints, halvings and mitres, housings and one of the most useful and versatile of joints, the dowel joint.

Chapter 3 presents some relatively simple woodworking projects — jobs like hanging a door and fitting door furniture (locks, latches and so on), panelling walls with timber cladding, and building basic box furniture. The last of these provides the key to a number of other projects involving using man-made boards, enabling you to reproduce almost any item of 'panel'-type furniture in your own workshop.

More advanced skills are introduced in Chapter 4, including detailed instructions for making more complicated joints like the mortise and tenon and the dovetail. There are also sections on using circular saws safely, and on getting the best from your router — perhaps the most useful and under-rated power tool available today. You will also find information on two unusual woodworking techniques — veneering and laminating. The former allows you to achieve expensive-looking results using cheaper woods for the construction of your furniture, and exotic veneers for the surface finish. Laminating wood opens up a whole new range of design possibilities, by allowing freer use to be made of curved shapes.

The book is completed by a whole range of projects for the more adventurous home carpenter to try out. They include adding doors and drawers to the basic boxes created in Chapter 3, building alcove cupboards and wardrobes, shelving and storage units, even beds and bunks. There is a section on making and fitting kitchen units which could help to cut pounds off the cost of a kitchen re-fit, and step-by-step instructions to help you carry out some of the less glamorous but just as important structural woodworking jobs — things like fitting a door frame, laying a timber floor or repairing the handrail and balustrade on your staircase. Finally, the aspiring Chippendale can even design and make a suite of dining chairs.

CHAPTER 1

CARPENTRY MATERIALS

The raw material of any carpentry project is wood – either one of
the many species of natural timber, or man-made board, but you
will also need fixings to help you assemble whatever you are
making, and some means of giving your workmanship an
attractive and durable finish.

SOFTWOODS

The do-it-yourselfer uses enormous quantities of wood every year for projects of all sorts, and the bulk of it is properly termed softwood. But what is softwood, and what do you need to know about it to be able to buy and use it successfully?

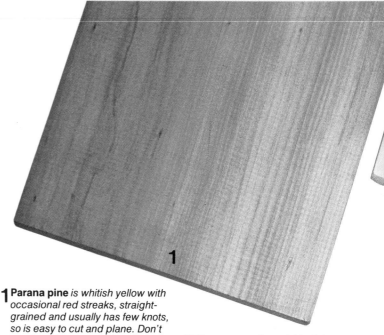

S oftwoods come from coniferous (cone-bearing) trees such as pine, spruce, fir and larch – evergreens with needle-like leaves. These grow in a well-defined belt running round the northern hemisphere, with the greatest reserves being found in Canada, Scandinavia and Siberia. Some species of softwood also grow at high altitude in tropical regions, but in nothing like the same quantities.

The name 'softwood' is generally rather misleading: yew, for example, is technically a softwood, yet is dense and quite difficult to cut, while balsa is one of the softest woods there is and is classified as a hardwood (see pages 10 and 11).

How they're grouped
Softwoods are divided fairly arbitrarily into two groups.

The first group is commonly called redwood, pine, red deal or yellow deal. There is actually no such thing as a deal tree; deal originally meant a piece of sawn wood 9 inches wide, not more than 3 inches thick and at least 6 feet long. Red deal comes from the Scotch Pine, yellow deal from the Yellow Pine. The second group is called whitewood or white deal (Norway spruce – the traditional Christmas tree).

Both generally have a very pale colour and weak grain pattern, and these properties are more pronounced in timber grown recently, with the accent on fast-growing species. You can see this clearly by comparing a plank of recently-cut softwood with the timber used in, say, a Victorian house, which will have a deeper colour and a closer, more noticeable grain.

Softwood is comparatively strong in the direction of the grain, weak across it. It is easy to saw, plane, chisel and sand, and holds screws well (nails can cause the wood to split along the grain). The wood is fairly porous, and is generally not durable enough to be used out of doors unless protected by paint, varnish or preservative. Western Red Cedar is the one commonly-available

exception to this rule, its red colour weathering to a pleasant grey if exposed to wind, rain and sunlight. Most softwoods are easy to treat with preservatives, however, since their porous nature means that the preservative penetrates deep into the wood to protect it by keeping rot and wood-boring insects at bay.

How softwoods are used
By far the greatest use for softwoods is in building houses – for floor and ceiling joists, roofs, doors and windows, wall cladding, staircases, floorboards, skirtings and a whole range of other smaller features. For the do-it-yourselfer softwood is the perfect material for jobs large and small, from building extensions and outbuildings to making free-standing or built-in furniture.

Sawn or planed?
Softwood is converted (sawn) into a vast range of sizes – see overleaf. The most important thing to remember is that these are nominal sizes, not actual ones. The wood is sawn to the nominal size, but then shrinks during seasoning. It may then also be planed, which reduces the wood's actual size still further – by about 3mm (⅛in) on each dimension with smaller sizes, more on larger timbers. Such wood is known as planed all round (PAR) or dressed all round (DAR), but is still described by its nominal size.

Use sawn timber (which is cheaper) where the wood will be hidden – in partition walls, for wall battening and so on. You should also buy sawn timber to plane down yourself if you want to produce wood of a particular cross-sectional size that is not available PAR (DAR). Alternatively, you can order it planed to 'finished' size from the next available sawn size – more expensive than PAR wood.

Softwood is also machined into an enormous range of mouldings, rounds ('broomsticks') and matchings (profiled tongued-and-grooved boards for decorative wall cladding).

1 Parana pine *is whitish yellow with occasional red streaks, straight-grained and usually has few knots, so is easy to cut and plane. Don't use it outdoors, and, since it tends to twist, for open shelving.*

The metric foot
Timber now leaves the sawmill in metric lengths, and so to save wastage many timber merchants sell wood measured in a contrived unit of 300mm – the so-called metric foot, actually measuring 11¾in. So if you order '6 feet' of wood, you may be sold a piece 6 metric feet – 1800mm or 5ft 10½in – long. If you actually need a full 6ft (1830mm) of wood, you may have to pay for 7 metric feet (2,100mm/6ft 10in) and waste the off-cut.

The sawing processes
It is much easier to understand wood as a natural material if you know how it is 'converted' – turned from logs into usable rectangular planks. The secret of the sawmill lies in producing the largest quantity of good-quality wood from each log, with the minimum of wastage. Three methods are commonly used.

Plain sawing means cutting the log into parallel planks. It yields pieces with two different grain patterns, depending on their position in the log, and those cut from the edge tend to curl and warp badly. This can be avoided

Brian Watson

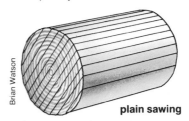

plain sawing

by *quarter* sawing – cutting the log along radial lines – and this also yields wood with a similar grain pattern throughout; it is,

2 European redwood *(deal) is a type of pine varying from dusty red to pale yellow. It can be used outside when preservative-treated. It's strong, hard and easy to work unless there's a lot of resin or knots.*

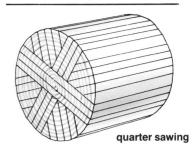

quarter sawing

however, more wasteful. The third method is *tangential* sawing, used to produce more wide planks from relatively small logs; wood sawn tangentially also has a plainer, more open grain pattern.

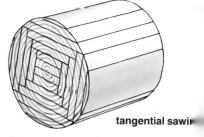

tangential sawing

Seasoning wood
Once wood is sawn, it has to be 'seasoned' at a controlled rate to dry out the sap and reduce the moisture content of the wood to around 10 or 12% – when felled wood can contain as much as twice its own weight of water. Seasoning makes the wood easier to work (anyone who has cut down a tree knows how difficult 'green' wood is to saw), lighter to handle and more

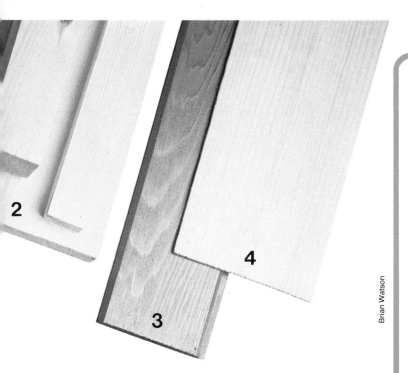

2

4

3

Most softwoods bruise and mark easily; take care when using your woodworking tools to avoid damage. In particular, always protect the wood surface with an offcut of scrap wood when tapping joints together or when pulling out nails with a claw hammer.

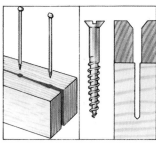

Splitting is likely to occur if you drive several nails in a row along the line of the grain – it's best to stagger them. Ideally you should use oval nails driven in with their flatter sides parallel to the wood grain. Drill clearance holes if using screws, countersinking if necessary to accommodate the screw heads.

Brian Watson

When you are using a plane you should work with the grain to get a clean finish; you will find that the plane cuts much more easily in one direction than in the opposite one. Always sand wood along the grain too, never across it.

Some softwoods have a high resin content and this may show up in sticky pockets. You can seal small pockets by drawing out the resin with a blow-torch, then brushing on knotting. If pockets are large, they are best cut out – so always choose timber with care at the start.

3 Western Red Cedar is rather oily, fragrant and pinkish-red to reddish brown. It's the most common type of cedar available. It can be used outdoors untreated – the weather will turn it silver grey.

resistant to attack by rot and insects. Carefully seasoned wood is also less prone to shrinkage and warping than unseasoned wood.

Faults in wood

Because wood is a natural material, it has its normal share of faults. One of the commonest is the knot, the cross-section of a branch exposed at the point where its starts growing from the trunk. Knots may be fresh (live) and tight-fitting, perhaps even oozing resin, or they may be dead, dark-coloured and loose – a sign that the branch was damaged before the tree was felled.

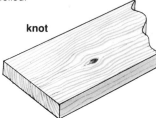

knot

Another common fault is the shake. Star shakes are caused by

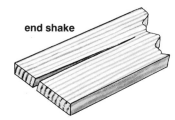

end shake

4 Spruce, also known as whitewood, is cream in colour. It's light and strong, physically easy to work and finishes well. It does not take preservatives well and so is restricted to interior use.

the outside of the log drying and shrinking more quickly than the rest, resulting in splits running from the centre to the outside of the log. Cup shakes occur when the inner part of the log dries

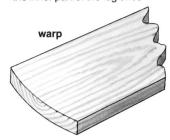

warp

more quickly than the outside, causing the wood to split between the annual rings. End shakes are caused by too speedy drying during seasoning.

Warping is caused by uneven drying during seasoning, and may

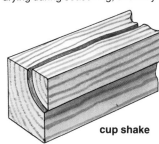

cup shake

occur across the grain (giving the wood a cupped cross-section) or along it as well (a twist, visible if you sight along the length).

You should look out for these faults when buying wood (except in the case of wood you want to be deliberately 'knotty') and reject any that is not sound and straight.

Quality control

Softwood is graded according to its quality when it leaves the sawmill in its country of origin. Wood from Scandinavia and Russia is divided into two broad categories called 'unsorted' (the better quality) and 'fifths'. Wood from Canada is usually sorted into 'clears' and 'merchantable' grades, with clears being somewhat better in quality than Russian or Scandinavian unsorted grade. Parana pine is

often graded into 'No 1' and 'No 2', both as good as the best Canadian wood.

Softwood may be further sorted by timber merchants into three grades – 'best joinery', 'joinery' and 'carcassing' (or building) grade. Best joinery grade is top-quality wood, virtually free of knots and suitable for use where the wood grain will be visible. Joinery grade is used for most general woodwork, carcassing grade for rough structural work where the wood will eventually be hidden from view.

Do-it-yourself shops usually sell only joinery grade wood. For other grades you will have to go to a timber merchant.

HARDWOODS

There's no mystery about hardwoods. Oak, walnut, mahogany, teak and many more well-loved timbers are readily available if you want to use their rich, varied shades and patterns in your home.

Most hardwoods really are harder than softwoods – but not quite all; the two classifications are named for botanical, not practical reasons, and hardwoods themselves vary widely in strength, toughness and weather-resistance. Their denseness can make accurate work easier, but it can also blunt tools faster; and you'll need to keep a sharp eye out for variable grain directions which make it hard to get an even surface with the plane.

Hardwoods do cost more, which is why softwoods are used for all rough house-carpentry. But your money buys a fascinating, inexhaustible variety of beautiful colours and grains. Once you have the confidence to work without paint to cover up your mistakes, and preferably with proper concealed joints rather than just screws and nails, you'll want to use hardwoods for all their subtle decorative possibilities, varnishing or polishing them to bring these out.

There are thousands of hardwoods, many strangely named and hard to get. Here we show only those you're most likely to find. But they give an idea of the tremendous range available. If your timber merchant shows you a piece of afzelia or jelutong, don't turn your nose up: it may be just what you want.

Many hardwoods are often used as thin sheets of veneer, to give the appearance without the cost. Sticking veneer down by hand is a fairly specialised operation, unless you buy the 'iron-on' real-wood veneers which are available in some of the more common timbers. Ready-veneered chipboard, or plywood with a decorative top layer, is another option.

Hardwood sizes

You can't buy hardwoods in standard sizes like nails, screws or even softwoods. Dimensions available depend on the supplier – and the wood. No-one can cut wide planks from narrow trees, or long straight pieces from short, twisted trees.

However, two groups of basic cross-sections are generally obtainable. Squarish pieces, for table and chair legs, panel edges, etc, can usually be found in sizes between 25 x 25mm (1 x 1in) and 50 x 50mm (2 x 2in); and wider, flatter boards, eg, for wall cladding or joining edge-to-edge to make tabletops, from 6mm (¼in) to 25mm (1in) thick, and 150-300mm (6-12in) wide.

But visit your timber merchant, discuss your requirements and see what he's got. Although you may have to consider alternative woods, he'll often be willing to cut wood specifically to suit your measurements. In fact, since hardwoods come in so many different types and sizes, he may well have to. Be prepared, however, to modify your design if he suggests a more economical way of cutting the timber. His advice will save you money.

1

Beech, *while not particularly decorative, is strong, and easy to work and finish because of its straight, close grain. Not durable enough for outdoor use, it is used in furniture, especially for chair-frames, and is sometimes given a pinkish colour by steaming.*

2

Mahogany *is either American (the Honduras variety is on the right; Brazilian is also common) or African, left – not the same species, but closely related and just as good. Mahogany is widely used for reproduction furniture. Its attraction lies in its rich colour and lustre.* **Utile** *(on top), another fine African wood, is very similar.*

Oak *can be red or, more commonly, white. Varieties of white oak come from Europe, America (underneath in the picture) and Japan. English oak (on top), the hardest, strongest and most durable, was universally used for hundreds of years. Imported European oak is now commoner, while Japanese oak is the lightest in weight of the three. Oak is not richly coloured, but it can have an attractive figure.*

6

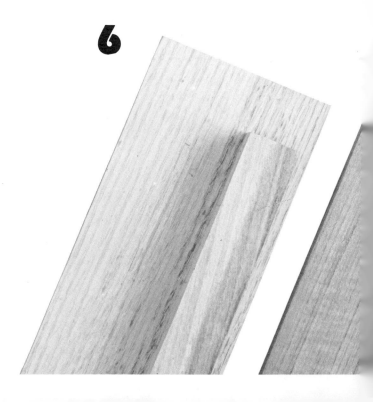

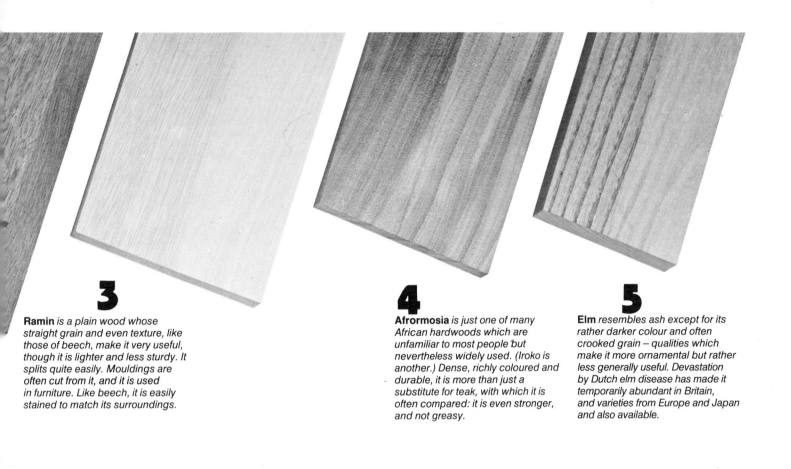

3

Ramin *is a plain wood whose straight grain and even texture, like those of beech, make it very useful, though it is lighter and less sturdy. It splits quite easily. Mouldings are often cut from it, and it is used in furniture. Like beech, it is easily stained to match its surroundings.*

4

Afrormosia *is just one of many African hardwoods which are unfamiliar to most people but nevertheless widely used. (Iroko is another.) Dense, richly coloured and durable, it is more than just a substitute for teak, with which it is often compared: it is even stronger, and not greasy.*

5

Elm *resembles ash except for its rather darker colour and often crooked grain – qualities which make it more ornamental but rather less generally useful. Devastation by Dutch elm disease has made it temporarily abundant in Britain, and varieties from Europe and Japan and also available.*

Teak *has long been celebrated for its great strength and extraordinary weather-resistance: it is ideal for all outdoor work. Its rich colour has been in demand for furniture in recent years, though it is not cheap. Its greasiness presents difficulties in glueing and for some finishing processes.*

Ash *is another strong, pale wood like beech, but with the coarse, open texture of oak. Its exceptional toughness and straight grain suit it for bending and for such things as tool handles. However, it is not a good outdoor timber.*

Walnut *was widely used in English furniture of the Queen Anne period. True walnut really comes from England (like the top piece in the picture) and other parts of Europe, as well as North America, but other similar woods are African (underneath), Queensland and New Guinea walnut. Its value lies in its depth and variety of colour and its nicely varied grain.*

Sycamore *is one of the most attractive types of maple, and has a lustrous creamy colour, sometimes nearly white. This, plus its compact grain and frequent rippling figure, give it a beauty of its own.*

7

8

9

10

COMMON SIZES FOR SOFTWOODS

Planed or dressed timber is sold in the same nominal dimensions as sawn timber but it is in fact roughly 3mm (¹/8in) smaller all round (the exact amount varies according to the cross-section). Thus the pieces of timber shown below are in fact slightly less in size than the dimensions by which they are sold. Not all planed timber sizes you can buy are shown here but the picture should give you some idea of the different sizes relative to each other.

The large sizes, eg 100 x 75mm (4 x 3in) or 150 x 75mm (6 x 3in) are used for structural work whereas the slim battens, eg 25mm x 12.5mm (1 x ¹/2in) are used for decorative work or situations where strength is not a necessary requirement. You can also see how timber may be offered for sale split, warped, bowed or with knots and you should look out for these faults when buying.

Jem Grischotti

The table below lists the range of sizes in which sawn and planed softwoods are sold and which you should find relatively easy to obtain. Softwoods are sold in other sizes by some stockists depending on the source of supply and the sawmill which processes the timber. You can also, of course, ask your stockist to plane a piece of timber for you from the next size up, though this is an expensive way of buying timber. All the PAR or DAR sizes listed here are available sawn but the reverse does not apply. A solid symbol means the size is available sawn or planed, an open one denotes a sawn size only.

Sawn and planed (dressed) sizes

thickness mm	12.5	16	19	25	32	38	50	75	100	125	150	175	200	225	300	thickness in
12.5	●			●		●	●	●	●		●					¹/2
16		●				●	●									⁵/8
19			●			●	●	●			●	●		●	●	³/4
25						●	●	●	●	●	●	●	●	●	●	1
32					●		●	●	●		●	●		●	●	1¹/4
38						●	●	●	●		●			●	●	1¹/2
50							●	●			●	○	○	●	○	2
75								●	●		●	○	○	●		3
100									●				○	●	●	4
	⁵/8	³/4	1	1¹/4	1¹/2	2	3	4	5	6	7	8	9	12		

width (in)

12

CHOOSING HARDWOODS

To help you select hardwoods for particular jobs, their properties are summarized in this table. All the woods listed will make fine interior furniture and fittings, and can be finished with oil, polish or varnish (teak is an exception, for it is too oily to varnish successfully). Woods in **bold type** are those you're most likely to find.

	Walnut	**Walnut (Afr)**	**Utile**	**Teak**	**Sycamore**	Sapele	Rosewood	**Ramin**	Obeche	**Oak**	Meranti	Maple	**Mahogany**	Iroko	Idigbo	**Elm**	Cherry	**Beech**	**Ash**	Agba	**Afrormosia**
Shade Woods range from light to dark. 1 = palest	2	2	1	1	2	2	2	2	2	1	★	2	1	1	3	2	1	2	2	2	3
Richness Some timbers look bland, while others glow with a deep lustre when sealed. 1 = plainest	3	2	2	1	2	2	2	2	3	2	2	2	3	1	3	2	2	3	2	3	3
Figure Grain patterns vary from straight to swirling (sometimes depending on how the wood is cut). 1 = plainest	2	1	2	1	1	3	1	2	3	2	2	2	1	1	3	2	2	2	1	2	3
Durability Some timbers need preservative treatment for outdoors. 1 = most perishable	3	3	1	1	1	1	2	3	2	1	3	3	1	1	3	3	1	3	3	2	1
Density Timbers vary greatly in heaviness and hardness. 1 = lightest/softest	3	2	2	3	2	2	2	3	2	3	★	3	1	2	3	3	2	2	3	2	3
Cost Timber prices change constantly, and rarity value has to be taken into account. 1 = cheapest	3	1	1	1	2	★	1	1	★	2	1	★	1	1	3	1	3	3	2	2	3

★ *depends on variety*

hints

Hardwoods have an outer layer of 'sapwood', usually removed because it's paler and less insect-resistant than the inner 'heartwood'. A 'waney-edged' or 'unedged' (UE) piece still has both sapwood and bark. However, hardwoods also come square-edged (SE) and planed on one or more edges. As with softwoods, look out for distortions in shape – and for knots, though these are sometimes desirable on the grounds of appearance.

Remember that different and even unrelated species may have the same name – 'walnut' can mean English, European (French or Italian), American, African, New Guinea or Queensland walnut. Also the same species may have several names.

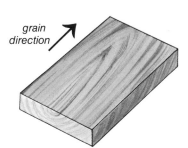

grain direction

Since hardwoods are hard and dense, you must know the grain direction of your piece, and if possible plane 'with' it. Planing against the grain is difficult and at worst tears out the wood. Some species have 'interlocked' grain, which goes both ways at once! In such cases you just have to go carefully.

Hardwood must be conditioned for at least 72 hours in the environment where it will eventually be used – indoors if you're making fine furniture – to prevent shrinkage or swelling from marring the finished work.

With hardwoods the finish is all-important. Ensure it's perfect by using a cabinet scraper (right). This is a metal rectangle whose edge is squared on the oilstone, then turned over with a burr so

that it will remove shavings far finer than any plane. Use it with a pushing or pulling action (below). Finally clean off dust and grease with turps.

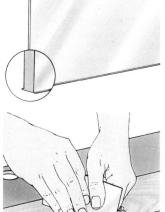

MAN-MADE BOARDS

Versatile, cheap and manufactured for uniform quality, man-made boards have become indispensable to all kinds of projects around the house. Here's a guide to the differences between them and what each is suitable for.

You only have to make some simple furniture or a few shelves from natural timber to realise just how expensive wood is. Man-made boards are the cheap alternatives. But they're not just substitutes for the real thing. In many situations, they have much more to offer than a low price. Most resist shrinking, swelling and warping better than natural woods. And because all are carefully manufactured for consistency in use, it's worth knowing exactly what each board can and can't do.

Fibreboards

Standard hardboard is the cheapest of all man-made boards and is produced by compressing wood fibre into hard, brown sheets. It is smooth on one side with a rough, mesh pattern on the other. Because it contains no adhesive, it's relatively weak, and if it gets wet it'll break up. But it's worth considering as a cladding, especially if you want something you can easily bend round curves.
● Thicknesses 2mm (5/64in) to 13mm (½in); 3, 5 and 6mm (⅛, ³/₁₆ and ¼in) are by far the most common.

Tempered hardboard is standard hardboard which has been treated to improve its strength and resistance to moisture, and is therefore suitable for use outdoors. It shouldn't be confused with oil-treated hardboard, which has only a short-lived and superficial moisture-resistance.

Decorative hardboards may be covered with PVC or melamine. They may also be factory-painted in a process known as 'enamelling'. Both types are easy to clean, but only their surfaces resist water. You can also get standard hardboard ready-primed for painting.

Moulded hardboards are often used as wall claddings. Some even have a paint or plastic finish. You can buy them with embossed and textured designs – woodgrain, tile and brick being among the most popular. But you'll probably have to order the less common types.

Perforated hardboard has holes or slots in it. It comes in a range of designs, including plain 'pegboard' (with regular rows of small holes).

Duo-faced hardboard is smooth on both sides.

Medium board is softer and weaker than the others, and this is the main reason why it's used in thicker sheets – 6-13mm (¼-½in). The denser type HM, also called 'panelboard', is used for cladding partitions in much the same way as plasterboard. The velvety grey/brown type LM is used for pinboards, etc. Both are available in versions made to withstand high humidity, and may also be flame-retardant, oil-treated, duo-faced or lacquered.

Softboard ('insulating board'), also made from fibres, is not compressed and is therefore even lighter and less dense than medium board. Apart from insulation, it too is used for pinboards.

MDF (medium-density fibreboard), although expensive and hard to obtain, is an extremely versatile material and can often be used instead of solid timber. It's far stronger than other fibreboards because it includes adhesive (like chipboard), and is highly compressed so that it's far denser than medium board. This means it not only does everything other man-made boards do, but also overcomes their two main problems – it doesn't flake or splinter, and when sawn it gives a smooth, hard edge which doesn't need disguising (it can even be stained to match a face veneer).
● Thicknesses 16mm (⅝in) to 35mm (1⅜in).

Chipboard

Chipboard is made by bonding wood chips with plastic resin. It's quite strong, and one grade is tough enough to be used for flooring. However, it's difficult to work it neatly or to screw into it effectively: the thread breaks up the chips so the screw pulls out under load. Few chipboards can withstand moisture, though grades for external use are available.
● In the simplest type of chipboard, all the chips are approximately the same size – but usually those nearer the surface are finer. The surfaces mostly come filled and sanded, ready for decoration, and some are even primed for painting. Much chipboard is sold with a wood or PVC veneer, or a melamine laminate. Plastic-faced boards come in a limited range of colours and wood effects.
● Thicknesses range from 4mm (³/₁₆in) to 40mm (1½in); 12, 18, 22 and 25mm (½, ¾, ⅞ and 1in) are commonest.

Plywood

Plywood is made by glueing wood veneers in layers. The grain of each veneer is laid at right angles to the ones on either side, the aim being to stop the sheet warping (though this isn't always completely successful). The sheet has an odd number of layers – hence the names, 'three-ply', 'five-ply' and so on. This ensures that the grains of the outside veneers always run in the same direction.
● Birch and gaboon are two of the main woods used for plywood.
Ideally, the veneers should be of the same wood and the same thickness. In fact, the outermost ones are always thin, and you'll often find thick veneers made of less dense timber in the centre.
● 'Stoutheart' plywood is the name given to a sheet where there is only one central thick veneer. This makes the edges of the sheet harder to work.
● Some plywoods have a decorative finish, which can range from a factory-applied paint or a plastic laminate to a particularly attractive wood veneer. Others are grooved to resemble match-board cladding.
● Two grading systems are used for plywood. The first indicates the number of knots, joins and other blemishes in the surface veneers. Its three grades are A (perfect), B, and BB for rough work. Where a board appears to have two grades (eg, B/BB), the first refers to one veneer the second to the other. The other system grades the

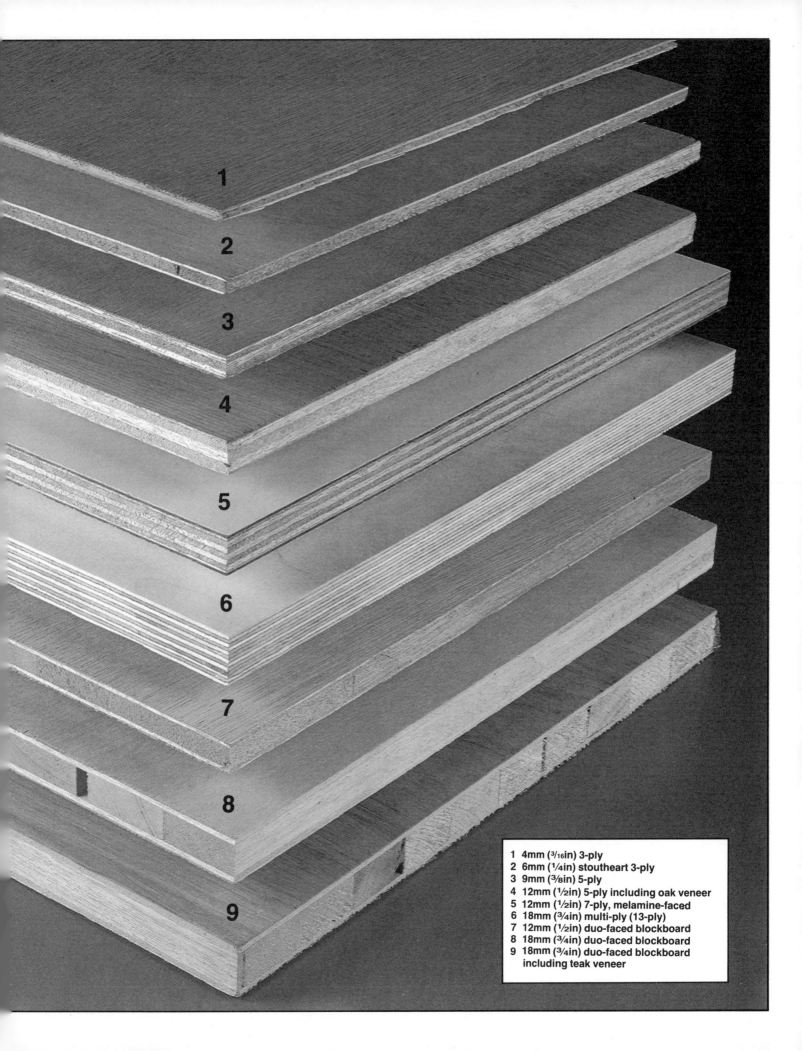

1   4mm (³/₁₆in) 3-ply
2   6mm (¹/₄in) stoutheart 3-ply
3   9mm (³/₈in) 5-ply
4   12mm (¹/₂in) 5-ply including oak veneer
5   12mm (¹/₂in) 7-ply, melamine-faced
6   18mm (³/₄in) multi-ply (13-ply)
7   12mm (¹/₂in) duo-faced blockboard
8   18mm (³/₄in) duo-faced blockboard
9   18mm (³/₄in) duo-faced blockboard
    including teak veneer

adhesive between the veneers. WBP (weather-and-boil-proof) will withstand severe weathering for at least 25 years; then, in order of durability, come BR, MR and INT, the last of which is only for dry internal use. The adhesive may outlast the veneers; but especially durable types of plywood (eg, marine plywood, used in boatbuilding) are also available.

● Thicknesses range from 3 to 6, 12 and 19mm (1/8, 1/4, 1/2 and 3/4in), but thinner and thicker types are made.

Blockboard

Blockboard is a bit like stoutheart plywood. It has a thick core of softwood slats glued side by side, and two outer hardwood veneers, one of which may be decorative. The veneer grain runs at right angles to the core grain. In more expensive (double-faced or five-ply) boards, two outer veneers are used on each face, which makes

the core joins less likely to show through.

● Blockboard is very useful where you need a relatively light, inexpensive slab, eg, for a tabletop or door. However, it's hard to get the edges neat, especially those where the core endgrain shows: there are often unsightly gaps between the slats, too. Fixing into these edges can be a problem for the same reasons.

● Surface veneers and adhesives are graded as for plywood, but no blockboard is really suitable for external use. There's no WBP grade (see above), and anyway the board contains too much softwood to be truly durable.

Laminboard is a superior blockboard. Its core is made from thinner, more uniform slats with no gaps between them. But it's hard to get.

● Thicknesses range from 12mm (1/2in) to 32mm (1 1/4in); occasionally up to 50mm (2in).

Buying boards

Say exactly what you want – name, grade, finish, thickness. A good timber merchant's catalogue helps a lot. Remember you can get a number of different veneers – from rosewood to oak – on chipboard, plywood and blockboard.

Think carefully how much you want. There are several 'standard' sheet sizes – commonest is 2400 x 1200mm (8 x 4ft). Buying a whole sheet is cheapest. If that's too much, or you have no power saw, small sheets may be available. Failing that, get it cut specially – but allow a little extra for trimming at home; shop sawing may not be very neat or accurate.

EDGINGS FOR MAN-MADE BOARDS

For the best finish, edge man-made boards with a timber 'lipping'. Often this can be bought or planed to the same width as the board thickness so it

fits flush on both the face and the underside. Use panel pins and PVA adhesive to fix it in place, and mitre the ends at the corners for a clean edge all round.

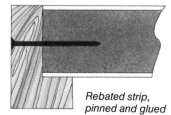

Rectangular-section strip, pinned and glued in place

Rebated strip, pinned and glued

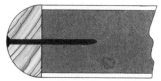

Half-round beading, pinned and glued in place

Tongue and groove – can be cut easily with power tools

Reeded moulding, pinned and glued

Another type of tongue and groove, slightly weaker

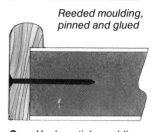
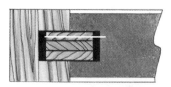

2 *Hockey stick moulding, pinned and glued*

Loose tongue of thin plywood in two matching grooves

Plastic edging strip

1 4mm (3/16in) pegboard
2 3mm (1/8in) hardboard, melamine-faced one side
3 3mm (1/8in) standard hardboard
4 9mm (3/8in) medium board, type LM
5 12mm (1/2in) canite board, painted one side
6 15mm (5/8in) MDF
7 12mm (1/2in) chipboard
8 15mm (5/8in) chipboard, wood-veneered and edged
9 15mm (5/8in) chipboard, melamine-faced
10 18mm (3/4in) chipboard

FINISHES FOR FURNITURE

There are many products you can use to give your furniture and fittings a fine finish. The range includes polishes, waxes and oils as well as lacquers or varnishes of various types.

Once furniture has been assembled it must be finished to seal its pores, protect its surface against heat, liquid and scratches, and to give it an attractive appearance. Before doing so, however, you might have to give it some preparatory treatment.

Preparing the wood

Restorer and cleaner contains refined alcohol and gum spirit of turpentine to dissolve old finishes. It should be applied gently using fine steel wool. A further application will probably be necessary, but don't overclean as you could mark the wood. To remove just oil or wax, apply restorer with a clean rag.

Wood bleach literally turns wood lighter in colour and also removes stains. It can only be used on bare wood and comes in two parts. You can make up to four applications, but after that many you'll have to accept any remaining stains.

Reviver contains pure boiled linseed oil that sinks into wood that has had its finish removed and appears dry and unattractive. It will prevent further drying and cracking and give some surface protection. Allow it to soak in for 24 hours.

Finishing the wood

The finish you select will depend on two factors. Firstly, the amount of protection the surface requires from water, heat and so on, and secondly, the degree of shine you want it to have.

French polish will give a superb finish with a mirror-like gloss provided it is correctly applied. However, the finish won't provide any real protection. It is made from the finest quality shellac and industrial alcohol, and you can use white or transparent polish to keep the wood a light colour, or flake orange or garnet for a darker finish. The secret of success lies in the application and the building up of several layers to get a beautiful, reflective surface.

White polish is french polish with bleached white shellac added. It is designed for use on light-coloured woods where the true natural appearance is to be maintained. It can also be used for sealing wood before waxing.

Button polish is applied like french polish but produces a harder, more orange-coloured finish.

Wax polish can be applied on its own, but it also makes an excellent surface covering for other finishes. It is not resistant to heat or scratches and needs frequent re-application. It is available in traditional wax blocks or as a liquid or spray.

Varnish (often called synthetic lacquer) provides a durable matt, eggshell or gloss finish that is highly water-resistant and can also cope well with spills and heat. It cannot be applied to wood that has been waxed or oiled unless all trace of the previous finish has been removed.

It comes in both one and two-part forms and can be sprayed, brushed or rubbed on. Follow the manufacturer's instructions closely as some lacquers require rapid application of coats to give amalgamation between layers, while others need 24 hours between each coat.

Plastic coating is a modern alternative to french polish that provides resistance to heat, liquids and scratches. It is available in clear, black or white, while other shades can be obtained by adding a small amount of wood stain. It requires a two-part treatment and can be given a matt finish by gentle rubbing down with wax polish and 0 or 1 grade steel wool. For a mirror finish, rub down with glass paper and apply a burnishing cream.

Using oil

Wood can also be sealed with oil but the treatment is best used only on hardwoods – softwoods become dirty and discoloured very quickly. The finish gives good resistance to moisture, but not to spills or heat. Rub the oil well in to the grain and repeat the application. Allow drying time between the coats and finish with fine grade steel wool, wax polish and a clean cloth.

Teak oil contains 'drying agents' to speed up the drying process, and gives an attractive seal to most hardwoods. It gives a minimal sheen.

Danish oil will not dry to a gloss if used on wood that has been already oiled. It gives a natural, open-grained lustrous finish, and can be lacquered over (unlike the other oils).

Linseed oil is slow-drying and forms a poor film. Heat-treated linseed oil, called boiled oil, is a better bet, and is easier to apply if mixed first with equal parts of turpentine.

Olive oil should be used to seal wooden articles, such as a chopping board, that will be used in food preparation.

KEY

1 *Preparatory treatments*
2 *Finishing in various forms*
3 *Oils for sealing hardwoods*
4 *French polish in liquid and solid form; shellac flakes are the main ingredient. Plastic coating is a modern alternative*
5 *Varnishes and synthetic lacquers.*

NAILS & SCREWS

To ensure the success of all your carpentry projects, be sure to choose the right nails and screws for the task.

Nails come in many guises for all sorts of different jobs, though some are easier to find than others. Before looking at them all, a few general points are worth considering.

The first is strength. Friction is what makes a nail grip, so long thick nails provide a better grip than short thin ones. Another factor is the shape of the nail's shank; on the whole, nails with specially shaped shanks are strongest, and cut nails are stronger than wire nails.

Cut nails cause fewer splits than wire nails because, being blunt, they break the wood fibres and create their own holes, while wire nails merely force the fibres apart.

Nails aren't very attractive. The standard method of hiding them is to punch their heads below the surface of the wood and fill the resulting hollows with stopping. But if you're securing such things as carpet, fabric or roofing felt, the large head found on most tacks and roofing nails is essential to hold the material in place.

Finally, think about rust. In most indoor work ordinary mild steel nails are fine but outdoors, you need a nail with more rust resistance. Normally this means a galvanised nail, but other rust-resisting finishes are available – and you can also get nails made entirely from metals that don't rust at all, such as brass, copper and even bronze.

Buying nails
When buying nails, remember they're described by length rather than diameter. Also, though it may be sensible (if more expensive) to buy small amounts in packets and boxes, it's more economical to buy loose nails sold by weight, not quantity.

General-purpose nails
Round wire nails (12) are used only for rough carpentry. They're available plain (12) or galvanised (15), in lengths from 20 to 150 mm (¾ to 6in).

Oval wire nails (14) are used in all types of general woodwork. Lengths are as for round wire nails; galvanised types are also available.

Lost head nails (16) are often used instead of ovals. Lengths range from 12mm (½in) to 150mm; you'll find plain or galvanised finishes.

Cut floor brads (11) are traditional fixings for floorboards. Lengths range from 20 to 150mm; they have a plain finish.

Cut clasp nails (17) are used for rough fixings in wood, and in masonry if it's not too hard. Lengths range from 25mm to 100mm (1 to 4in).

Masonry Nails (4) are specially hardened to make a reasonably strong fixing in brickwork and the like. Twisted shanks grip better than plain ones. They come in various gauges (thicknesses) and in lengths from about 12 to 100mm (½ to 4in).

Plasterboard nails used for fixing plasterboard to ceilings and stud walls, are similar but have a jagged shank for extra grip.

Panel pins (6) are slim versions of the lost-head nail, used in fine work for fixing mouldings and the like. Lengths range from 12 to 50mm (½ to 2in).

Moulding pins (9) and **veneer pins** (7) are still thinner lost-head nails and are used for fixing thin lippings and mouldings. Lengths range from 12 to 25mm (½ to 1in).

Specialised nails
Hardboard pins (8) are for fixing hardboard. Their diamond-shaped heads burrow into the surface as the pin is driven home. Most have a coppered finish; lengths are from 10 to 38mm (⅜ to 1½in).

Sprigs (5), also called cut brads, are mainly used for holding glass in window frames. Normally plain, lengths range from 12 to 19mm (½ to ¾in).

Cut tacks (2) have large flat heads for holding fabric and carpet in place. Finishes are blued, coppered or galvanised; lengths range from 6 to 30mm (¼ to 1¼in).

Roofing nails are used for fixing corrugated roofing sheets. One (1) is used with curved washers; the other has a special sprung head. Both are usually galvanised. Lengths range from 63 to 112mm (2½ to 4½in).

Staples (3) are used to fix wire fencing, upholstery springs and the like, and are either galvanised or plain. Lengths range from 12 to 40mm (1½ to 1⅝in).

Annular nails (10) have ribs along the shank to prevent them pulling out, and are used for fixing sheet materials. Lengths range between 25 and 75mm (1 to 3in); finishes are plain steel or coppered.

Clout nails (13) have extra-large heads which make them ideal for fixing roofing felt, slates, sash window cords and so on. Lengths range from 12 to 50mm (½ to 2in); most are galvanised.

To be able to pick exactly the screw you need for a particular purpose, it helps to know what each part of the screw does.

The thread is the spiral that actually pulls the screw into the wood and holds it there. Most have the same profile, but chipboard screws combat the material's crumbly quality with their shallower spiral; some screws have a double thread, which means the screw won't wander off-centre and can be driven more quickly. Most wood screws have about two-fifths of their length unthreaded, forming the shank, but chipboard screws are threaded all the way up to head for better grip.

Screw heads come in three main shapes. Countersunk is the commonest. The name describes how the screw head fits into the surface of what you're fixing – into a hole with sloping sides. This hole is made in wood with a special countersink bit; many metal fittings such as hinges have their screw holes already countersunk.

The raised countersunk head looks more handsome, and is often used with exposed metal fittings. The round head is used for fixing metal fittings without a countersink to wood.

On wood screws the Pozidriv recess has now given way to the similar-looking Supadriv type. Each has its own screwdriver shape, but you can use a Pozidriver for both.

Screws for special purposes include the clutch-head screw, which can't be undone once driven. The coach screw, used for heavy framing work, has a square head and is tightened with a spanner. The mirror screw is inserted in the usual way; then a chrome-plated dome is screwed into the head, making it a decorative feature.

Sizes and materials
How big is a screw? Its length ranges from 6 to 150mm (¼ to 6in). The gauge – the diameter of the shank – has a number from 0 (the smallest) to 32; 4, 6, 8, 10 and 12 are the commonest. Remember that you can have the same screw length in different gauges and the same gauge in different lengths.

And what are screws made of? Steel is the commonest and cheapest material, but isn't very good-looking and rusts easily. Luckily there are several alternatives. Steel itself comes with various coatings, from nickel plate to black japanning. Of other metals, brass (available plain or chromium-plated) is fairly corrosion proof but weak. Aluminium (also weak), stainless steel and silicon bronze are virtually corrosion-free. Stainless steel is the strongest of the three, but is expensive.

Remember when buying screws to give all the relevant details – length, gauge number, head type, material, recess type and finish.

HEADS AND THREADS
1 The commonest head profile is countersunk, with a flat top and sloping sides.
2 Raised countersunk heads have a slightly domed top, and are used with metal fittings.
3 Round-head screws are used to fix metal fittings without countersunk screw holes.
4 The screw thread usually extends to about three-fifths of the screw length, but chipboard screws are threaded all the way up.
5 Most screws have a slot in the head.
6 Supadriv recesses need a special screwdriver.

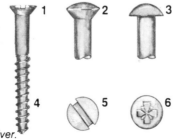

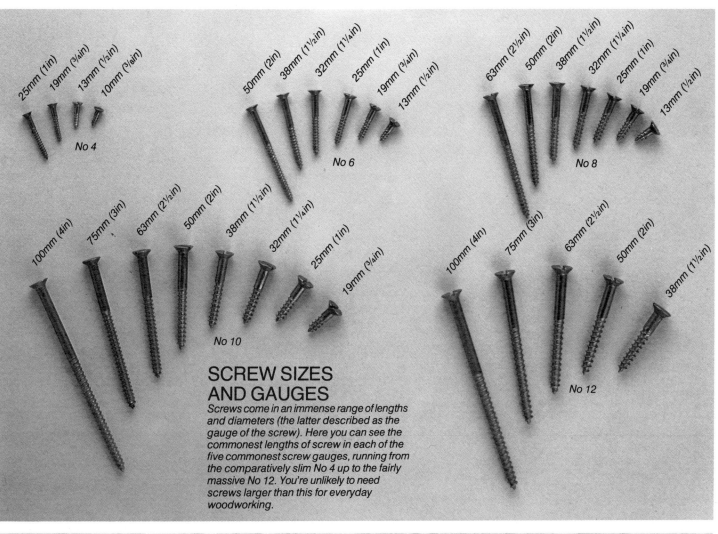

25mm (1in) 19mm (¾in) 13mm (½in) 10mm (⅜in)
No 4

50mm (2in) 38mm (1½in) 32mm (1¼in) 25mm (1in) 19mm (¾in) 13mm (½in)
No 6

63mm (2½in) 50mm (2in) 38mm (1½in) 32mm (1¼in) 25mm (1in) 19mm (¾in) 13mm (½in)
No 8

100mm (4in) 75mm (3in) 63mm (2½in) 50mm (2in) 38mm (1½in) 32mm (1¼in) 25mm (1in) 19mm (¾in)
No 10

100mm (4in) 75mm (3in) 63mm (2½in) 50mm (2in) 38mm (1½in)
No 12

SCREW SIZES AND GAUGES

Screws come in an immense range of lengths and diameters (the latter described as the gauge of the screw). Here you can see the commonest lengths of screw in each of the five commonest screw gauges, running from the comparatively slim No 4 up to the fairly massive No 12. You're unlikely to need screws larger than this for everyday woodworking.

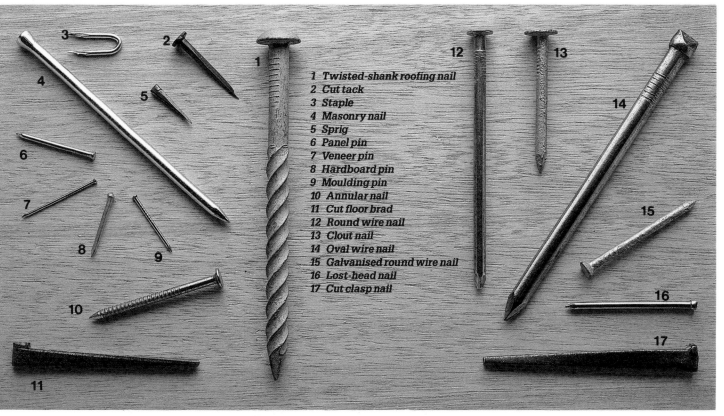

1 Twisted-shank roofing nail
2 Cut tack
3 Staple
4 Masonry nail
5 Sprig
6 Panel pin
7 Veneer pin
8 Hardboard pin
9 Moulding pin
10 Annular nail
11 Cut floor brad
12 Round wire nail
13 Clout nail
14 Oval wire nail
15 Galvanised round wire nail
16 Lost-head nail
17 Cut clasp nail

HINGES

There's a very wide range of hinges available, in all sorts of sizes and materials. Some are general-purpose types, while others are designed to do just one specific job, so it's important that you select the correct one.

When choosing a hinge, the first essential is to know what kind of door or flap you're fitting – what it's made of, and whether it's lay-on or inset (see Adding doors to basic boxes).

The second is to know how wide a choice you have. For most applications there are three or four suitable hinges. In all, there are scores of variations: here we show the main types you're likely to use.

Most hinges are made of steel, brass and white nylon, singly or in combination. Chromium and nickel plate, and brown plastic, are also used.

Butt hinges

Butt hinges, the traditional type, are still used constantly. They consist of two rectangular *leaves* (except on a flush hinge, these are the same shape), joined by a *knuckle* with a pin through it. Butt hinges come in sizes from 25mm (1in), for use on furniture, to in excess of 100mm (4in) long for hanging room doors. Materials include steel, brass and nylon.

● Some butt hinges (usually brass) have ornamental *finials* at each end of the knuckle; on some of these, such as the **loose-pin** type (4), the finials unscrew so you can tap out the pin. This makes fitting them a lot easier, because you can fasten one leaf each to door and frame separately before hanging the door by assembling the two.

● A **piano hinge** (8) is simply a narrow butt hinge sold as a continuous length of up to 1800mm (6ft), and originally designed to hinge the keyboard cover on a piano. You can easily cut it with a hacksaw to any length you need.

● The **back flap hinge**'s wide leaves (5) equip it for the task of holding table and desk flaps.

● **Rising butts** (6) are widely used on room doors. They enable the door to be lifted off at any time

– and the spiral in the knuckle pulls the door closed automatically. You may have to remove the inner top corner of the door to prevent it catching on the doorstop as the door swings home.

● The **flush hinge** (7) isn't strictly a butt hinge, because one leaf closes within, rather than against, the other. It's unsuitable for heavy doors, but – unlike ordinary butt hinges – it doesn't need to be recessed. Instead, its leaves are simply screwed onto the meeting surfaces – the smaller one to the door. The thickness of the leaves equals the clearance around the door.

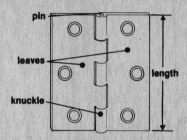

pin — leaves — knuckle — length

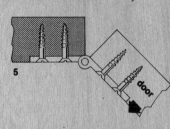

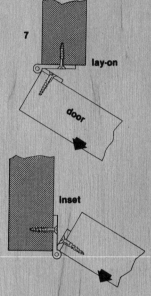

Butt hinges

Probably still the commonest type, these come in many varieties. When fitting, it's important to get them in line vertically.

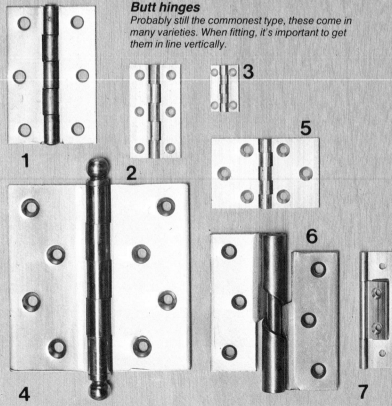

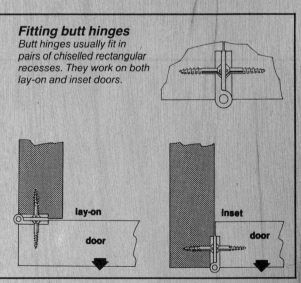

Fitting butt hinges

Butt hinges usually fit in pairs of chiselled rectangular recesses. They work on both lay-on and inset doors.

lay-on   door

inset   door

Decorative hinges

These hinges, also surface-fixing (9, 10 and 11), are of course used for their ornamental effect. Note that the front frame or edges of the cabinet must be fairly wide to accommodate them.

There's also a much smaller and less ornamental type of surface-fixing hinge which looks rather like (14) and is suitable for light doors.

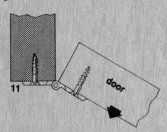

Pivot hinges

Pivot hinges are so called because all or part of each leaf lies in a horizontal plane and so needs only a small pivot, rather than a long knuckle, to connect it to the other.
● **Centre hinges,** the traditional type (12), can only be used on inset doors. A door hung with these has one hinge on its top edge, and one at the bottom; one leaf of each hinge is recessed into the door, one into the cabinet.

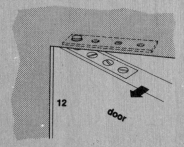

This hinge is hidden when the door is closed – and it's handy if for any reason you can't attach butt hinges to the door or cabinet or both.
● The more modern type (sometimes confusingly called 'semi-concealed') is *double-cranked.* On a cranked hinge, one leaf is bent into a right angle. On a double-cranked hinge this is true of both leaves.

Either way, the door swings from a different point to that on a non-cranked hinge – ideal for a lay-on door, because it will open fully (ie, to 90°) without passing beyond the cabinet side. If the cabinet is beside a wall, or next to

another cabinet of the same or greater depth, this is essential.

The other good point about cranked hinges is that they're easier to fit accurately, because their angles locate over the edges of timber or board.

The cranked pivot hinge shown here (13) and on page 106 requires a small saw cut to be made in the edges of the door and cabinet to take its neck. Other types are simply fitted to the top and bottom edges of the door, without the need for cuts. All can be bought for left- or right-hand opening doors.

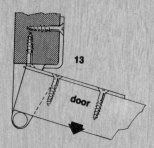

● Not shown is the **lift-off pivot hinge,** for lightweight lay-on doors, half of which screws bodily into the door and half into the cabinet. One half incorporates a pin and the other a socket, so you can hang the door after fitting them, as with a loose-pin hinge. (Lift-off butt hinges are also available.)

Cranked hinges

The main family of cranked hinges have knuckles rather than pivots. They give you several further options for fitting lay-on doors. Their main disadvantage is that they're highly visible on the edge of the door.
● The **cranked surface-fixing hinge** (14) will only take light weight doors because it isn't recessed. The one shown accommodates 6mm (¼in) thick plywood.

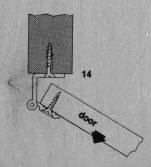

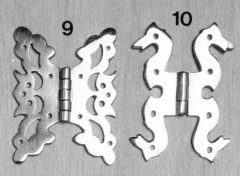

Decorative hinges

Because they're surface-fixing, and the knuckle is short compared to the leaves, these are useful where the meeting edges of door and cabinet aren't straight.

● The **lift-off cranked hinge** (15) combines the advantages of a cranked hinge with the ease of fitting given by separable leaves (see page 585). It is recessed like a butt hinge.
● 16 is similar except that it lacks the lift-off facility. This particular model is very solidly made in brass.

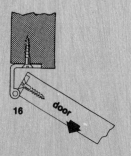

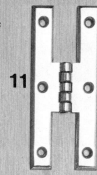

Cranked hinges

Always try these out (like pivot and concealed hinges) on scraps of timber or board before buying, to see how they work.

Pivot hinges

Traditional pivot hinges have two flat leaves. Modern types, which are cranked, differ in being especially easy to fit.

Invisible hinges

Invisible hinges are especially neat little devices. Although completely hidden when the door is closed, they have intricate mechanisms which allow it to open to 180°. They work on both inset and lay-on doors.

● The **cylinder hinge** (17) simply fits into a pair of drilled holes.

● The mechanism of the **Soss** or **invisible mortise hinge** (18) fits into a mortise, while its face plate sits in a shallow recess like the leaf of a butt hinge.

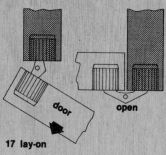

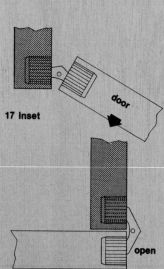

17 lay-on

17 inset

Concealed hinges

An enormous amount of work has gone into the development of concealed hinges, and many different models are available.

While most are designed, like cranked hinges, to allow lay-on doors to open within the overall width of the cabinet, some will fit inset doors, and some both – those for lay-on doors varying according to the amount of overlap they give. Often the thickness of timber or board is important. You'll also find variations in how far the hinges open. And some concealed hinges, such as the two shown here, have a positive spring action which serves instead of a catch to keep the door closed.

The concealed hinge can't be seen, because it's fixed entirely inside the door and cabinet. As a rule, the part fixed to the door includes a threaded cylindrical section which fits into a wide, shallow circular recess bored in the surface, where it's held in position by screws.

● This recess is readily and accurately milled out by industrial machines, but less so by the home woodworker. That may lead you to choose a surface-fixing type like (19), which fixes in the easiest possible way – by screwing onto both surfaces.

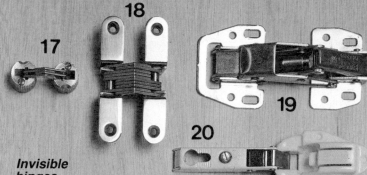

18

17

19

20

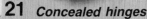

21

Invisible hinges

Invisible and concealed hinges both have clever mechanisms which pull the door clear of the cabinet instead of letting it swing. With invisible hinges this is completely hidden.

Concealed hinges

The great attraction of these is their adjustability and variety. Many models, too, don't require a separate catch to be fitted.

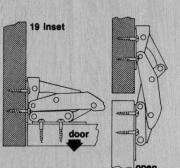

19 inset

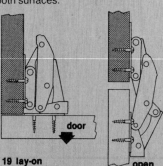

19 lay-on

This model also has a spring to keep the door firmly open, as well as closed. The action is so sure that it will even hold up a light flap without the need for a stay.

● (20) is the **recessed** type, (21) is its **mounting plate,** which is screwed inside the cabinet; the thin end of the hinge is screwed, in its turn, to the plate. This arrangement, like that of a lift-off or loose-pin hinge, makes for easy door hanging; but it's also unique in allowing easy adjustment of the door's position after it's been fitted.

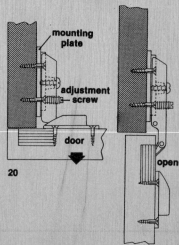

mounting plate

adjustment screw

door

20

open

FITTING HINGES

In essence, the fitting procedure is the same for all hinges.

1 Make sure the door fits.

2 Work out exactly how the hinges will be positioned, including the dimensions of any recesses.

3 Mark out the hinge positions on the door, plus recesses if any.

4 Fix the hinges to the door.

5 Position the door accurately, and fix the hinges to the cabinet.

Fitting butt hinges is dealt with in greater detail on pages 45-47 and 110-113

All doors need at least two hinges, unless you're using a piano hinge. The very tallest and heaviest need four; intermediate ones need three.

There are no rules about the spacing of hinges. However, with butt and similar types, the top hinge is often placed a distance equal to its own length down from the top of the door and the bottom one up from the bottom by the same or twice the distance. On framed doors, the upper end of the top hinge is often lined up with the lower edge of the top rail in the frame, and the lower end of the bottom hinge with the upper edge of the bottom rail.

All hinges will work in any material. But they have to take a lot of stress, so you need to make sure they're secure. Don't use small, light hinges for a large, heavy door. Recesses usually make for greater strength than surface fixing, provided the hinges fit into them tightly.

But surface fixing is stronger in veneered or plastic-faced chipboard, because breaking through the facing weakens the material. If using butt hinges in this type of board, get round the problem by recessing them to twice the depth in the other material.

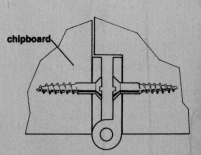

chipboard

In chipboard, too, you should use chipboard screws. Fixing into its edges is not, however, to be recommended.

CHAPTER 2

BASIC TECHNIQUES

Whether the woodworking job you are planning to carry out is a simple or a complicated one, you will not get far without first mastering the basic carpentry skills.

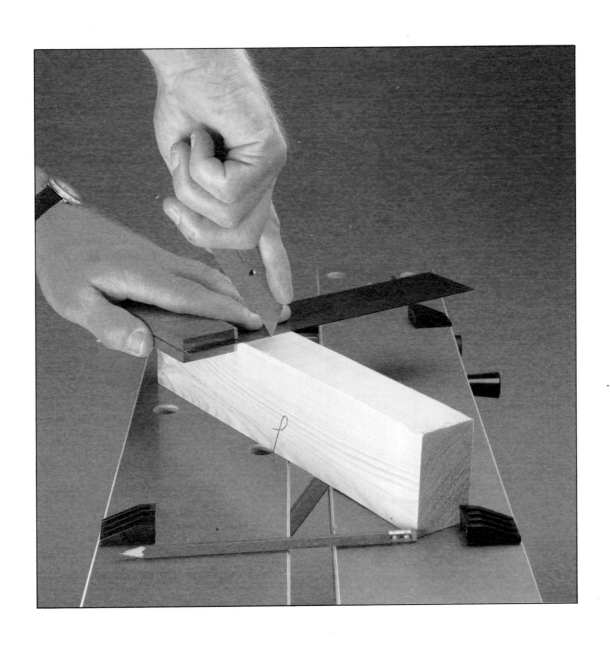

A GUIDE TO WOODWORK JOINTS

If there were no joints, there could be very little woodwork. They come in a great many varieties. This guide helps to remove the confusion from picking the right joint for the job.

C arpentry without joints is a miserable affair, depending solely on adhesive, nails, screws, bolts and other fittings.

Though all these have their places, and are often needed for reinforcement, proper joints provide a wholly different source of strength and stability. Made by shaping the pieces themselves, they frequently (and traditionally) need no fixing hardware at all. Because of this, they usually contribute neatness too, and sometimes save money. They can even supply ornament.

General principles
Accurate cutting is absolutely basic to good jointing. Apart from looks,

it's often vital for strength, since components which meet squarely and snugly help adhesives to do their work (especially PVA, which isn't much good at filling gaps).

Some joints, especially in building carpentry, need no adhesive, relying instead on weight and/or on being part of a large, solid structure. For the rest, the rule is that larger glued areas mean more strength. A mortise-and-tenon joint, for example, is stronger than a halving joint largely because it has two pairs of main meeting faces instead of one. Shoulders, too, aid location and rigidity.

Remember, however, that cutting any joint exacts its own price in

L-JOINTS FOR FRAMING

A mitred front (2) makes a halving joint (1) look neater; you can also include it in a corner bridle joint (3).

Haunches (4 and 5) stop a tenon piece from twisting.

A plain mitre (8) is quite weak. Keys (9) or a spline (10) reinforce it; both are planed flush after assembly. The spline can be of either thin plywood or solid timber. In the latter case the grain should run across it, for strength, instead of along it as you'd normally expect.

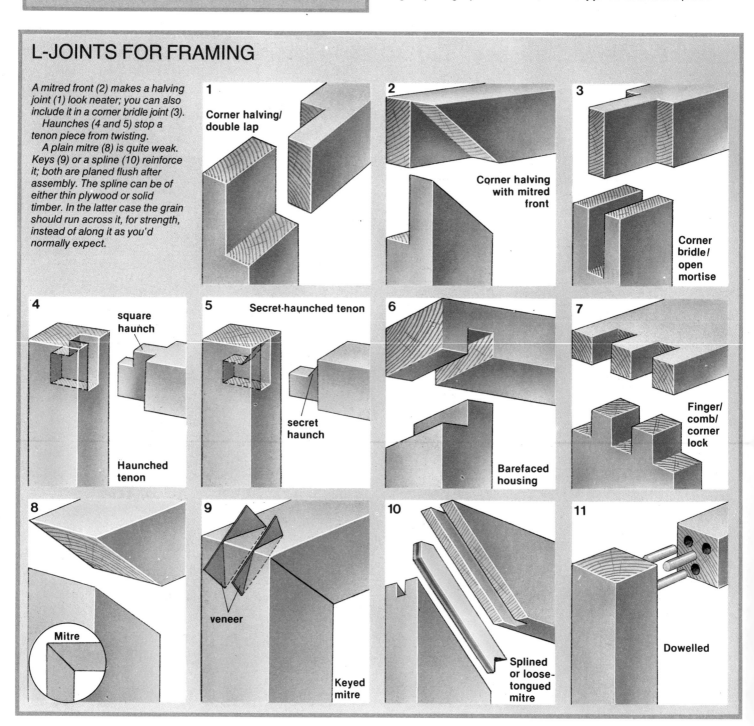

1 Corner halving/ double lap

2 Corner halving with mitred front

3 Corner bridle/ open mortise

4 square haunch — Haunched tenon

5 Secret-haunched tenon — secret haunch

6 Barefaced housing

7 Finger/ comb/ corner lock

8 Mitre

9 veneer — Keyed mitre

10 Splined or loose-tongued mitre

11 Dowelled

terms of strength. A halving effectively reduces (say) a 50x50mm (2x2in) piece to a 50x25mm (2x1in) piece. This point is often forgotten. The second piece, tight-fitting and well glued though that may be, won't lessen the fact. You must be sure your choice of joint justifies any overall reduction in size and therefore strength.

Choosing joints

Framing joints are used with lengths of timber, both softwood and hardwood. Board joints are for flat pieces, often of man-made materials. Broadly speaking, the two groups are separate, though

some joints (eg, the finger joint) can be used in either situation. Both groups include corner joints, T-joints and a few X-joints. Three-way framing joints are usually combinations of simple corner joints.

Note that there's another category we don't show, namely 'scarf' joints. These join timber end-to-end. Though many ingenious patterns have been devised, they take some cutting, and none is as strong as a piece of wood which is long enough to start with. In new work that's not hard to come by, and the scarf joint is usually used only for localised repair work where a complete length of timber cannot be easily replaced.

On the whole, the joints in common use – of which a good selection appears here – are popular for good reasons, and serve most purposes. Common sense and growing familiarity with them will reveal these in more detail. Very often, of course, there's more than one joint for a particular task – and different people have their own favourites. In many cases, further information about individual joints is given in other sections of this book.

But, whatever you do, don't think that these illustrations tell the whole story. Probably thousands of other joints have been used at one time and another – and there's still

nothing to stop you from inventing your own variants if you want and need to. But it's wise, first of all, to check that an ordinary joint won't do. This may save you trouble – and the search for one will concentrate your mind on the exact qualities you're looking for. Usually strength, appearance and ease of cutting are what it all boils down to.

Consider, too, exactly what you want the joint to do. In which direction, or directions, is each piece likely to sag, twist, be pushed or be pulled? Make sure you combat exactly the stresses you expect – and not others which are unlikely, or you risk making the joint unnecessarily complicated.

L-JOINTS FOR BOARDS

On wider pieces like these, the grain must always run the same way on both halves of the joint, so they can shrink and swell freely across it even when glued. For the same reason, use a glued spline (16) only with man-made boards.

Joints 12 to 16 are all best made with a router – or on a saw table, tilting the blade for the mitre cuts. You could use a rebate plane for the first four, but power tools are pretty well essential for 16 (a neat, strong joint).

20 represents the ultimate in Western joints. As its name implies, its complex innards are entirely hidden. Don't attempt to cut it unless you're very keen indeed – even many tradesmen would have difficulty.

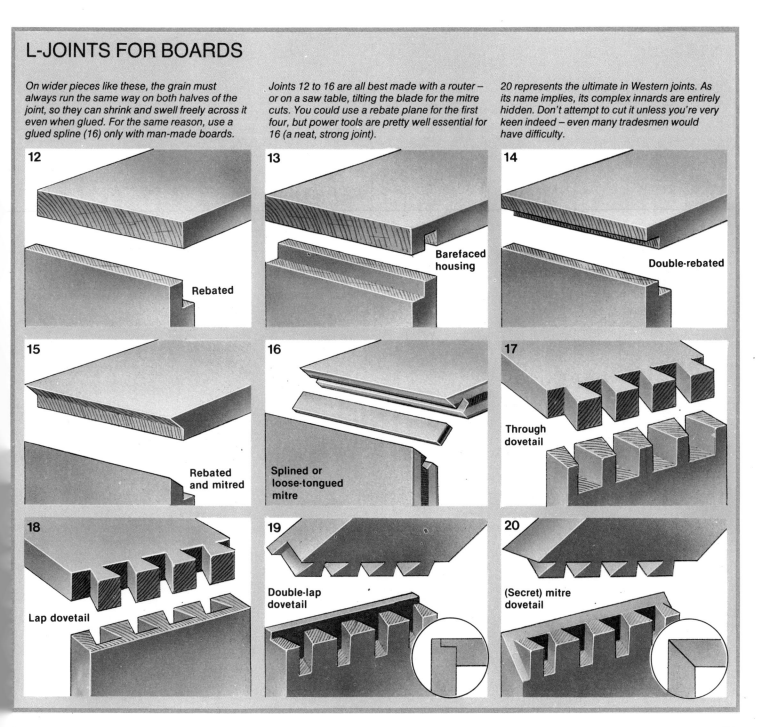

12 Rebated

13 Barefaced housing

14 Double-rebated

15 Rebated and mitred

16 Splined or loose-tongued mitre

17 Through dovetail

18 Lap dovetail

19 Double-lap dovetail

20 (Secret) mitre dovetail

T-JOINTS FOR FRAMING

There's a mortise-and-tenon joint for almost every purpose. Pegs and wedges (29 to 31) add strength and can be very attractive, especially in a contrasting wood. You can even wedge pegs. When using double wedges (30), drive them in with alternate strokes so that they enter the cuts evenly.

31 can be a knock-down joint if unglued.

As a general rule, make mortises one-third the thickness of the piece (24 to 31, 33, 34 – and see also 3, 4, 5). This avoids both weakening the tenon and splitting the mortise piece.

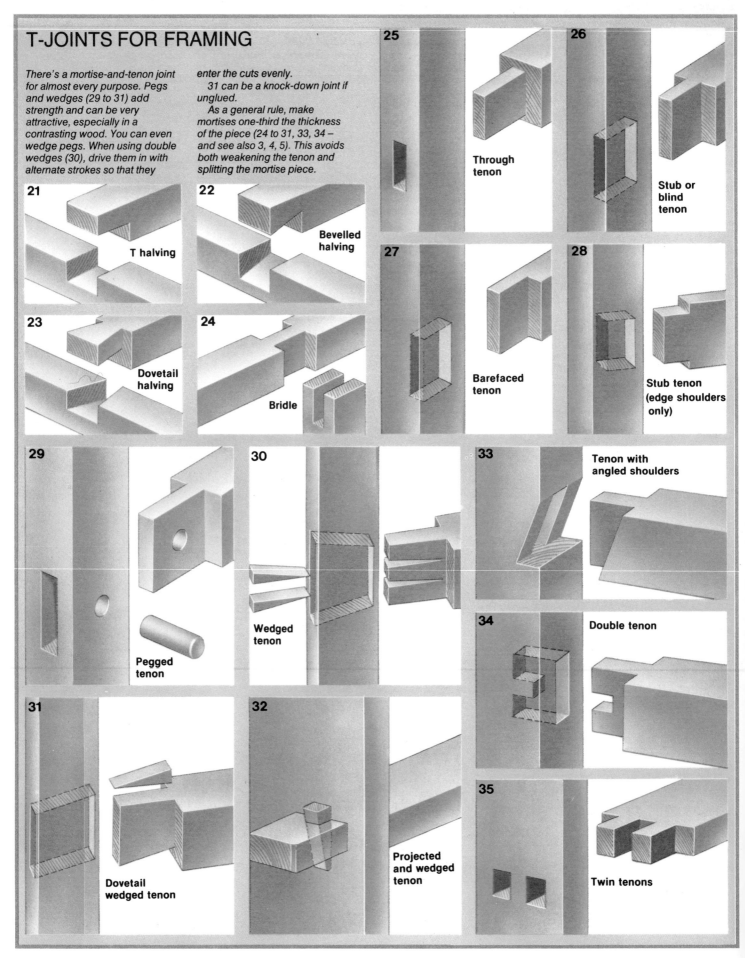

21 T halving

22 Bevelled halving

23 Dovetail halving

24 Bridle

25 Through tenon

26 Stub or blind tenon

27 Barefaced tenon

28 Stub tenon (edge shoulders only)

29 Pegged tenon

30 Wedged tenon

31 Dovetail wedged tenon

32 Projected and wedged tenon

33 Tenon with angled shoulders

34 Double tenon

35 Twin tenons

IMPLE JOINT

It's often thought that only elaborate joints give good results in woodwork. It isn't true. There are simple ways to join timber, and one of the simplest is the butt joint. It's easy to make, can be used on natural timber or man-made boards, and it's neat. What's more, given the right adhesive and the right reinforcement, a butt joint can also be strong enough for most purposes.

The great thing about butt joints is their simplicity. You can use them on any kind of timber or man-made board, provided it isn't too thin – not under 6mm (¼in). The only problem you will run into is where you are joining chipboard. A special technique is needed here to get the screws to grip, as is explained later.

Although it is possible simply to glue two pieces of wood together, unless you add some kind of reinforcement the result won't be very strong. So in most cases, the joint should be strengthened with either screws or nails. The question is which? As a rule of thumb, screws will give you a stronger joint than nails. The exception is where you are screwing into the endgrain of natural timber. Here, the screw thread chews up the timber to such an extent that it has almost no fixing value at all. Nails in this case are a much better bet.

Choosing the right adhesive
Even if you are screwing or nailing the joint together, it ought to be glued as well. A PVA woodworking adhesive will do the trick in most jobs, providing a strong and easily achieved fixing. This type of adhesive will not, however, stand up well to either extreme heat or to moisture; the sort of conditions you'll meet outdoors, or in a kitchen, for example. A urea formaldehyde is the glue to use in this sort of situation. It isn't as convenient – it comes as a powder that you have to mix with water – but your joints will hold.

Choosing the right joint
There are no hard and fast rules about choosing the best joint for a particular job. It's really just a case of finding a joint that is neat enough for what you're making, and strong enough not to fall apart the first time it is used. And as far as strength is concerned, the various kinds of butt joint work equally well.

Marking timber
Butt joints are the simplest of all joints – there's no complicated chiselling or marking out to worry about – but if the joint is to be both strong and neat you do need to be able

to saw wood to length leaving the end perfectly square.

The first important thing here is the accuracy of your marking out. Examine the piece of wood you want to cut and choose a side and an edge that are particularly flat and smooth. They're called the face edge and face side.

Next, measure up and press the point of a sharp knife into the face side where you intend to make the cut. Slide a try-square up to the knife, making sure that its stock – the handle – is pressed firmly against the face edge. Then use the knife to score a line across the surface of the timber. Carry this line round all four sides of the wood, always making sure that the try-square's stock is held against either the face edge or the face side. If you wish, you can run over the knife line with a pencil to make it easier to see – it's best to sharpen the lead into a chisel shape.

Why not use a pencil for marking out in the first place? There are two reasons. The first is that a knife gives a thinner and therefore more accurate line than even the sharpest pencil. The second is that the knife will cut through the surface layer of the wood, helping the saw to leave a clean, sharp edge.

Sawing square

One of the most useful – and easiest to make – aids to sawing is a bench hook. It'll help you to grip the wood you want to cut, and to protect the surface on which you are working. You can make one up quite easily, by gluing and screwing together pieces of scrap timber (see *Ready Reference*).

You also need the ability to control the saw, and there are three tips that will help you here. Always point your index finger along the saw blade to stop it flapping from side to side as you work. And always stand in such a way that you are comfortable, well balanced, and can get your head directly above the saw so you can see what you are cutting. You should also turn slightly sideways on. This stops your elbow brushing against your body as you draw the saw back – a fault that is often the reason for sawing wavy lines.

Starting the cut

Position the piece of wood to be cut on the bench hook and hold it firmly against the block furthest from you. Start the cut by drawing the saw backwards two or three times over the far edge to create a notch, steadying the blade by 'cocking' the thumb of your left hand. Make sure that you position the saw so that the whole of this notch is on the waste side of the line. You can now begin to saw properly using your arm with sort of piston action, but keep your left (or right as the case may be) hand away from the saw.

As the cut deepens gradually reduce the angle of the saw until it is horizontal. At this point you can continue sawing through until you start cutting into the bench hook. Alternatively, you may find it easier to angle the saw towards you and make a sloping cut down the edge nearest to you. With that done, you can saw through the remaining waste holding the saw horizontally, using the two angled cuts to keep the saw on course.

Whichever method you choose, don't try to force the saw through the wood – if that seems necessary, then the saw is probably blunt. Save your muscle power for the forward stroke – but concentrate mainly on sawing accurately to your marked line.

Cleaning up cut ends

Once you have cut the wood to length, clean up the end with glasspaper. A good tip is to lay the abrasive flat on a table and work the end of the wood over it with a series of circular strokes, making sure that you keep the wood vertical so you don't sand the end out of square. If the piece of wood is too unmanageable, wrap the glasspaper round a square piece of scrap wood instead and sand the end of the wood by moving the block to and fro – it'll help in keeping the end square.

DOVETAIL NAILING

This is a simple way of strengthening any butt joint. All you do is grip the upright piece in a vice or the jaws of a portable work-bench, and glue the horizontal piece on top if it – supporting it with scrap wood to hold the joint square – and then drive in the nails dovetail fashion. If you were to drive the nails in square, there would be more risk that the joint would pull apart. Putting them in at an angle really does add strength.

The only difficulty is that the wood may split. To prevent this, use oval brads rather than round nails, making sure that their thickest part points along the grain. If that doesn't do the trick, try blunting the point of each nail by driving it into the side of an old hammer. This creates a burr of metal on the point which will cut through the wood fibres rather than parting them.

Once the nails are driven home, punch their heads below the surface using a nail punch, or a large blunt nail. Fill the resulting dents with wood stopping (better on wood than ordinary cellulose filler) and sand smooth.

1 *Drive nails at angle: first leans to left; next to right, and so on.*

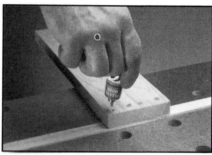

3 *Fill resulting dents with stopping compound to cover up nail heads.*

THE OVERLAP

This is the simplest of all and is one you can use on relatively thin timber. The example shown is for a T-joint, but the method is the same if you want to make an X-joint.

Bring the two pieces of wood together as they will be when joined, and use a pencil to mark the position of the topmost piece on the one underneath. To reinforce the joint, countersunk screws are best, so mark their positions on the top piece of wood, and drill clearance holes the same diameter as the screw's shank – the unthreaded part – right the way through. The screws should be arranged like the spots on a dice (two screws are shown here, but on a larger joint where more strength is needed five would be better) to help stop the joint twisting out of square. Enlarge the mouths of these holes with a countersink bit to accommodate the screw heads, and clean up any splinters where the drill breaks through the underside of the wood.

Bring the two pieces of wood together again using a piece of scrap wood to keep the top piece level. Then make pilot holes in the lower piece using either a bradawl or a small drill, boring through the clearance holes to make sure they are correctly positioned. Make sure the pilot holes are drilled absolutely vertically, or the screws could pull the joint out of shape. Finally, apply a thin coating of adhesive to both the surfaces to be joined (follow the adhesive manufacturer's instructions), position the pieces of wood accurately and, without moving them again, drive home the screws.

3 *Reassemble joint and bore pilot holes in bottom piece with bradawl.*

2 With nail punch or large blunt nail, hammer nail heads below surface.

4 When stopping is dry, sand flush with surface of surrounding timber.

CORRUGATED TIMBER CONNECTORS

Another simple way of holding a butt joint together is to use ordinary corrugated timber connectors. Simply glue the two pieces of wood together, and hammer the connectors in across the joint. Note that they are driven in dovetail fashion – the fixing is stronger that way.

For strength, hammer in connectors diagonally rather than straight.

Ready Reference

MAKING YOUR OWN BENCH HOOK

This a very useful sawing aid to help grip the wood when cutting. Hook one end over the edge of the workbench and hold the wood against the other end. Make it up from off-cuts and replace when it becomes worn.

You need:
● a piece of 12mm (½in) plywood measuring about 250 x 225mm (10 x 9in)
● two pieces of 50 x 25mm (2 x 1in) planed softwood, each about 175mm (7in) long. Glue and screw them together as shown in the sketch. Use the bench hook the other way up if you're left-handed.

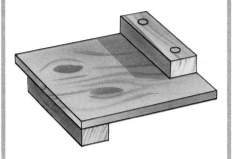

TIP: SAWING STRAIGHT

● hold wood firmly against bench hook and start cut on waste side of cutting line with two or three backward cuts
● decrease angle of the saw blade as cut progresses
● complete cut with saw horizontal, cutting into your bench hook slightly

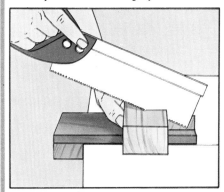

1 Bring pieces squarely together. Mark position of each on the other.

2 Drill and countersink (inset) clearance holes for screws in uppermost piece.

4 Apply woodworking adhesive to both pieces and press them together

5 Carefully drive in screws. If they're tight, remove and lubricate with soap.

TIP: TO SMOOTH CUT END

● rub with a circular motion on glasspaper held flat on the workbench, so you don't round off the corners
● on large pieces of wood, wrap glasspaper round a block of wood and rub this across the cut end

For handsaws see FACTFINDER 1.

FIXING INTO CHIPBOARD

Because neither nails nor screws hold well in chipboard, how do you hold a butt joint together? The answer is that you do use screws, but to help them grip, you drive them into a chipboard plug. Chipboard plugs are a bit like ordinary wall plugs. In fact, you can use ordinary plugs, but you have to be careful to position the plug so that any expanding jaws open across the board's width and not across the thickness where they could cause the board to break up.

The initial stages of the job are exactly the same as for the overlap joint – marking out, drilling the clearance holes, and so on. The difference is that instead of boring pilot holes in the second piece of wood, you drill holes large enough to take the chipboard plugs. Pop the plugs into the holes, glue the joint together and drive home the screws.

Incidentally, if you can't use any sort of plug at all – for example, when screwing into the face of the chipboard – the only way to get the screw to hold properly is to dip it in a little woodworking adhesive before you drive it home.

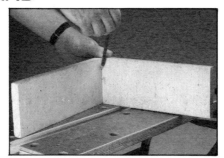

1 Bring pieces together and mark position of overlap with a pencil.

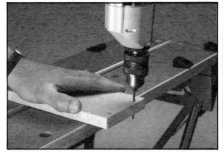

2 Drill and countersink clearance holes in overlapping piece.

3 Mark screw positions through holes onto end of second piece.

4 Drill chipboard to take plugs, then glue and screw joint together.

REINFORCING BLOCKS

The joints described so far are fairly robust, but if a lot of strength is needed it's worth reinforcing the joint with some sort of block. The simplest is a square piece of timber.

First drill and countersink clearance holes through the block and glue and screw it to one of the pieces you want to join so that it's flush with the end. To complete the joint, glue the second piece in position, and drive screws through into that. You can arrange for the block to end up inside the angle or outside it. Choose whichever looks best and is easiest to achieve.

With the block inside the angle, you'll have a neat joint and the screw heads won't be openly on display. However, in most cases it means screwing through a thick piece of wood (the block) into a thin piece (one of the bits you want to join), so it's not as strong as it might be. If greater strength is needed work the other way round, driving the screws through the pieces to be joined, into the block. You can neaten the result to a certain extent by using a triangular rather than a square block.

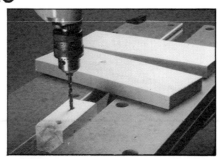

1 Drill and countersink clearance holes through reinforcing block.

2 Glue and screw block in place level with end of one piece of wood.

3 Glue second piece in place and drive screws into it through block.

4 In some cases this joint looks better with block outside angle.

JOINTING BLOCKS

Made from plastic, these are just sophisticated versions of the wooden blocks you can make yourself, and they're used in similar situations. Their only real advantage is that they tend to give a neater result when you're working with veneered or melamine covered chipboard, but only because they come in the right colours. There are basically two kinds to choose from.

The simplest is just a hollow triangular 'block' that comes with a snap-on cover to hide the screws. More complicated versions come in two parts. You screw one half of the block to each piece of wood, and then screw the two halves together using the machine screw provided. It's essential here that both halves of the block are positioned accurately, and since the blocks vary from brand to brand in the details of their design, you should follow the manufacturer's instructions on this point.

1 *Screw half of block to one piece of wood and mark position on other.*

2 *Next, screw second half of block in place on second piece of timber.*

3 *Finally, connect both halves of block using built-in machine screw.*

4 *Treat blocks that come in one piece as wooden reinforcing blocks.*

ANGLE IRONS

If still greater strength is needed, use either an angle iron or a corner repair bracket to reinforce the joint. These are really just pieces of metal pre-drilled to take screws and shaped to do the same job as a reinforcing block (the angle irons) or to be screwed to the face of the two pieces of timber across the joint (the flat T-shaped and L-shaped corner repair brackets).

In either case, bring together the pieces of wood to be joined, position the bracket, and mark the screw holes. Drill clearance and pilot holes for all the screws, then screw the bracket to one of the pieces before glueing the joint together and screwing the bracket to the second piece. They don't look very attractive, so use where appearance isn't important, ie, at the back of a joint, or where the joint is going to be concealed in some other way.

1 *Corner joints strengthened with plywood and an angle repair iron.*

2 *T-joints can be simply made with angle irons or repair brackets.*

SKEW NAILING

There'll be some situations where you cannot get at the end of the wood to use dovetail nailing. Here you must use skew nailing instead. This means glueing the two pieces securely together and then driving a nail into the upright piece of wood at an angle so it also penetrates the horizontal piece. Put a couple of nails into each side of the upright so that they cross. To stop the upright moving, clamp a block of wood behind it or wedge it against something solid.

Stop movement while driving nails with scrap wood block and G-cramp.

HALVING JOINTS & simple mitres

Getting joints to fit snugly is one of the major objectives in carpentry, and nothing introduces the techniques so well as the halving joint. As for the perfect finish, that's the role of the mitre.

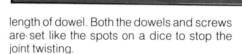

There are many situations in woodwork when you need a joint that's fast and simple, but also neat and strong. And this is where halving joints come into their own. Despite their simplicity, they're very effective joints because the two pieces of wood are cut so they interlock together, either face to face or edge to edge, making the joint as strong as — if not stronger than — the timber itself. They are used almost exclusively for building frameworks, joining the rails (side pieces) either at a corner or in a cross absolutely flush. You end up with a frame that's neat enough to be on show and sturdy enough to need no reinforcement.

Mitre joints, though not strictly speaking considered halving joints as there's no interlocking, are halved to make up a perfect 90° angle. In this section, only the simple mitre is dealt with — the more complicated forms (eg, mitred secret dovetails) are covered in another section.

Strength of joints

There are three things that affect the strength of a halving joint — the size of the timber, the quality of the timber, and any reinforcement you add.

The size of timber is important because it governs the amount of adhesive in the joint; the greater the areas glued together, the stronger the joint will be. Usually problems only arise when you are trying to join thin pieces of timber together — it's almost impossible to get the joint to stay rigid. Regarding timber quality, hardwoods rarely present a problem, but with softwoods, splitting can occur which will seriously weaken the joint. You should, therefore, reject timber containing knots, cracks and other potential weak spots.

In many cases, the correct adhesive is all the reinforcement you need — use a good quality PVA woodworking adhesive, or, if the joint will be subjected to heat or moisture, a urea formaldehyde woodworking adhesive. If still greater strength is required — this is more likely on corner halving joints than on cross halvings — you should drive screws through the overlaps, or, for a more natural look, drill a hole right through and glue in a

length of dowel. Both the dowels and screws are set like the spots on a dice to stop the joint twisting.

Simple butt joints (see pages 27-31) must be reinforced in some way to have strength, but with mitred butt joints this would defeat the decorative aim. Because of this, they are normally reserved for situations where strength is not required — picture frames and decorative edgings, such as door architraves for example.

Marking corner halving joints

Having sawn the ends of the two pieces of wood to be joined perfectly square (see pages 27-31) place one piece on top of the other, and mark the width of the top piece on the one below. Carry this mark right round the timber using a knife and a try-square, then repeat the process, this time with the bottom piece of wood on top.

Next divide the thickness of the timber in two. You need a single-tooth marking gauge for this: it consists of a wooden shaft with a sharp metal pin called a spur near one end, and a block of wood (the stock) which can be moved along the shaft and be fixed at any point with the aid of a thumbscrew.

Position the stock so that the distance between it and the spur is roughly half the timber's thickness, and place it against one edge of the wood. Use the spur to dent the surface of the timber, then repeat with the stock against the other edge. If the dents co-

incide, the gauge is set correctly. If they don't, reset the gauge. Don't try to make small adjustments by undoing the thumbscrew and moving the stock — you'll go on for ever trying to make it accurate. Instead, with the screw reasonably tight, tap one end of the shaft sharply on a hard surface. Depending which end you tap and how hard you tap it, the setting will increase or decrease by the merest fraction.

With the setting right, wedge one end of the timber into the angle of a bench hook, place the stock of the gauge firmly against the timber's edge and holding it there, score the wood from the width line to the end. You'll find this easier if, rather than digging the spur right into the wood, you merely drag it across the surface. Score identical lines on the other side and the end.

Use a pencil to shade the areas on each piece of wood that will form the waste (the top of one, the bottom of the other), then grip the first piece upright in a vice. The lower down you can get it the better. If you can't get it low, back it with a piece of scrap wood to reduce vibration. Using a tenon saw, carefully saw down until you reach the width line — the first one you marked. The golden rule of sawing any kind of joint is to saw on the waste side of the marked line (it's *always* better to saw or chisel off too little rather than too much since you can always take off a little more but you can never put it back). And remember that the closer the fit, the

MAKING A CORNER HALVING JOINT

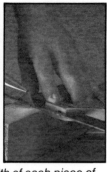

1 *First mark the width of each piece of wood on the other. Then, using a knife and square, continue these width lines round all four sides of each piece.*

2 *To mark the thickness line, set a marking gauge to half the thickness of the wood and, holding the stock firmly against one edge, scribe the line.*

3 *It's easier to start sawing at an angle, then gradually bring the saw to the horizontal. Keep the wood gripped firmly in the vice until you're finished.*

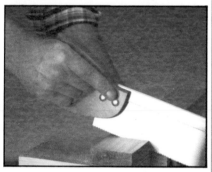

4 *Transfer the wood to a bench hook and cut down along the width line to remove the waste wood. Be sure to cut on the waste side of the guide line.*

5 *Smooth both parts to be joined with glasspaper and apply adhesive. Clamp together with a G-cramp until dry, protecting the wood with scrap timber.*

6 *When the adhesive has set, drill holes for reinforcing wood screws or dowels. If using screws, countersink the hole to take the screw head.*

stronger the joint will end up. Basically, it should fit like a hand in a glove.

Remove the wood from the vice, put it on a bench hook and cut down along the width line to release the waste wood. Again make sure you cut on the waste side of the line and be prepared to make final adjustments with a chisel. Treat the second piece of wood in exactly the same way, then bring the two together and check the fit.

You can use either a chisel or a piece of glasspaper to take off any unevenness in the timber, although it'll be quicker to use a chisel to clear out the edges so that the corners are absolutely square. When the pieces finally fit neatly, spread adhesive on both faces of the joint and hold them in place with a G-cramp (protecting the wood's surface with scrap timber) until the glue has set. Remove the cramp, and add any re-

Ready Reference

WHERE TO USE HALVING JOINTS

Halving joints are usually used for making frameworks. Here you can see which joint to use where, and how each one is assembled.

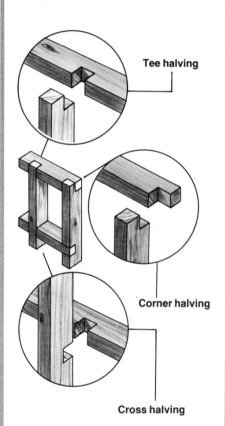

Tee halving

Corner halving

Cross halving

TOOLS FOR HALVING JOINTS

For measuring and marking: use a *handyman's knife* rather than a pencil for marking; use a *marking gauge* on each face of the joint – it'll be more accurate than using a tape measure; a *try-square* ensures accurate squaring off.
For cutting: use a *tenon saw* and a broad-blade *chisel* (25mm/1in) for cutting out cross halvings.

TIP: LABELLING JOINT PARTS

Avoid mixing up the pairs of joints by labelling the two parts with a letter and a number as soon as you cut them.

MAKING A CROSS HALVING JOINT

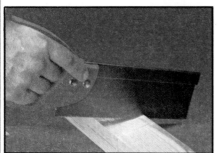

1 *First mark out the waste area to be removed, then cut down the width lines with a tenon saw.*

2 *Hold the timber in a vice or against a bench hook and remove the waste by chiselling at a slight upward angle.*

3 *Do the same on the other side until there's a 'pyramid' of waste in the middle. Gradually flatten this.*

4 *When nearing the thickness line, hold the cutting edge at an angle to the wood grain. Trim fibres in the corners.*

inforcing screws or dowels that may be needed, drilling pilot holes first.

Making cross halving joints
The difference between cross halving joints and corner halving joints is that you cannot remove the waste using only a saw. You have to make a 'housing' and for this you need a chisel (see pages 40-43 for more details of halving joints).

Saw down the width lines to the halfway mark and make additional saw cuts in between to break up the waste — these can be the same width as the chisel blade to make chipping out easier. Grip the work in a vice, or on a bench hook, and now use the chisel to remove the waste. This is done in four stages. Guiding the chisel blade bevel uppermost with one hand and striking the handle with the palm of your other hand — for this job your hand is better than a mallet — reduce the edge of the timber nearest to you to a shallow slope ending a fraction above the halfway line. Don't try to remove all the wood in one go or it will split. Remove just a sliver at a time.

The next step is to turn the wood round and slope the other edge to leave a sort of pyramid of waste. With that done, pushing the chisel through the wood rather than hitting it, gradually flatten off the pyramid until you have brought it level with the halfway lines. You'll get a neater finish here if, in the final stages, you work with the chisel's blade flat but at an angle to the grain of the wood. Finally, again pushing the chisel, remove any ragged fibres lodged in the angles of the housing.

Once you've sawn and chiselled out the housing in the second piece of wood, the next step is to try fitting the two together. Don't try forcing them if they don't quite fit — you're in danger of splitting the wood. Instead, carefully chisel off a fraction more wood, bit by bit, until you can fit the pieces together without undue force. If, on the other hand, you've cut the housing too wide so the fit is very loose, you'll have to add some re-inforcement like screws or dowels, and fill in the gaps with a wood filler, stopping or a mixture of fine sawdust and PVA adhesive. It's not worth trying to add a wedge unless the gap is very wide (over 6mm/¼in) because the result can be very messy.

Making a mitre joint
With wood that's square or rectangular in section, the first job is to make sure that both pieces are absolutely squarely cut. Use the try-square to check this — if they're not, it's better to cut another piece of wood than attempt to make adjustments. Next, place one piece on top of the other to form a right angle. Mark an internal and external corner on both, then take them apart and carry the marks across the edge with a knife and try square. Join up the marks on each piece of wood — this will give sawing lines at 45°. Mark the waste side of each with a pencil.

Wood that is raised on one side (eg, mouldings for picture frames) cannot be marked in the same way as the pieces won't sit flat on each other. The easiest way is to mark the

MAKING MITRES

1 *With square or rectangular wood, cut ends absolutely square and stack to form a right angle. Then mark the inner and outer corners on both pieces.*

2 *Carry lines down each edge with knife and try square, and score a line between corner marks to create an angle of 45°. Shade waste in pencil.*

3 *Press the wood against the bench hook and keep the saw at a shallow angle. Cut the diagonal, using the line on the edge to keep the saw vertical.*

THE SIMPLE MITRE

1 *The ends of two battens are cut to 45° and, when fixed together, make a 90° angle in this simplest of mitre joints, ideal for picture framing.*

2 *With thick timber frames, use corrugated steel fasteners driven into the back of mitre joints, where they will not be seen from the front.*

3 *Another method of strengthening a fairly thick mitre joint from behind is to pin triangles of plywood across the corner, out of sight.*

4 *Ready-made angle brackets with pre-drilled, countersunk screw holes make a quick, rigid and hidden fixing for two mitred battens in a frame.*

point of the mitre (the corner point) and then to use a simple *mitre block* to cut the angle. A mitre block not only helps you support the piece of wood (like a bench hook) but also has saw cuts at 45° in the back face to guide the saw. Then you only have to line up the mitre point on the wood with the saw now set at the correct angle. You can make a mitre block yourself — see *Ready Reference*.

Mitre aids

There are other devices available to help you cut mitres accurately. A proprietary *jointing jig*, for example, guides the saw either at right angles or at 45°; a *mitre box* is like a mitre block but has an extra side so that the whole length of the saw is kept in line.

Without these devices, getting the angles right isn't easy — but if necessary you can use a bench hook, driving in two nails so the wood is held against the block and the line of cutting is free of the bench hook. This is not as easy as using one of the other methods. Mark the wood so you know the sawing line, then place it in the mitre block, box or jig, to line up with the appropriate groove to guide the saw. If the wood you are cutting is very thin, put some blocks of scrap wood under the device to bring it up to a reasonable height. Insert a tenon saw into the guide slot and, holding it level, saw away.

There are only two things that can go

wrong. If the block is old, the 'guide' cut may have widened, resulting in an inaccurate cut. A larger tenon saw may help, but really the only answer is to hold the saw as steady as possible. The other common error when cutting mouldings and the like is to cut two mitres the same — that is two right-handed or left-handed angles, instead of one of each. This can be avoided by always marking the waste on the wood, and checking that the saw is in the correct guide slot before you begin.

Clean up the cut ends with glasspaper, taking care not to alter the angle, and glue and cramp the joint together. For frames, special mitre cramps are available, but you again make up your own. From scrap wood, cut four L-shaped blocks, and drill a hole at an angle through the point of each L. Feed a single piece of string through the holes of all four blocks, position the blocks at the corners of the frame and tie the string into a continuous loop. To tighten up, twist the string around a stick, and keep twisting the stick to draw the blocks together. You can then wedge the stick against the frame to stop it untwisting until the adhesive has set.

There are three ways to strengthen mitres — with timber connectors, plywood triangles or metal angle repair irons. For frames they should be fitted from behind, either by glueing, or glueing and pinning (see the photographs above).

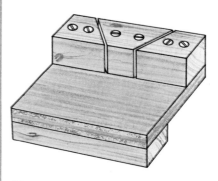
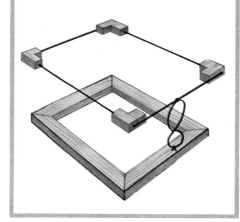

MAKING JOINT WITH DOWELS

Called wood pins or pegs, dowels are lengths of hardwood with an important role to play in simple carpentry. They can be a decorative part of joints made with them, or be there for strength alone. Few tools are needed but the secret of success lies in using them accurately.

There are two basic ways in which you can use dowels in woodworking joints. You can drive a dowel through such joints as a half lap instead of using a nail or screw, or you can use them to make joints in their own right by drilling holes in one piece of wood, glueing in dowels, and then slotting these into corresponding holes in the second piece.

The dowel joint proper is used mostly in furniture making where it provides a neat joint of great strength without intricate cutting and without the need for unsightly reinforcement. Dowels can also be used to repair furniture.

In any joint, the size of the dowel is very important. Use a small one in a big joint and it won't have sufficient strength; use one that's too large and the holes you drill to accommodate it will weaken the wood. Ideally you should choose dowels which are no more than one third the thickness of the timber into which they will be fixed.

The thickness of the wood must be considered, too, for the dowels must have sufficient space between them and at each side otherwise when they're hit home or pushed into their corresponding holes the wood will split. So follow the carpenter's 'one third rule' and mark the width as well as the thickness into three (ie, a 9mm/³⁄₈in dowel will need at least the same amount on both sides of it). And don't forget that planed wood can be up to 5mm less all round than the dimensions you ordered, and three into this size might not give you enough room for a successful joint.

Types of joints

There are different types of dowel joint. The simplest and easiest to make is the *through* dowel joint in which the dowel peg passes right through one piece of timber and into the other, sometimes passing through this as well if it's thin enough. Because in either case the ends of the dowels show, they are often used as a decorative feature of the article you're making.

If you don't want the ends of the dowels to be seen, you must make a *stopped* joint. In

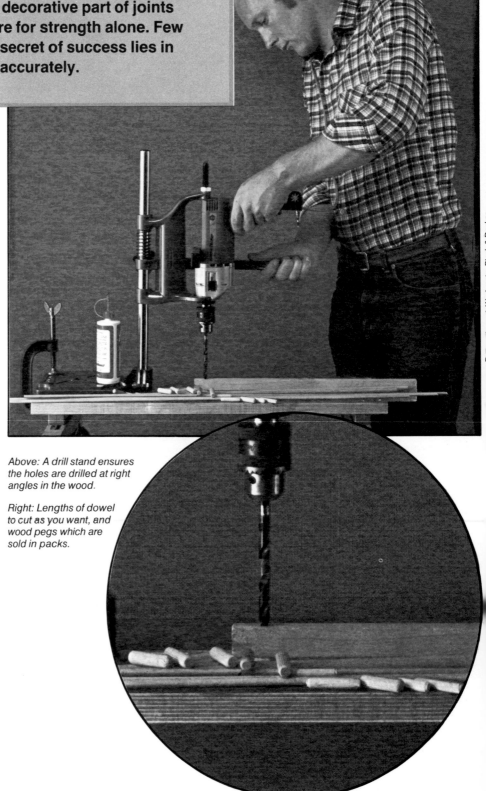

Above: A drill stand ensures the holes are drilled at right angles in the wood.

Right: Lengths of dowel to cut as you want, and wood pegs which are sold in packs.

JOINTS MADE WITH DOWELS

The through dowel joint ready for assembly. The dowels are firmly embedded in one piece and will pass right through the other.

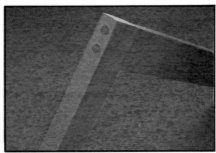

When assembled the through joint shows up the dowels. Cut them a little longer so after cramping they can be planed flush with the wood.

The stopped joint has dowels in one piece which will go into the other far enough to ensure rigidity but won't be seen on the other side.

A close fit for the finished stopped joint. When drilling the holes they should be slightly deeper than the dowel to hold any excess adhesive.

Mitred dowel joints can be tricky to make as you can't use the 'pin' method (see next page) for marking up because of the 45° angle.

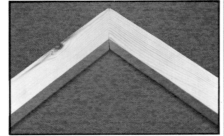

The hidden strength in this joint is the two different lengths of dowel. Very effective for frames where you don't want reinforcement to be seen.

A halving or half lap joint made at a corner can either be glued and screwed or, if it will be on show, made secure with dowels which fit into holes placed like spots on a dice.

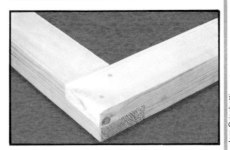

The completed dowelled halving joint gives one overall look of wood. The same effect can be achieved by topping countersunk screws with dowel pellets cut from an offcut of the wood.

Jem Grischotti

Ready Reference

BUYING DOWELS

Dowel lengths from timber merchants are sold in these diameters:
● 6mm (¼in)
● 9mm (⅜in)
● 12mm (½in)
Larger diameters – 16mm (⅝in) and 19mm (¾in) – can be softwood rather than hardwood.

TIPS TO SAVE TIME

● Buying grooved dowel saves you having to groove it yourself.
● **Pre-packed dowels** are bought in packs containing short lengths of diameters such as 4mm, 8mm and 10mm. They are fluted (finely grooved) and the ends are chamfered.
● **Dowel pellets** finish woodwork where screws have been countersunk. They should fit the hole exactly but be fractionally deeper so they can be planed back when the adhesive has set. Buy pre-packed, or cut your own from offcuts using a special plug attachment for an electric drill.

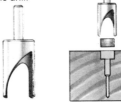

TOOLS

● **try-square and marking gauge** are essential for accurate marking up
● **electric drill** held in a drill stand for perfectly plumb holes
● **mallet** for tapping in the dowels
● **block or ordinary plane** for finishing a through joint
● **cramp** to hold the joint until the adhesive has set

CHAMFER DOWEL ENDS

If cutting your own dowels rub the cut ends with medium-grade glasspaper to give a gentle chamfer (it makes the dowel go in more easily).

Apply woodworking adhesive to the meeting faces of the wood as well as brushing or squirting it into the holes.

MARKING UP

1 *With wood that's rectangular or square in section, use a marking gauge to make the central line on the edge where the dowels will go.*

3 *Lightly tap small panel pins into the wood at the two centre points. Snip off their heads leaving about 3mm (1/8in) protruding.*

2 *Divide this central line into three, then draw two lines at right angles.*

4 *Holding the second piece of timber firmly against a bench hook or edge of the try-square, press the pins in to mark the drill positions (inset).*

Leave the pins slightly proud of the surface and snip off their heads with pliers. Bring the two pieces of wood together in the correct joint position, and the heads of the pins will mark where the holes are to be bored in the second piece of timber. Remove the pins with pincers before drilling.

Where you are joining two horizontal rails to an upright at a corner, you should stagger the holes, otherwise the dowels will clash inside the upright.

Cutting holes

Holes for the dowels can be made either with a hand drill or an electric drill. In each case, obviously, the bit used must match the diameter of the dowel. The main difficulty is that you must ensure the bit is truly at right angles to the timber you are drilling, or a dowel that protrudes from one hole will not fit snugly into the hole in the matching timber.

You can use an electric drill held in a drill stand to guarantee that the bit is truly at right angles to the timber. Or where the timber is too large for this you can use a dowelling jig to ensure accuracy. Where you are cutting a through dowel joint, you can avoid this problem by cramping both pieces of wood together in a vice and boring through both.

For stopped joints, the hole you bore should be slightly deeper than the depth to which the dowel penetrates, to leave a small reservoir for any excess glue that is not squeezed out along the groove. A depth gauge ensures this. Various types for both hand and electric drills are available but you can improvise by making your own. Either stick a bit of tape on the bit's shank, carefully positioned so that the distance between its lower edge and the end of the drill exactly equals the depth of the hole required. Or you can take a length of timber – 25mm (1in) or 38mm (1½in) square according to the diameter of the dowel – and bore a hole right through its length. Cut this timber to length so that when it is slipped onto the bit's shank, the part of the bit left protruding will cut a hole of the right depth. In both cases you should take your measurement to the cutting end of the drill only – not to any threaded or shaped lead-in point.

For a stopped dowel joint, drill holes so the dowels will penetrate each piece of timber by between one-half and two-thirds of the timber's thickness.

Fixing and finishing dowels

Always check first that the joint is a good fit and is accurately square before applying PVA adhesive. You can then squirt adhesive into the holes, but since you risk applying too much this way, it is better to brush the

this the peg doesn't go right through either piece of timber. This is perhaps the most common dowel joint.

Joint shapes

Dowels can be used to make joints of various types, including L-joints, T-joints and X-joints between rails or boards, and three-way joints between rails and posts, as in furniture-making. They can also be used to reinforce edge-to-edge joints between boards, for example when making a drawer.

Cutting dowels

Cut dowels to length with a fine-toothed tenon saw, holding the dowels in a bench hook or a vice. For through joints, cut one dowel slightly longer than the combined thicknesses of the timbers, so that the ends can be trimmed flush after the joint is assembled. For stopped joints, cut the dowels slightly shorter than the combined depths of the holes into which they fit, and lightly chamfer the ends using glasspaper, a chisel or a proprietary dowel sharpener (which works just like a pencil sharpener).

Dowels need a shallow groove cut in their sides to allow excess adhesive to squeeze out as the joints are assembled. With much

practice you can do this with a chisel or tenon saw (having cramped it lengthways in a workbench), but it is probably easier to buy grooved dowel in the first place – in lengths you cut to size yourself, or for small jobs as pre-packed pegs. If buying pegs make sure you choose ones that correspond with the bit size for your drill.

Marking hole positions

First, use a try-square to check that the meeting faces or ends of the timber to be joined are cut perfectly square and are of the same thickness. You can then mark the positions for the dowel holes. Set a marking gauge to half the width of the timber, and mark a line down the middle of the end of one length of timber. Determine exactly where on this line the centre of the holes will be – the ideal is that they should be from 25mm (1in) to 50mm (2in) apart and never nearer than 19mm (3/4in) from the edges. Using a try-square, draw lines across the gauge line to mark the exact centres of the holes.

To mark matching holes in corresponding positions on the second piece of timber use the following method to ensure accuracy. Drive small panel pins into the first piece at the positions you've marked for the holes.

Jem Grischotti

DRILLING HOLES

1 *To ensure that holes will be in exactly opposite positions on a through joint, drill both pieces of wood at the same time.*

2 *The depths you have to go to for a dowel joint can be marked on the bit with a piece of tape, allowing a little extra at both ends for glue.*

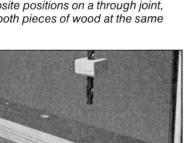

3 *Another way of making sure you don't go too deep is by making a depth gauge from a scrap of timber. Or you can buy a proprietary gauge.*

4 *A dowelling jig has holes for different sized bits. When you cramp it over the wood use spare timber to prevent the screw marking the wood.*

adhesive onto the dowel before tapping it into place with a mallet — you can use a hammer but you should protect the dowel with a block of wood. You should also apply adhesive to the meeting faces of the timber.

The glued joints should be cramped until the adhesive has set.

With through joints and halving joints, you now saw off the bulk of the protruding dowel and use a block plane to trim the end flush. You can use an ordinary plane for this, but it must be set for a very fine cut. Smooth off any remaining roughness with glasspaper.

If using dowel pellets, hit them into place over the countersunk screws (with the ones you've cut yourself make sure the grain follows that of the wood). Plane off excess after the adhesive has dried.

MAKING THE JOINT

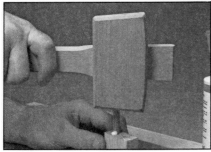

1 *First check that the dowel fits snugly, but not too tightly. Then apply adhesive and gently tap it into place with a mallet.*

2 *After cramping to allow the adhesive to set, finish off a through joint by planing away the excess along the side of the wood.*

Ready Reference

RULES FOR DRILLING HOLES
● make them the same diameter as the dowels
● they should be a little deeper than the dowel's length
● slightly countersink these where the pieces of wood meet

TIP: DOWELLING JIG
With a drill use a dowelling jig so the holes will be straight and square.

WHAT CAN GO WRONG?
The most common problems are:
● the dowels being too tight. Forcing the joint together causes the wood to split – so always check the fit first
● the joint being forced out of alignment because the holes were drilled out of line with one another – always check the alignment before finally applying the adhesive

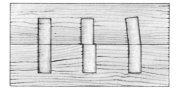

MITRED DOWEL JOINTS
● use a mitre box for accuracy
● place mitred pieces together in a cramp and mark them at the same time
● the dowel at the outer corner should be shorter than the one at the inner corner

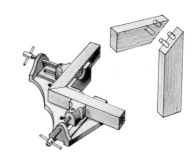

HOUSING JOINTS

If you're putting together a bookcase or installing shelves in any other sort of furniture, then housing joints are the ones to use for attaching the shelves to the uprights. Here's how to make them.

Housing joints are very useful in constructing drawers, door frames and partition walls, among other things: but they're indispensable for fixing shelves neatly into uprights. The joint gets its name because the end of the shelf fits into a square-bottomed channel or 'housing' across the upright. A basic housing joint is as simple as that, and very easy to cut and assemble. What's more, it's ideal for supporting the weight of a shelf and its contents – it resists twisting, and it looks much more professional than the metal brackets or other fittings which can do the same job.

Such fittings are readily available and often easy to use, but if your design is modern, they'll tend to spoil its clean lines; and if it's traditional, they'll naturally be inappropriate. They will never give the unobtrusive and craftsmanlike finish which you can obtain from carefully designed and made housing joints.

Types of housing joint

There are a few variations, and each has its own purpose. A 'stopped' housing joint is completely invisible; you can't see the connection between shelf and upright at all, because (unlike the basic 'through' housing joint) its housing stops about 20mm (¾in) short of the front of the upright. You can also cut out a step in the front of the shelf to allow it to fit flush with the upright just as in a through housing joint, and so get the best of both worlds.

A 'barefaced' housing joint is a little more complicated. You still slot the shelf into the upright – but this time you also cut away a step or 'rebate' across the end of the shelf to form a sort of tongue (with one 'bare face'). So the housing into which it fits has to be correspondingly narrower than the shelf thickness. This type of joint is used at corners, where you can't cut an ordinary housing; and its stepped shape helps to keep the structure rigid. It can also be used with the rebate in the upright where you want unbroken woodgrain across the top surface of the horizontal.

Strongest of all is the dovetail housing

joint. For this one, the housing has sloping (undercut) sides, and the end of the shelf is shaped to fit – which means it can't be pulled out sideways. This is an attraction where you expect furniture to come in for rough treatment, (eg, being dragged across the floor). However, it's tricky to cut without power-tool assistance, and in practice the do-it-yourselfer will seldom find it really necessary.

It's worth saying here that even the best-made housing joint is only as strong as the shelf. If you're planning shelf storage, you have to think about what the shelf is made of, its thickness, its length and how much weight you want it to carry. A thin shelf bends easily, and it's unwise to try to span a gap of more than 1,200mm (4ft), at the very most, without some support in the middle. Even then, a full load of books will cause sagging.

Making a housing joint

Even with hand tools, housing joints are among the easiest to cut. For a basic through housing joint, you don't need to touch the shelf at all. You just mark out the position of the housing in the upright, cut down the housing sides with a tenon saw, and pare

away the waste with a chisel and wooden mallet (see pages 32-35 for details). The only difficulty, as in all carpentry, is to make sure that your marking, sawing and chiselling are always careful and accurate.

A stopped housing takes a little longer to cut, but only because you need to hollow out its stopped end first, to make sawing easier. You may also need to remove a small notch or 'shoulder' from the shelf, which is easily done with a tenon saw and perhaps a chisel too.

For a barefaced housing joint, the housing is cut in the same way as a basic housing. Cutting the rebate in the shelf is another job for tenon saw and chisel.

Using power tools

A power router is an integral tool with a chuck that accepts a wide range of special bits for cutting grooves and mouldings quickly and accurately. It saves a lot of time when making housing joints, and eliminates both sawing and chiselling. Or you can use a circular saw, setting it for a very shallow cut and running it across the upright where you want the housing to be – first clamping on a batten to act as a guide. Because the saw-

Jem Grischotti

40

BASIC HOUSING JOINT

1 Use your knife and try-square to square a mark across the inner face of the upright where the top of the shelf is to go.

2 Measure up the full shelf thickness with a carpenter's rule or a flexible tape measure. As always, try for absolute accuracy.

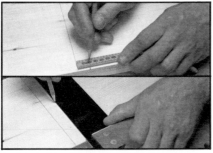

3 Mark this distance on the upright, working down from the first line to give the housing width; square the mark across in pencil only.

4 Place the shelf between the two lines to check them. If necessary, re-draw the second. When that's right, go over it with knife and try-square.

5 Use a rule to set your marking gauge to 1/3 the thickness of the upright, which is the usual depth of a housing for a strong and rigid joint.

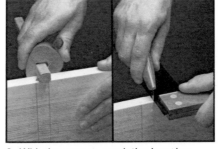

6 With the gauge, mark the housing depth on the upright's edges. Then use a knife to square the marks for the housing sides to depth across the edges.

7 When cutting the sides to depth, cramp on a batten to prevent the saw from wandering sideways.

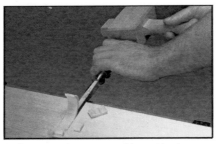

8 Remove the waste with a chisel, working from both ends on long housings. Pare along the sides if necessary to clean them up.

Ready Reference

WHICH HOUSING GOES WHERE

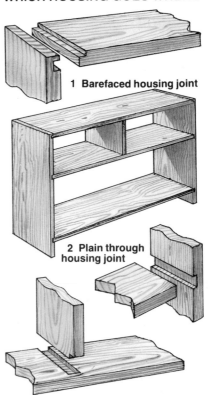

1 Barefaced housing joint

2 Plain through housing joint

3 Stopped housing joint with shoulder

THE TOOLS YOU'LL NEED

A tenon saw: for cutting the sides of housings, rebates and shoulders.
A bevel-edged chisel: the same width as the housing, plus a wooden mallet.
A hand router: is useful for smoothing the bottom of the housing.
Marking gauge, knife, pencil and try-square: for accurate setting-out.

POWER TOOL OPTIONS

A power router: ideal for cutting all types of housing quickly and easily.

A circular saw will cut an ordinary housing very well – but you'll need to make several passes with it across the timber to cut the housing.

Jem Grischotti

STOPPED HOUSING WITH SHOULDER

1 *After marking out the housing on the upright (except on the front edge), mark where it stops, about 19-25mm (³/4-1in) inside the front edge.*

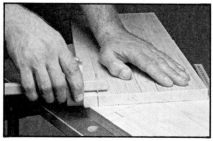

2 *With the marking gauge still at the same setting, mark the shoulder depth across the shelf end and a little way down each of its faces.*

3 *Set the gauge to ¹/3 the thickness of the upright, and mark the housing depth on its back edge only. Bring the side marks down to meet it.*

4 *Use the same setting to mark the shoulder width on the front edge and both faces of the shelf, meeting the marks you've made for the depth.*

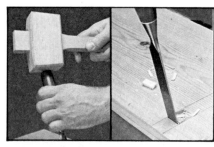

5 *Roughly chisel out the first 25mm (1in) or so of the stopped end of the housing – across the grain and up to.the sides, then back towards the end.*

6 *Cut the sides of the housing with a tenon saw. You'll need to use short careful strokes so as not to bang against its inner end.*

7 *Clear out the housing with a mallet and chisel, inching forwards at an angle if the chisel won't reach all the way in when held flat.*

8 *Saw down into the front edge of the shelf until you reach the marked depth of the shoulder, being careful not to overshoot.*

9 *Chisel into the endgrain to remove the waste and complete the shoulder; or you can use a saw – but again, don't cut too deep.*

blade is narrower than the housing you're cutting out, you'll need to make several parallel, overlapping cuts.

Putting it together

When you assemble the joint before glueing, to see if it fits, you may think that it's too tight and you need to pare away wood from the housing or the shelf.

But be sure not to overdo this – and be careful where you remove it from. A shaving off the wrong place can allow the end of the shelf to rise or fall so that it's no longer level.

If, on the other hand, the joint turns out to be very loose, you'll need thin slivers of wood or veneer to pack it out.

For maximum tightness, strength and squareness, a housing joint should really be glued, then cramped together while the adhesive sets. Where a shelf or shelves fit between a pair of uprights, as usually happens, your best plan is to glue and cramp the whole structure up at once, so as to get it all square in one go. Use sash cramps (long bars of steel with two adjustable jaws) and simply place the structure between them, with the shelf running along their length, and blocks of scrap wood positioned on the outside of the uprights to protect them from the pressure of the jaws. You'll probably have to borrow or hire the sash-cramps. When using them, you need to

check the structure constantly for squareness, as cramping, unless done correctly, can cause distortion.

You can always reinforce a housing joint by nailing through the outside of the upright and into the endgrain of the shelf, concealing the heads by punching them in and plugging the holes with wood filler.

On the whole, screws are best avoided, since they grip badly in endgrain; but for a chipboard shelf you can use special chipboard screws – or ordinary wood screws each driven into a special plastic plug, or 'bush', which is pressed into a pre-drilled hole in the end of the shelf. You can disguise screwheads with plastic covers.

BAREFACED HOUSING JOINT

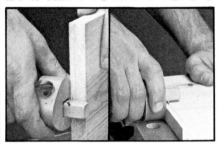

1 At ¹/₃ the shelf thickness, mark the rebate depth along its end and across its edges; likewise mark across the upright's edges and inner face.

2 At ¹/₃ the upright thickness (very likely the same as the shelf thickness), mark your rebate width across the top face and both edges of the shelf.

3 Saw out the rebate depth across the shelf with a tenon saw, using careful strokes to keep it the right side of the line.

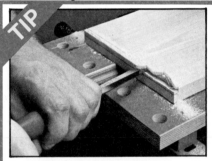

4 Chisel out the rebate width along the endgrain. You'll get a more accurate result if you do it in several goes rather than all at once.

5 Measure the full shelf thickness and set your marking gauge to that measurement by holding it against the rule.

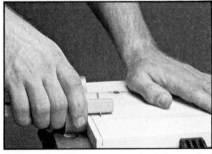

6 Pressing the gauge against the end of the upright, mark across its face and edges where the bottom of the shelf will be positioned.

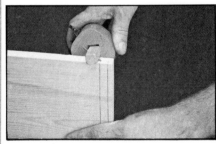

7 Mark the depth of the housing on the back edge of the upright, only ¹/₃ of the way across: any further and you'll weaken the joint.

8 Cut the housing just like the basic one, taking care not to break off the end. After glueing, nail through into the tongue for extra rigidity.

Jem Grischotti

Ready Reference

TIPS FOR BETTER HOUSINGS
● a cramped-on batten is useful as a saw guide
● a third saw-cut down the centre of a wide housing will help the removal of waste

● for short housings in narrow wood, set the piece on edge and chisel vertically for greater accuracy

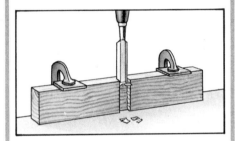

● use a rule or try-square to check that the housing has a level bottom

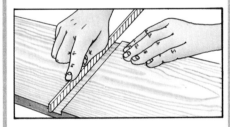

● for pairs of uprights, use the housings in the first to mark out those in the second; this will ensure a level shelf

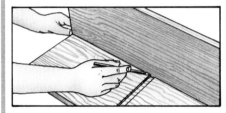

● a chipboard shelf can be secured with chipboard screws driven into special plastic plugs.

CHAPTER 3

BASIC PROJECTS

There are a whole host of comparatively simple woodworking jobs likely to need doing in any household, and completing these successfully will pave the way towards tackling more complicated projects such as simple furniture.

HANGING A DOOR

Ill-fitting doors are irritating to use, ungainly to look at, and ineffective at keeping out draughts. Knowing how to adjust the frame, straighten the door, or, if need be, how to replace it entirely, may sound complicated. In fact, the techniques required – planing, chiselling and sawing – are nothing more than basic carpentry.

Replacing old doors that squeak, stick or let in draughts is one of the quickest ways of improving your home. And whether you're changing a bedroom door, cupboard door or front door, large or small, the techniques are the same. They involve nothing more complex than planing, chiselling and sawing.

Recently there has been greater awareness of how doors can make or mar a house, and there are now many different styles to choose from. There are, however, only two basic types for rooms or entrances to houses: the traditional panelled door, and the flush door. Though plain, the flush offers a wide choice of finishes – including adding your own mouldings to make up panels!

Doors described as external are thicker, heavier and tougher, more resistant to weather and burglars. Unless you want to soundproof a room, you'll only waste money if you buy an external door for use inside the house where a lighter one will do – and you might even damage a light partition wall by overloading it with a door that's too heavy.

Sometimes local building regulations insist on a fire-resistant internal door: normally where it opens onto the stairwell of a modern three-storey building (or an old two-storey one with a loft conversion), and where it separates your home from a built-on garage. If you have to put these in you have to make adjustments to the frame and change the hinges as well.

Look first at the frame

Before you do anything at all about a new door, you should take a long hard look at the frame in which you intend hanging it. If it's badly damaged or out of square by more than 25mm (1in) you should consider replacing it altogether. This is not as difficult as it sounds, for if you shop around you can find sections of framing, and even complete frames, ready shaped to blend with every style and accommodate every type of door.

On the other hand, the frame may only need surface blemishes repaired to be in good enough shape to take the new door. Taking off the old door may prove tricky if the screws are stuck fast; but, once it's done,

Jem Grischotti: Sapele plywood door: W H Newson

you can make good the frame with wood or cellulose filler so it will look as good as new when painted. It makes life easier if you can reuse the old hinge recesses, but if they're too chewed-up you'll need to pin and glue in bits of wood (as with other large holes) before filling them.

You may have to renew the doorstop – (draught-excluder) the part which the front of the door actually hits when it closes – if the new door is a different thickness from the old or won't lie flush with the outside frame. You can buy suitable planed wood in various thicknesses. If the old doorstop isn't removable (it may be made all in one with the frame) you'll need to add another piece, flush with it, before attaching a new doorstop bead. This should only be lightly nailed until the door is hung, for its position may have to be altered.

The hanging process

Even once you've got the frame right, and you've chosen your new door for the exact size of opening, it may still not quite fit. This could mean offering it up to the door-frame, marking it with a pencil and planing or sawing it down to make adjustments. As this can be time-consuming, and demanding on the arms, it's best to work on it next to the place where it'll be hung. Panel doors, especially, are heavy; and another pair of hands can be very useful at strategic points – for example, when the hinges need to be held exactly in the right place to be screwed in.

Chocks and wedges are also very handy for holding the door steady when planing and chiselling, and for supporting the door in the opening when you're marking it so the clearance is right above and below. Luckily these are made from scraps you'll probably have around – small pieces of 3mm (1/8in) hardboard, for example, can be stacked to give the right thickness for the space that should be above and below the door.

Ready Reference

DOOR TYPES

Panel doors have two vertical stiles and horizontal rails that enclose panels of plywood, solid timber or glass. **Moulded panel doors** have the classic look but each face is shaped from a sheet of wood, fibreboard or plastic which is bonded to a timber frame.

Flush doors have a narrow timber frame around a solid, semi-solid or cellular core. They are faced with plywood or hardboard; many have thin lipping; some are reinforced where hinges and locks are to be fitted. **Fire-resistant doors** are usually flush, but are thicker and more robust. They should be used with hardwood one-piece rebated frames.

HINGE POSITIONS

Internal doors 125mm-150mm (5in-6in) from the top. 175mm-230mm (7in-9in) from the bottom; use 75mm (3in) or 90mm (3½in) steel or brass butt hinges.
Heavy doors or external doors need a third hinge halfway between the other two. Use 100mm (4in) steel or brass butt hinges.

HANGING A DOOR

1 *To check the height, wedge the door against the hinge side of the frame using an offcut that gives the correct clearance at the bottom.*

2 *Mark the area that has to be removed using a try-square for accuracy, then saw off. On a panel door, take equal amounts from top and bottom.*

3 *To check the width, offer the door to the frame against the hinge side and wedge with offcuts that give the correct clearance top and bottom.*

4 *Hold the door steady when planing: saw and chisel a housing in scrap wood and press in a wedge.*

5 *On the latch edge hold your finger under the side of the plane to prevent it rocking. On top and bottom, plane inwards so end grain doesn't splinter.*

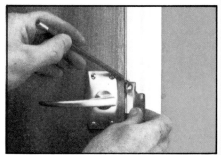

6 *When the door hangs properly, put in the handle. Rub the tongue with chalk, then open and shut it till the frame is marked with keep plate's position.*

Jem Grischotti

Plane: Stanley Tools

Altering dimensions

Enlarging a door, by adding a strip of wood, carries the risk both that it will be too obvious and that it will eventually fall off. But the job can be tackled fairly easily if you first plane the edge of the door straight – keeping your finger at the side of the plane will prevent it falling off the narrow surface. Next, cut your strip to length and plane it to the exact extra size you require – making sure it's a little proud of the door thickness on both sides. Glue and nail it on, and lastly plane it flush with the door face so that when painted it makes an inconspicuous join.

More commonly, however, you'll have to make your door smaller. To take off large amounts you'll need a ripsaw or a powered circular saw; guide it along a batten firmly cramped to the door. After sawing, plane the edge smooth.

Alterations like this are relatively easy on panel doors – but remember to saw similar amounts off both opposite edges to avoid lopsidedness, and be careful not to destroy the joints. A flush door, unless the core is solid, is a very different proposition. A cellular core (made of wood strips laminated together or a honeycomb of kraft paper), a narrow timber frame, and the hardboard or plywood faces are all there to

make the door lightweight. And you risk mutilating any or all of them if you try to alter the width (the height's all right, for you can make a new piece to glue and nail in at the top or bottom if you need to).

So, if you need to take off more than a little, buy a panel door. If you must have a flush door and you can't get one that fits or is about 10mm (⅜in) larger, buy one slightly undersize and add lippings all round to make up the extra height and width.

A fitting finish

Once the door fits the frame you can add the hinges. If you're re-using the existing hinge recesses in the frame, support the door in the opening parallel to the upright and mark on it where their tops and bottoms are. If you're cutting new ones, mark their positions on both door and frame.

Remove the door and, using a try-square and marking-gauge, mark out all new recesses – a hinge should fit flush with both the door edge and the edge of the frame. Carefully chisel out the recess and screw one side of the hinges to the door, checking that they lie neatly in place.

The standard steel or brass butt hinges you need can be bought anywhere. Another option is self-closing 'rising butts' which will

carry the door clear of the floorcovering as it opens, and enable it to be lifted off if necessary without unscrewing them – good if you're redecorating. If the door's not going to have a lot of weight put on it (eg, on a cupboard) light and shorter hinges are best. Choose those that can be surface-mounted and you won't have to chisel out recesses.

Support the door in position again, and fix the hinges to the frame with one screw each. See whether the door swings and closes properly; if not, you can take it off again and make various adjustments to the way the hinges sit in the frame.

The final step is to fill any defects, to sand the door down, and to paint or varnish it. On an external door in particular, make sure you include the top and bottom edges in your treatment (the bottom will have to be dealt with before the door is hung) so that damp cannot penetrate and swell or rot the door.

Hinges should not be painted as this can interfere with the pivot action – and the constant friction of the door will cause the paint to chip anyway. If made of ferrous metal, they can rust, so they should either be primed with a metal or rust-inhibitor primer or coated with a clear lacquer. A non-ferrous metal like brass won't rust but it can tarnish, so clear lacquer is a good idea in this case.

PUTTING ON THE HINGES

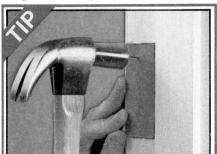

1 If old hinge positions are unusable fill in with 3mm (¹/₈in) hardboard or ply. Nail in place, fill with wood filler.

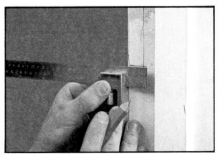

2 Mark up the new hinge positions on the frame using a combination square to get the width measurement right.

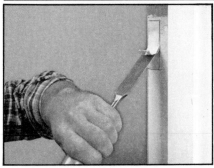

3 Make the first shallow cut with the chisel bevel down. Turn it bevel up to smooth the recess.

4 Wedge the cut-to-fit door in the frame with correct clearance at side, top and bottom. Mark hinge positions.

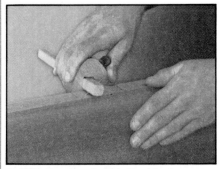

5 With the door held in the block cramp, use a marking gauge, then a try-square to mark recesses.

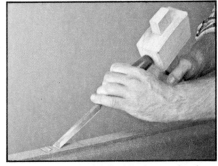

6 Use a 25mm (1in) chisel to make the recess (the hinge must lie flush). Drill holes, screw hinges to door.

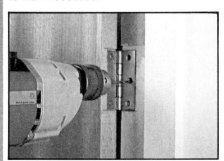

7 Wedge door so the hinges fit the recesses in the frame. Mark, then drill the central holes only.

8 Put screws in central holes, then check that the door closes properly. Adjust if necessary, add other screws.

Jem Grischotti

Ready Reference

TIPS: REMOVING OLD SCREWS
● use a screwdriver that fits the slot exactly (scrape out any paint first)
● if the slot is damaged make a new one with a hacksaw at right-angles to the old
● if the screw won't budge put the screwdriver in the slot and tap it with a hammer or mallet; or heat the screw with a blow-torch, then leave to cool and contract before trying to remove
● the last resort is to drill out the screw using a power drill.

PROBLEM CHECKLIST
If the door swings open or closed by itself the hinges are not taking the weight equally. To do this they must be vertically above each other, so you'll have to move one of them either backwards or forwards across the frame.

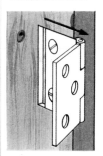

If the door sticks at the lock edge you can either deepen the hinge recesses in the frame or shave a little off the lock edge.

If the door springs open when you shut it the hinge recesses are too deep. Pack the back of the hinge with a piece of cardboard cut to the shape of the recess.

If the bottom of the door isn't parallel with the floor glue and pin on a wedge-shaped lipping. When planed flush and painted it should not be seen.

Remember to make all the adjustments while each hinge is held only by its central screw. Only when the door fits well should you drive in the rest.

FITTING FRONT DOOR FURNITURE

A door looks naked without the right fittings. These make it attractive, and help it do its job. Installing them requires few special skills – just some careful planning and accurate workmanship.

When you buy a door, it comes without 'furniture' – as tradesmen call handles, letter plates, street numbers, knockers and the rest. You'll have to obtain and fit these yourself; there is an immense variety of styles available.

But the most important items, though they don't strictly come under the same heading, are of course locks and latches. First of all, let's run over the most important difference between the two. A latch has a bolt which is kept closed – ie, protruding – by a spring. It's opened by turning a handle, but closes again the instant this is released. A lock, on the other hand, has no spring, and is both opened and closed by a key or handle, or both.

A mortise lock (or latch) is so called because it fits into a deep mortise which you cut in the edge of the door. This far-from-impossible task is the most demanding you're likely to face when fitting out a door: if you can tackle it successfully, you should certainly be equal to the others.

It involves carefully marking the position of the mortise, drilling out the bulk of the waste to the right depth, cleaning up the hole with chisels, and chiselling a larger shallow recess to take the 'forend' of the lock or latch (plus the faceplate which is screwed over it).

You'll also need to cut a hole for the handle spindle, or for the key – drilling in either case, and elongating the keyhole with a padsaw. In the case of a 'sashlock', which combines a lock with a latch, you'll need both these holes.

Moreover, some types of mortise lock have a cylinder mechanism (round, oval or 'dual-profile' – pear-shaped) which passes through the door, so you need a hole for that instead of a keyhole. An ordinary round cylinder needs a sizeable hole, which – like a mortise – will require a bit and brace, or a spade bit in a power drill. Pear-shaped and oval holes can also be made with twist bits; enlarge them with a padsaw or chisel.

The body of a rim lock (or latch), on the other hand, is screwed to the inside of the door. It doesn't require a separate hole for a key or handle. But all except the cheapest rim locks have a cylinder mechanism, which again needs a hole through the door face.

Choosing and fitting locks and latches

For internal doors, a mortise latch – or even just a catch – is usually enough, and it's unobtrusive. An external door needs a latch, too, so you can open it from inside without a key. But, of course, it also needs at least one lock.

In many homes, it carries a cylinder lock called a 'nightlatch', which is halfway to being a latch. A rim nightlatch (the usual type) opens from inside with an integral handle as well as from outside with a key.

Though sprung, it can be retained in the open or closed position with a locking knob on the inside called a snib. However, a nightlatch isn't secure unless it's a 'deadlatch': that is, unless the bolt can be 'deadlocked' immovably in the closed position from outside. This is either done with a key – a procedure usually known as double-locking – or else happens automatically as you close the door. Often the handle can be deadlocked too.

A nightlatch, therefore, should be accompanied by a good mortise lock – preferably a five-lever model.

All locks and latches also have a part which goes on the door jamb – see *Ready Reference*. In the case of mortise fittings, it's a 'striking plate' (usually flat, with a rectangular hole in the centre) which is screwed into a recess cut to fit. More secure types have a sort of box on the plate, which is mortised

into the timber of the door frame. Rim fittings have a 'staple' or 'keep', which again incorporates a box for the tongue, and is usually partly recessed. In both cases, you fit these components after the main lock – closing the door and using the lock itself to mark the right position on the jamb with the aid of a square.

Apart from security and convenience, there's one thing to bear in mind when choosing locks and latches: the construction of the door they are fitted to. A panel door should present no problem unless its stiles (uprights) are exceptionally narrow, in which case you need a special narrow-stile lock or latch. It's wise, too, not to cut mortises in or near timber joints.

A flush door, unless it's solid throughout, will have at least one solid 'lock block' in its largely hollow core – the position or positions of which should be indicated on the door itself. For a secure fixing, it's important that the lock or latch should be sited there and nowhere else.

Fitting a letterplate

Apart from locks and latches, the only item of door furniture whose installation could remotely be described as complicated is a letterplate.

This consists of a metal surround with a hinged and sometimes sprung flap to cover the hole, plus maybe a knocker and/or a handle. Its siting demands some thought.

On a flush door, it too will have to be placed over a special block. A panel door usually affords more choice – but, if there's no rail (cross-member) at a height which is suitable from the point of view of looks and the post-man's comfort, you may have to position it vertically.

If the rear of the plate lies flat against the door and the flap opens outwards, your best plan is to position the plate accurately, lift the flap and draw round the inside to give the outline of your intended hole. Otherwise, you'll have to rely on careful measurement to determine the hole's size and position.

If you have a jigsaw with a blade long enough to pass through the door, cutting the hole is straightforward. If not, you'll probably have to resort to a wide, robust chisel and mallet, perhaps after drilling a series of holes closely spaced round the edge. A padsaw is an alternative, but cutting the hole with it will be a long, hard job.

Finish the inside of the hole (and any mortises) in the same way as the rest of the door to stop moisture from penetrating.

The actual fixing of the plate will be via bolts or machine screws which pass through holes drilled right through the door. If these are overlong, shorten them with a junior hacksaw.

A useful accessory for the inside of the door is a letterbox to catch your post – thus protecting it from children, pets and feet, and saving you from stooping.

Other items

Handles are fitted (and usually sold) separately from the mortise latches which they operate, and almost always in pairs. They're simply screwed to the door face in the same way as the escutcheon plates which cover keyholes. A square-sectioned steel spindle, cut to length if necessary with a hacksaw, passes through the door between handles.

For a sashlock, you can use the type of handle which incorporates a keyhole as well.

A common adjunct, especially for internal doors, is a finger-plate – often decorative – which prevents dirty finger-marks on the door itself. It too is screwed on. Knockers and house numbers are bolted, screwed, nailed, self-adhesive or secured by spikes protruding from the back.

A door viewer – the wide-angle lens which enables you to eye callers without their seeing you – comes in two halves, which are simply screwed together through a single pre-drilled hole.

For doors by which you don't leave the house, such as most back doors, bolts are an extra security measure. The mortise bolt, a simple type of mortise lock usually operated by a serrated key, is better than the traditional 'barrel' or 'tower' bolt, which can be more easily forced open.

FITTING A CYLINDER RIM LOCK

1 Drill a hole for the cylinder after marking its position from the lock's mounting plate, or with a template if one is supplied by the manufacturer.

2 Fit the cylinder and 'rose' through the hole, and mark where to cut off the connecting bar (including any extra length required). Cut with a hacksaw.

3 Screw on the mounting plate, after marking the screw positions (from the fitting or template) and making pilot holes with a drill or bradawl.

4 Insert the cylinder and rose through the hole again, and make sure the connecting bar engages in the slotted pivot in the mounting plate.

5 Insert the connecting screws through the mounting plate and into the threaded lugs in the back of the cylinder, and tighten them to hold it in place.

6 Screw the main body of the lock to the mounting plate via the screws in the case. Fit the keep to the door jamb (see Ready Reference, page 51).

FITTING A LEVER MORTISE LOCK

1 Decide the height at which you want the lock to go, place it on its side on the door edge, get it square, and mark the height of the casing.

2 Set a mortise gauge to the thickness of the casing, centre it on the door edge, and score along. Alternatively, use an ordinary marking gauge.

3 Choose a spade or auger bit that matches the thickness of the casing, and use tape to mark on it the lock's depth from the front of the faceplate.

5 Using chisels, turn the row of holes into a clean, oblong mortise. Insert the lock to test the fit, and shave the mortise further if necessary.

6 Insert the lock casing fully into the mortise (being careful that it doesn't jam) and mark all round the fore-end with a sharp pencil.

7 To chisel the recess for the fore-end and faceplate, first make a series of cuts across the grain. Work very carefully while doing this.

9 Position the faceplate and fore-end back to front, to check whether your recess is the right depth. Chisel it a little deeper if necessary.

10 Position the lock accurately against the face of the door, and mark through the keyhole (plus the spindle hole, if there is one) with a bradawl.

11 Drill the hole (or holes) right through the door, and enlarge the keyhole with a padsaw. Fit an escutcheon plate (keyhole plate) over it.

4 Drill a row of holes to depth, being sure to stay exactly between your height and thickness marks. At all costs, you must keep the drill vertical.

8 Chisel vertically along the sides of the recess (gently, so as not to split the timber) and then remove the waste with the chisel bevel-upwards.

12 Insert the lock again, position the faceplate and drive in the screws. Sometimes the lock and faceplate each have a separate pair of screws.

LETTERPLATES

1 Measure the size of the cutout you'll need to make in the door. It may have to be off-centre – for example, if it must include room for the flap mechanism.

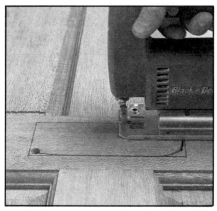

2 Mark your measured rectangle on the door, drill a hole inside the line, and cut it out – using a jigsaw for speed if you have a long enough blade.

3 Finish the hole neatly, and cut out recesses for the threaded lugs if necessary. Then drill holes for the bolts, fit the plate and tighten the nuts.

Ready Reference

DOOR JAMB FIXINGS

For a **mortise** fitting: extend the bolt (if any), push the door to, and mark where each tongue comes on the frame (A). Then square the marks across to the doorstop, position the striking plate, mark round it, and chisel a shallow recess plus one or two mortises (B). Screw the plate on.

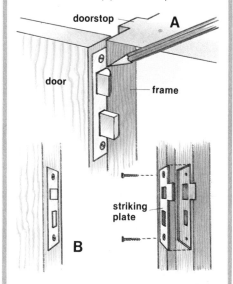

For a **rim** fitting: mark the frame opposite the edges of the case (C). Position the keep, mark round it, chisel a recess and screw it on (D).

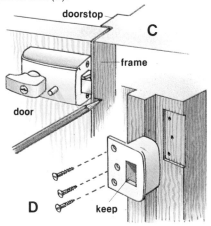

TIP: BEWARE 'HANDING'

Latches (and some handles) only fit one way round. Before buying, know which 'hand' you want. A door that's hinged on your **left** and opens towards you ('anti-clockwise closing') takes a **left-hand** latch with a **left-hand** handle on your side, and a right-hand latch and handle on the other.

SHELVING: THE BASICS

There are lots of ways of putting up shelves. Some systems are fixed, others adjustable – the choice is yours. Here's how both types work, and how to get the best from each.

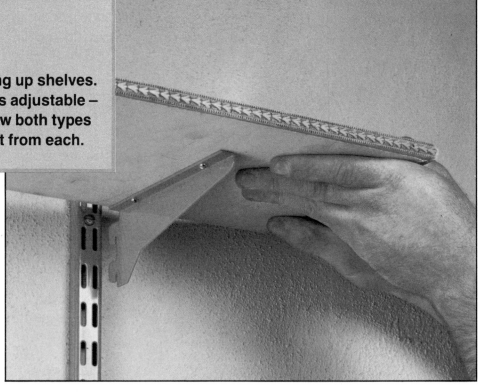

Deciding how much shelving you'll need is always tricky – because, the more shelves you have, the more you'll find to go on them! So it's always wise to add an extra 10 per cent to the specification when you start planning.

Think carefully about what you want to store and display, and try to categorise it by size and weight. The size part is fairly easy. Concentrate first on the depth (from front to back) and length; a collection of paperback books, for instance, might need 3.5m (10ft) of 150mm (6in) deep shelves. Having the shelves a bit deeper than you really need is always worthwhile, and if you add 10 per cent the length should look after itself.

Next, the heights in each grouping will tell you roughly how far apart the shelves must be. Most paperbacks are 175mm (7in) high – allow an extra 25mm (1in) for easy access and removal.

Finally, weight. The trouble here is that, even if you weigh what you'll be storing, you can't translate the result into shelf, bracket and fixing materials or sizes. Instead, think in terms of light, moderately heavy and very heavy. Items such as the TV and stereo, while not especially weighty, are best treated as very heavy, because it would be nothing short of disastrous if a shelf did give way under them!

Shelf design

Where you put the shelves affects the amount of storage you can gain, how you build them, and the overall look of the room itself. This last may not be important in a workshop, for instance, but in a living room, where the shelves may well be the focal point, a bad decision can be serious.

The obvious spot for shelving is against a continuous wall. This offers most scope to arrange the shelves in an interesting and attractive way. An alcove is another possibility. Shelving here is neat, and easily erected; it is a very good way of using an otherwise awkward bit of space. A corner has similar advantages if you make triangular shelves to fit – though they're really only suitable for displaying plants or favourite ornaments.

Planning it out

If appearance matters and you're putting up a lot of shelves, a good way to plan is by making a scale drawing of the whole scheme to see how it looks. Then check for detail. If your TV has an indoor aerial, make sure you have room to adjust it. With stereo systems, ensure the shelf is deep enough to take all the wiring spaghetti at the back. And do think about the heights of the shelves from the floor (see *Ready Reference*).

Finally, make sure you provide adequate support for the shelves and the weight they'll be carrying. There is no very precise method of gauging this, but you won't go wrong if you remember that for most household storage a shelf needs support at least every 750mm (30in) along its length. This will usually be enough even with chipboard, which is the weakest of shelving materials. But bowing may still be a problem, so for items in the 'very heavy' category it's advisable to increase the number of supports by reducing the space between them.

Which material?

Chipboard is usually the most economical material, and if properly supported is strong enough for most shelving. It can be fairly attractive, too, since you can choose a type with a decorative wood veneer or plastic finish. These come in a variety of widths – most of them designed with shelving in mind.

Natural timber, though more costly and sometimes prone to warping, is an obvious alternative. You may have difficulty obtaining some timber in boards over 225mm (9in) wide, but narrower widths are readily available. For wider shelves, another way is to make up the shelf width from narrower pieces. An easy method is to leave gaps between the lengths and brace them with others which run from front to back on the underside, forming a slatted shelf.

Blockboard and plywood (see pages 14-16) are also worth considering. They are both a lot stronger than chipboard and have a more attractive surface which can be painted or varnished without trouble. However, in the thicknesses you need – at least 12mm (½in) – plywood is relatively expensive; blockboard is cheaper, and chipboard cheaper still. All these man-made boards need to have their edges disguised to give a clean finish. An easy yet effective way to do this is just to glue and pin on strips of timber moulding or 'beading'. Also remember that the cheapest way to buy any of these boards is in large sheets (approximately 2.4m x 1.2m/8ft x 4ft), so it's most economical to plan your shelves in lengths and widths that can be cut from a standard size sheet.

Shelves needn't be solid, though. If you want them extra-thick, for appearance or strength, you can make them up from a timber frame covered with a thin sheet material. Hardboard is cheap, but thin plywood gives a more attractive edge; alternatively use a timber edging strip.

BRACKET SHELVING

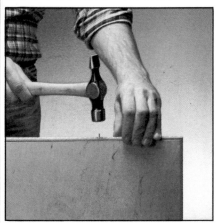

1 *If your shelves are of man-made board, a good way to give them neat edges is to pin on decorative 'beading', mitred at the corners.*

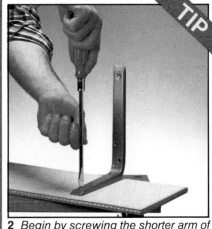

2 *Begin by screwing the shorter arm of the bracket to the shelf. Position it squarely and in such a way that the shelf will lie snugly against the wall.*

3 *Using a spirit level as a guide, mark a pencil line along the wall at the height where you want the top of the shelf to be positioned.*

4 *Hold the shelf, complete with brackets, against this line, and mark with a pencil through the screw holes in the brackets, so you know where to drill.*

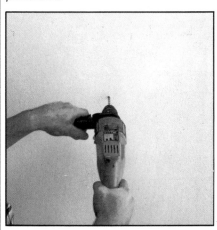

5 *Drill holes in the wall with a power drill, using a masonry bit if necessary, and being sure to keep the drill straight. Then insert plastic plugs.*

6 *Hold the shelf in position, insert one screw in each bracket and tighten it halfway; then insert the others and tighten the whole lot up.*

Ready Reference

PLANNING SHELVES

When you design storage, plan ahead and think about *how* you're going to use it.

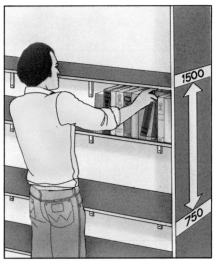

Height. Keep everyday items well within reach. That means between 750 and 1500mm (30 and 60in) off the ground.
Depth. Shelves that are deepest (from front to back) should be lower, so you can see and reach to the back.
Spacing. An inch or two over the actual height of the objects means you can get your hand in more easily.

HOW TO SPACE BRACKETS

Space brackets according to the shelf thickness. Heavy loads (left) need closer brackets than light loads (right).

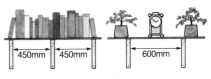

12mm (½in) chipboard

12mm (½in) plywood
19mm (¾in) chipboard

19mm (¾in) plywood

ADJUSTABLE SHELVING

1 Metal uprights come in a range of sizes, but occasionally they may need shortening. If so, you can easily cut them down with a hacksaw.

2 After using your level to mark the height for the tops of the uprights, measure along it and mark out the spacings between them.

3 Hold each of the uprights with its top at the right height, and mark through it onto the wall for the position of the uppermost screw hole only.

4 Remove the upright, drill the hole and plug it if necessary. Then replace the upright, and fit the screw – but don't tighten it completely.

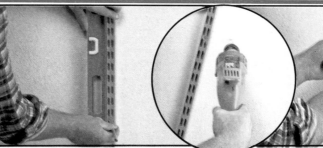

5 With the upright loose, hold a level against it and adjust it till it's vertical. Then mark through it for the other screw positions.

6 Hold the upright aside and drill the other holes. Plug them, insert the screws and tighten them all up – not forgetting the topmost one.

7 Now you can screw the bracket to the shelf, aligning it correctly and taking particular care over how it lines up at the back edge.

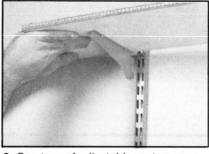

8 One type of adjustable system uses brackets with lugs at the back. It's easiest to let these lugs project behind the shelf when screwing on brackets.

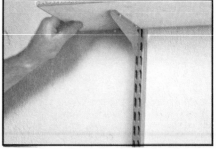

9 The lugs simply hook into the slots in the uprights. Changing the shelf height is just a matter of unhooking them and moving them up or down.

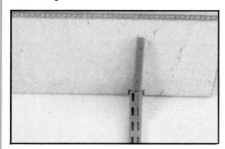

10 If you want the back edge of the shelf right against the wall, notch it with a tenon saw and chisel to fit round the upright. Inset the bracket on the shelf.

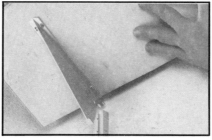

11 The channel system is different. First of all, you engage the bracket's upper lug in the channel and slide it down, keeping the lower one clear.

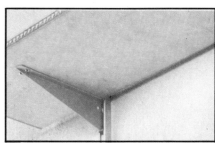

12 When you reach the position you want, level the shelf and the bracket, so as to slide its lower lug into one of the pairs of slots down the upright.

Fixing shelves

The simplest method of fixing shelves is directly to the wall, using brackets. L-shaped metal brackets of various sizes and designs are available everywhere – some plain and functional, some with attractive lacquered or enamelled finishes. It's just a question of choosing ones about 25mm (1in) less than the shelf depth, spacing them the right distance apart and screwing them to both shelf and wall.

If you're filling up your shelves with books, the support brackets won't be seen. But if you're using the shelves for ornaments, the brackets will be visible, so choose a style that blends. Alternatively, you can make up your own brackets from two pieces of timber butt-jointed into an L shape and braced with a diagonal strut or triangular block.

The fixing technique is the same either way. First you draw a line on the wall where the shelf is to go, using a spirit level. Next, fix the brackets to the shelf and put the whole assembly up against the line. Mark on to the wall through the pre-drilled screw holes in the brackets; then take the shelf away and drill holes in the wall, filling each with a plastic plug. Lastly, drive in one screw through each bracket; then insert the rest and tighten them all up.

Because the accuracy of this method relies largely on your ability to hold the shelf level against your line, you may find it easier to work the other way round. By fixing the brackets to the wall along the guide line, you can then drop the shelf into place and screw up into it through the brackets. This works, but you must position the brackets with great care, and avoid squeezing them out of position as you screw them into the wall. That isn't always easy. For one thing, many brackets don't have arms which meet at a neat right angle. They curve slightly, which makes it hard to align the top of the shelf-bearing arm with the line on the wall.

Making a firm fixing

Remember that the strength of all brackets depends partly on the length of their arms (particularly the one fixed to the wall) and partly on the strength of your fixing into the wall. The longer the wall arm in proportion to the shelf arm, the better; but it's also important to use adequate screws – 38mm (1½in) No 8s or 10s should do – and to plug the wall properly. In a hollow partition wall you really must make sure you secure the brackets to the wall's wooden framework and not just to the cladding. Even if you use plasterboard plugs or similar devices, a lot of weight on the shelf will cause the brackets to come away from the cladding and possibly damage the wall.

Of course, there is a limit to how much weight the brackets themselves will take.

Under very wide shelves they may bend. With shelves that have heavy items regularly taken off and dumped back on, and shelves used as desk-tops, worktops and the like, the movement can eventually work the fixings loose. In such cases it's best to opt for what's called a cantilevered shelf bracket. Part of this is set into the masonry to give a very strong fixing indeed. Details of its installation vary from brand to brand, but you should get instructions when you buy.

Alcove shelving

All proprietary brackets are expensive. However, for alcove shelving there's a much cheaper alternative, and that is to use battens screwed to the wall. All you do is fix a 50 x 25mm (2 x 1in) piece of softwood along the back of the alcove, using screws driven into plastic plugs at roughly 450mm (18in) centres. Then screw similar ones to the side walls, making sure that they line up with the first. In both cases, getting the battens absolutely level is vital. In fact, it's best to start by drawing guidelines using a spirit level as a straight edge.

A front 'rail' is advisable where the shelf spans a wide alcove and has to carry a lot of weight. But there's a limit to what you can do. With a 50 x 25mm (2 x 1in) front rail and battens, all on edge, 1.5m (5ft) is the safe maximum width.

A front rail has another advantage because, as well as giving man-made boards a respectably thick and natural look, it also hides the ends of the side battens. So does stopping them short of the shelf's front edge and cutting the ends at an angle.

The shelf can be screwed or even just nailed to the battens to complete the job.

Movable shelves

Unfortunately, both brackets and battens have one big drawback: once they're fixed, they're permanent. So you might consider an adjustable shelving system which gives you the chance to move shelves up and down. Such systems consist of uprights, screwed to the wall, and brackets which slot into them at almost any point down the length.

There are two main types. In one, brackets locate in vertical slots in the uprights. The other has a continuous channel down each upright. You can slide brackets along it and lock them at any point along the way, where they stay put largely because of the weight of the shelf. With both types, brackets come in standard sizes suitable for shelf widths, and there's a choice of upright lengths to fulfil most needs.

Many proprietary shelving systems of this sort include a number of accessories to make them more versatile. These include book ends, shelf clips and even light fittings.

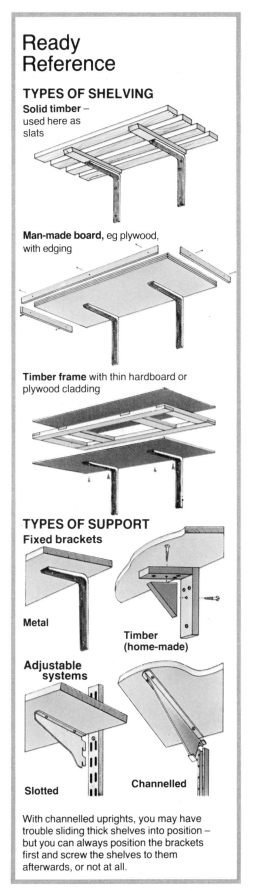

Ready Reference

TYPES OF SHELVING

Solid timber – used here as slats

Man-made board, eg plywood, with edging

Timber frame with thin hardboard or plywood cladding

TYPES OF SUPPORT

Fixed brackets

Metal

Timber (home-made)

Adjustable systems

Slotted

Channelled

With channelled uprights, you may have trouble sliding thick shelves into position – but you can always position the brackets first and screw the shelves to them afterwards, or not at all.

PANELLING WALLS WITH TIMBER

Natural timber panelling can transform your walls like no other material, bringing warmth and atmosphere to even the least promising room. Yet the technique of installing it is easily mastered.

Cladding interior walls with natural timber is an age-old decorative technique. Nowadays, it's most popular in the form of narrow boards.

They look extremely attractive and have other advantages too. Panelling is a perfect cover-up for plaster in poor condition, and for lumpy walls often found in older houses. Moreover, it has excellent insulation properties.

If you plan to panel one or more of your walls, go and see what the timber merchant has to offer. Cedar, ramin, mahogany and meranti are all possible woods for the purpose. But by far the most popular is 'knotty pine' – softwood of various species with knots that would be unacceptable in ordinary joinery work. It's available from almost all suppliers. The commonest size is 100 × 12mm (4 × ½in), in lengths up to 3m (about 10ft). Width and thickness, as usual, are nominal: since the timber is planed smooth, these dimensions will actually be smaller.

Most boards used for panelling have a protruding tongue along one edge, and a groove in the other, so that each piece fits into the next. Quite often both outer edges are chamfered, forming attractive V-shaped grooves when the boards are interlocked; hence the name 'TGV' — tongued, grooved and V-jointed.

Boards with concave faces are also obtainable as in 'shiplap', which has one edge rebated to overlap the thin edge of the next board. It's almost always used horizontally. Horizontal cladding creates the optical illusion that the wall is wider than it really is: vertical cladding makes it seem taller.

Battening the wall

All cladding is normally fitted onto 50 × 25mm (2 × 1in) rough sawn softwood battens, which are themselves nailed or screwed to the existing solid wall.

They're unnecessary if the wall is a hollow partition construction which is framed with vertical studs and horizontal noggins to which the cladding can be nailed. But be quite sure you're nailing through into the timber frame and not just into its covering, which is usually plasterboard and thus won't hold the nails well.

If cladding the inside of an external wall, you can keep out damp with a vapour barrier such as polythene sheeting. You simply place it under the battens before you fix them to the wall. Even if you don't include a vapour barrier, it's wise to treat the battens and the back of the cladding with wood preservative, in case condensation leads to rot. And the job also offers a unique opportunity to fight heat loss, for you can easily place insulating material between the wall and the cladding.

Buying the timber

If the shop prefers to supply panelling in assorted lengths, it will be cheaper to buy it that way, rather than in the exact dimensions you want; but many suppliers now sell TGV in pre-cut bundles, containing timber in lengths of 1800mm (just under 6ft), 2400mm (8ft) or 3000mm (10ft).

To work out how many lengths of vertical cladding you need, divide the wall width by the board width – remembering that the board's face will be only about 90mm (3½in) wide if it's nominally 100mm (4in).

For horizontal cladding, divide the wall height by the board width. For board length, just measure the wall – though on wide walls you may have to fit boards end-to-end.

Before buying boards always check them – especially knotty pine – for splits, loose knots, discolouration and twisting. Don't be afraid to reject bad ones.

Battens should run at right angles to cladding; in the case of diagonal panelling, either vertically or horizontally. They should be spaced about 600mm (24in) apart, except that the first and last in a row of vertical battens should be at either end of the wall. And you'll always need battens next to doors, windows and other fitments, and under any butt joints between the ends of boards.

Buy your cladding at least two weeks before use, and keep it inside the house. This is because your home will be warmer than the place the timber has been stored. The heat will reduce the amount of moisture in the wood, which will make it shrink. You should therefore give this time to happen *before* you fix the cladding in place; otherwise it will shrink afterwards. That may result in tongues coming out of grooves, which will leave unsightly gaps.

As soon as you get the cladding home, lay it flat on the floor (provided the floor is dry) in small piles, with boards face to face. Leave it for a fortnight, shuffling the boards around every few days. Don't attempt to dry them out artificially, as this will be sure to warp them.

FIXING THE BATTENS

For a professional finish, the wall battens to which the cladding boards are fixed should not follow any undulations in the surface. You can test whether your wall surface is uneven by holding a timber straight edge against it horizontally and vertically; you will then be able to see at a glance where lumps or hollows fall. The examples here are for vertical cladding; the hollows are exaggerated.

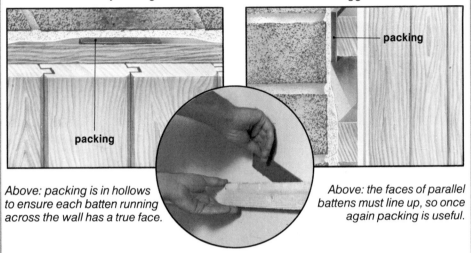

packing

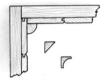

packing

Above: packing is in hollows to ensure each batten running across the wall has a true face.

Above: the faces of parallel battens must line up, so once again packing is useful.

Inset: hardboard is an ideal packing material

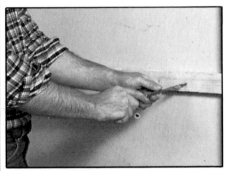

1 Fix battens with No 8 screws, 600mm (2ft) apart and 63mm (2½in) long – long enough to go through the plaster. Masonry nails are an alternative.

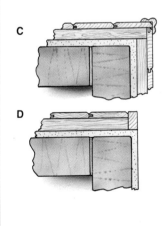

2 To form a neat link between the bottom of an existing cornice and the top edge of the cladding, use scotia moulding. Butt the cladding up to it.

Fixing the cladding

If the wall is solid, use masonry nails, or screws in plastic plugs, to fix the battens. Take care not to drive them into cables or pipes; be especially careful round electrical fittings. The important thing is to get the battens at a constant level, both vertically and horizontally. Insert pieces of hardboard, plywood or scrap timber behind them where necessary. On a slightly concave wall, for example, you'll have to pack behind the centres of the battens to get them truly vertical, whereas on a convex wall you'll have to pack behind the top and bottom of each batten.

Then position a piece of cladding as the first in the row – usually against a side wall (against the ceiling for horizontal cladding). If the side wall isn't vertical, or is uneven, you'll have to scribe the board – see page 370 — and cut to the resulting pencil line.

Place the first board so the tongue is ready to fit into the next piece, and nail the board to the battens. Another method, which avoids your having to conceal the nail heads, is to fix this first board in position over the battens using a contact adhesive. This will hold it firmly in place straight away without nailing or cramping. (Note: no other adhesive will achieve this.)

You can nail the next board through its tongue, angling the nails inwards. The heads will be covered by the groove in the following board. Use this 'secret' nailing for all the other boards too, except the last. With cladding other than tongue-and-groove, such as shiplap, there is no tongue; so secret nailing means

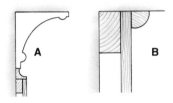

FIXING THE CLADDING

1 *Hold the first board vertically against the side wall – or its skirting, if the cladding goes that far down. Lightly pin the board to the battens.*

2 *Scribe the board with a pencil pressed against a block of wood 50mm (2in) wide and run down the side wall. The mark follows the wall profile.*

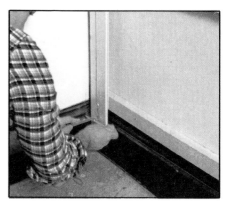

3 *For a neat result, scribe around the shape of the skirting too. A second pencil can take the place of scrap timber as a guide for this.*

6 *Then fix the first board to the battens permanently by driving 25mm (1in) panel pins through its face. (On stud partitions you'll need 38mm/1½in pins.)*

7 *Before nailing each subsequent board, ensure a snug fit by tapping an offcut held against it. Check with a spirit level, and adjust it if necessary.*

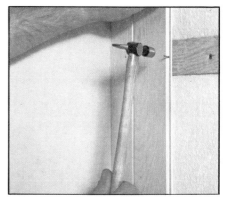

8 *Nail at an angle through the board's tongue – but not too near the end, or you'll split the wood. The groove in the next board will cover the pin heads.*

placing the nails where the rebated edge of the next board will cover their heads.

Repeat the fitting and nailing process right across the wall, checking that each board is still vertical (or horizontal). When you get to the end, it's unlikely that the last board will fit exactly, so you'll probably have to scribe it.

Even once you've cut it to shape, you may have trouble squeezing it in if you've already nailed all the other boards in position. There are two ways of dealing with this. One is to fit the last three or four boards at the same time, inserting the tongues in the grooves and then springing them into place, before nailing through their faces. The other is to plane or chisel off the back of the groove in the last board, and simply lay the board onto the battens – fixing it either with impact adhesive, or nails.

An external corner (eg, the end of a chimney breast) means planing off the tongue, at least from the last board. If the cladding continues round the corner, give the angle a neat finish by butting the grooved edge of the next board

at right angles against the tip of the last one, perhaps pinning a length of right angle or 'birdsmouth' (L-shaped) moulding neatly over the join. If the cladding ends there, your best bet is to nail a small rectangular-sectioned piece of planed timber (say 32 × 13mm/1¼ × ½in) to the ends of the battens so that it covers the edge of the last board as well. This method will also work at a door frame.

At an internal corner, just butt the boards together, or butt the last one against the next wall if the cladding ends there.

A quadrant, triangle or scotia moulding will give added neatness; you can use this along the junction with the ceiling too, or below a ceiling moulding.

Skirtings and other features

If the wall you're panelling has an existing skirting board, it's best left on and used as a batten, nailing the cladding to it. If it's thinner than the other battens, you'll need to pack it out first. So nail on a strip of timber, hardboard or thin ply-

wood, to bring it to the right thickness.

You can also use it as a recessed plinth. This will prevent the bottom of the cladding from being scuffed or damaged. Stop the cladding short of the floor, so that it ends some way up the skirting. Or fix the bottom of the cladding to a batten nailed immediately above the skirting, leaving the whole of the skirting exposed.

Alternatively, you can put new skirting over the cladding. With horizontal cladding, back the skirting with short lengths of board, nailed one to each batten, rather than wasting a whole board behind the skirting. Another form of skirting is a quadrant moulding (nailed to the cladding, not the floorboards, in case of timber movement).

If the old skirting is thicker than the battens you'll have to take it off carefully, or it will prevent you from nailing the cladding flat. If it's an obsolete pattern, removing it has the advantage that you can still match the room's other skirtings, because you can put it back on top of the cladding.

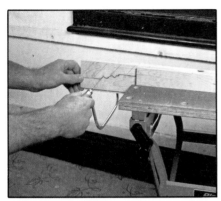

4 Take down the board and cut out the skirting profile with a coping saw or power jigsaw. Then cut along the rest of the board with a rip saw.

5 To prevent heat loss through the wall, place polystyrene insulation board, of the same thickness as the battens, between them.

9 At a window, door or end wall, pin the last board to the second last and use an offcut of cladding to scribe it. Then remove it, cut it to shape and fit it.

10 You'll need to cut short boards for some places, such as under a window. The bottom edge of the cladding can often be nailed to existing skirting.

Ready Reference

MORE FINISHING TOUCHES
Finishing off cladding neatly at a doorway, skirting boards and round electrical accessories can be tricky. Here are some solutions.

DOOR FRAMES
Fit cladding up to the door frame, then pin a vertical strip to the ends of the battens and add new door architrave moulding.

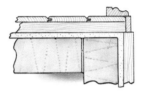

SKIRTING BOARD

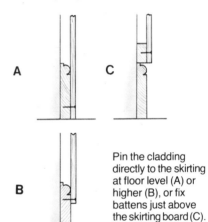

Pin the cladding directly to the skirting at floor level (A) or higher (B), or fix battens just above the skirting board (C).

ELECTRICAL FITTINGS
Pin battens round surface-mounted fittings (D) and cut the cladding to fit flush with the edges of the mounting box (D). The face plate may not be exactly flush with the cladding surface.

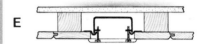

Remove flush fittings, and refix to the cladding with a new box and proprietary fixing lugs (E).

Like skirting, the architrave round doors and windows can either be removed or left. If you remove it, finish the cladding with strips of wood, in the same way as for any external corner where panelling ends; for decoration fit architrave (new, or old if it's in good condition) on top of the boards. If you leave the old architrave, fit battens up against it where necessary, nail the cladding to those, and cover its edge with a right-angle, birdsmouth or rebated moulding, planed to fit.

Electrical sockets also need battens next to them. A surface-mounted box generally needs no further treatment, since its face will end up more or less level with the surface of the cladding.

The simplest way of dealing with a flush-mounted box is to re-fix it to the wall surface, put battening and cladding next to it, and screw the face plate back on to overlap the cladding. If a flush-mounted box is too deep or shallow for this, use it as if the cladding were plasterboard. That is, attach special metal lugs to the sides of the box, so that screwing on the face plate clamps the box to the cladding.

Wall-mounted light fittings can usually be dealt with by re-fixing them onto the cladding, having drilled a hole through it for the wires. The cladding, of course, will need to be cut round all projecting features.

Surface finishes
As you fix the cladding, punch any visible nail heads below the timber surface. Then, when you've finished, you can fill the holes with a matching-coloured wood filler. Next, sand the entire timber surface with fine grade abrasive paper. An orbital sander will take much of the hard work out of this job.

When you've prepared the surface in this way, you can apply a stain, if you want to give the wood a deeper, richer or brighter colour. Follow this with a clear varnish in a matt, satin or gloss finish according to your taste. For fuller information on finishing natural timber, see FINISHES FOR FURNITURE page 17.

BUILDING BASIC BOX FURNITURE

Almost all storage furniture today is built on the box principle, which is also the quickest and easiest method when you're doing it yourself. Here are the joints and techniques you need to make hard-wearing, good-looking pieces.

Apart from tables and chairs, just about all furniture is used to contain things. You can make a very good container in the obvious way: by taking five boards – a top, a bottom, two sides and a back – and joining them together at the corners. That's the essence of what is called box construction.

According to its size and how you fit it out with shelves, partitions, drawers, hinged or sliding doors, and so on, you can turn your box into almost anything: for example, a wardrobe, a sideboard, a chest, a cupboard, a bedside or bathroom cabinet, a kitchen unit, a set of bookshelves or a hi-fi unit.

Using chipboard
The box method is ideal for modern man-made boards (see pages 14-16). Natural timber, especially hardwood, has the drawback that it's very difficult to get in widths over 225mm (9in), so you can only use it to build shallow cabinets. With chipboard, plywood and blockboard there's no such restriction.

Because it combines cheapness with good looks, veneered or plastic-faced chipboard is the most popular material for box furniture construction. Useful thicknesses are 12, 15 and 18mm (½, ⅝ and ¾in). Boards are normally 2440 or 1830mm (8 or 6ft) long, and come in widths from 150mm (6in) to 1220mm (4ft). Naturally, it's most economical to make items in sizes which utilise standard-size boards with the minimum waste.

Chipboard edges are unsightly, so boards are veneered or plastic-covered on the two long edges as well as on both faces. But you'll still have to conceal the bare short edges, plus any which you expose when cutting up the board. You can often do this by choosing the right joints. Otherwise, you can buy iron-on self-adhesive edging strip at the same time as the board. Or, for greater durability, use a timber lipping (ie, a suitable strip of plain wood or a decorative timber moulding glued, pinned on and stained to match if necessary).

Plastic-faced chipboard (which can be covered in either relatively soft PVC or more durable plastic laminate) needs no finishing treatment, but it's usual to varnish or oil wood-veneer boards. You can paint the latter if you prefer. Both materials give even the simplest box furniture a really professional look. In fact, they're so easy to work with that you need a very good reason to choose anything else.

You can of course buy chipboard without veneer or plastic facing, but after the necessary finishing processes for furniture its cost would end up about the same anyway.

A disadvantage of chipboard is that it's the weakest of man-made boards. Across a horizontal span of about 900mm (3ft) it will even sag under its own weight. So you need to support it at a maximum of 750mm (30in) intervals – even less, if it's to carry heavy objects. Remember that books, records, hi-fi and video equipment, and the TV set, are very heavy indeed.

Other materials
The strongest alternative is blockboard, which comes in standard sheets of 2440 x 1220mm (8 x 4ft) and is usually 19mm (¾in) thick. It's also the most expensive of the boards, but because of its great strength you can use it unsupported over spans twice as great as chipboard. Its main disadvantage is that the ends of the core, which is made of battens, present an unattractive appearance and need to be disguised like the edges of chipboard.

A good substitute for blockboard is 12mm (½in) thick plywood, which is almost as strong yet somewhat cheaper. In addition, its edges are neater than those of blockboard. For a smaller piece of furniture – say, a tiny bathroom cabinet – you might get away with plywood 9mm (⅜in) or even 6mm (¼in) thick. Plywood comes in standard sheets the same size as blockboard, but is also often available in smaller pieces.

Both plywood and blockboard usually require some finishing treatment. You can always add your own plastic laminate (using a contact adhesive). This is rather expensive, but will give you an extremely attractive and hard-wearing result. Veneered or plastic-faced plywood, and blockboard, is also obtainable.

Joints for boxes
Having chosen your material, you need to decide what type of joint to use at the corners of the box. If you have little or no

FROM BOXES TO FURNITURE

The box idea is enormously useful, because you can develop it in so many ways. Just by adding to it, and mixing

the different features, you can turn a box into almost any item of furniture you want.

Think of a box

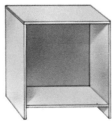

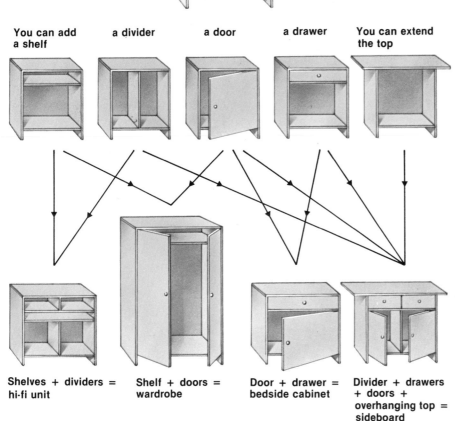

You can add a shelf   **a divider**   **a door**   **a drawer**   **You can extend the top**

Shelves + dividers = hi-fi unit

Shelf + doors = wardrobe

Door + drawer = bedside cabinet

Divider + drawers + doors + overhanging top = sideboard

Ready Reference

POWER TOOL JOINTS

With a router, or even a circular saw, you can cut several strong corner joints in man-made boards, reinforcing them with strips of wood if necessary. Cut edges need veneering.

rebate   double rebate

mitre   mitre with loose tongue of 4mm (3/16in) plywood

FITTING A BACK

You can nail a back to the edges of the box – or to strips of wood which are screwed inside it.

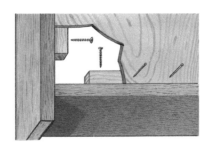

MAKING A PLINTH

You can easily make the 'toe recess' type of plinth with a strip of 100 x 25mm (4 x 1in).

expertise with power tools, the glued butt joint – where the edge of one board meets the face of another – forms the basis every time (see pages 27-31).

You can use it by itself, but usually it's reinforced. There are several ways of doing this. Firstly, you can use nails, by punching their heads below the surface and filling the holes with wood stopping. Secondly, you can use screws – either double-threaded or chipboard screws, or ordinary screws driven into plastic bushes which have been previously inserted into holes drilled in the thickness of the board. Conceal the screw

heads with plastic tops.

Thirdly, and for a stronger fixing still, you can use dowels (see pages 36-39 for details), glueing them in after lining the pieces up carefully and drilling appropriate holes. Here again there are two options. You can drill right through the outer piece in the same way as for screws, leaving the heads of the dowels to be sanded smooth as a decorative feature. Alternatively, use stopped dowels: in other words, drill only part of the way through the outer piece, so the heads are concealed.

A dowelled or plain glued butt joint will

BASIC BUTT JOINTS

1 First cut all the pieces to size, after carefully marking them out with a try-square and straight edge. A power saw with a fine blade cuts fast and cleanly.

2 To avoid mix-ups during assembly, mark each piece with its name, and mark both halves of each joint with appropriate matching letters or numbers.

3 The simplest board joint is the plain glued butt joint. The cut edge must be straight and square, and the joint needs careful cramping to keep it aligned.

5 Chipboard screws are even stronger. First of all, place the edge half of the joint carefully against the face half, marking its position if necessary.

6 Mark screw positions as well. If the joint isn't at a corner, you may have to measure their distances in from the edge for a really accurate result.

7 Drill holes, a little smaller than the screw diameter, through both pieces before inserting the screws. Use No 8 screws on 18mm (³⁄₄in) thick board.

need to be cramped while the glue is drying if it's set square and tight. You can use sash cramps, or improvise your own cramping arrangements.

But there are other and even simpler ways of improving a butt joint; they involve placing reinforcements inside the angle. The easiest of all is to use plastic jointing blocks (see pages 27-31 again), which you screw to both pieces. They make a very rigid fixing even without glue. Stronger still is a square- or triangular-sectioned strip of wood, glued on and nailed or screwed to both pieces. Either of these reinforcements can be used in addition to screws, nails, dowels or glue alone.

Design features
Cut your pieces so that any existing edging strip will be where you want it on the finished box, and so that the grain of the face veneers

will run in the same direction up the sides and across the top. The latter will give the box a more unified look.

Bear in mind that even the cleanest cut may damage the face veneer on the underside of a board, so you'll want that side to be the less visible of the two.

Usually the top of the box sits on the sides, which thus support the top corner joints. It can even overhang them, giving a larger and more useful surface. However, either type of construction does mean you'll have to conceal the edges at each end of the top. The problem doesn't arise with the bottom or with intermediate shelves, for their ends will be concealed by the box's sides.

If you are adding a door or drawer to your box, think carefully at the design stage to make sure you get the details right. There's more information about these on pages 110-113 and 132-135.

For a really neat job, shelves and dividers can be fitted in housings (see pages 40-43 for details). However, you can't cut housings in plastic-faced boards, and in any case you may find plastic jointing blocks, or other proprietary fittings such as shelf supports, easy to use and just as effective.

Even the best-jointed and most substantial box is quite easily distorted into a lozenge shape. That is, until you fit the back. This need only be made from hardboard of 4mm (³⁄₁₆in) plywood, and can be glued and pinned onto the back edges of the boards. It's best to make it about 3mm (¹⁄₈in) too small all round, so that it's less easily seen from the top or sides. Alternatively, you can inset it – either in stopped rebates in all four edges, or against narrow strips of wood which are themselves screwed a little way inside the box.

A plinth is another feature on many pieces.

4 Nails are one way of reinforcing a glued butt joint. Always have a wet rag handy to wipe off any excess adhesive which is squeezed out during assembly.

8 A square-sectioned strip of wood is another good reinforcement. Position, mark, drill and glue it; then drive chipboard screws both ways.

STOPPED DOWEL JOINTS

1 Draw a line down the face of one board in exactly the position where you want the centre line of the other board's edge to meet it.

3 Drill dowel holes in both pieces, positioning them accurately on the marks. Adhesive tape round the drill bit warns you when it's gone far enough.

2 Mark the dowel positions along this line, on both pieces, making sure each pair of marks matches exactly. Dowels should be 150-225mm (6-9in) apart.

4 Put the pieces together, having first inserted glue and dowels into the set of holes you've drilled, and having spread adhesive along the joint.

The word covers two different things. One is the traditional cabinet base, built separately out of four lengths of 100 x 25mm (4 x 1in) planed softwood used on edge, which fits over the bottom of the box. The corners are mitred or butt-jointed and reinforced with triangular wooden blocks, glued or screwed in place, which also serve as supports for the box when it's located inside the plinth. This type of plinth is mainly for decoration.

The other type is really a toe recess. It's formed by raising the bottom of the box and fitting a piece of timber below it, along the front. The timber is fixed at each end into notches cut in the bottom corner of each side. The fixing can be done by any of the jointing methods already described. This type of plinth helps to prevent stubbed toes and damage to the cabinet, and is particularly common on kitchen base units and living-room wall units.

FINISHING TOUCHES

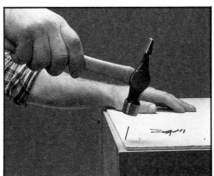

1 4mm (³/₁₆in) plywood makes a good back for a box. Drive panel pins through it at an angle, so that they don't come through the board faces by accident.

2 Glue and pin beading onto the edges, for decoration and to hide those which you've cut. The shelf and bottom are inset to conceal the beading's ends.

CHAPTER 4

ADVANCED TECHNIQUES

Once your confidence has grown, you can begin to extend your repertoire by acquiring some of the more advanced woodworking skills.

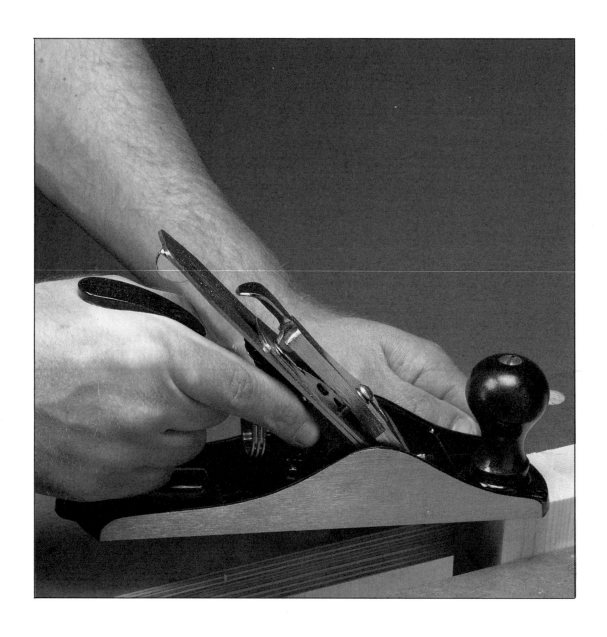

MORTISE & TENON JOINTS

Mortise and tenon joints are indispensable if you're making furniture that's both strong and good-looking, and are particularly useful for making the most popular pieces of furniture – tables and chairs.

Take a piece of wood, shape the end to form a 'tongue', then fit the tongue into a matching slot in the side of another piece, and you've made a mortise-and-tenon joint.

The tenon is the tongue and the mortise is the slot, and the joint has proved its usefulness over centuries in all kinds of wooden frameworks because of its strength and resistance to movement. It's the best joint for fixing horizontal pieces of wood – 'rails' – into uprights such as table and chair legs.

Once you've got the knack of cutting it cleanly, you've mastered a joint which will stand you in very good stead. Whenever you're joining two lengths of wood in a T or L shape, and you want something stronger and more elegant than a halving joint, go for a mortise and tenon joint. The only time it won't work is on thin, flat pieces – boards, planks and panels: use housing joints instead.

There are numerous types of mortise-and-tenon joint at your disposal. Think carefully about the job the joint has to do before deciding which to use.

Choosing the right joint

A *through tenon* passes right through the mortise piece (which makes it easier to cut the mortise). Because you can see its endgrain, it's used in rougher work or as a decorative feature. It can also be wedged from the outside for strength and/or visual effect.

A *stub tenon* is one which doesn't pass right through, but fits into a 'blind' mortise – a hole with a bottom. The most familiar kind, especially in furniture, has shoulders all round which conceal the joint.

A *barefaced tenon* has the tenon cut with only one side shoulder instead of two – useful if the tenon piece is already very thin; or the tenon may be reduced in width by having edge shoulders cut in it – see *Ready Reference*.

A *haunched tenon* is a compromise often used at the corner of a frame to keep it from twisting. The haunch – an extra step between the tenon and the piece it projects from – can

be square or sloping. A sloping haunch is hidden and easier to cut – see *Ready Reference* again.

A *double tenon* is just a pair of tenons cut on one piece of wood – used if the piece is very wide and you don't want to cut a single enormous mortise to take one wide tenon.

An *offset tenon* is simply one which isn't in the centre of the tenon piece.

Making the joint

Let's assume you're making a basic stub tenon joint. It doesn't really matter whether you start by making your mortise or your tenon; the important thing is to get them to fit together. However, cutting the tenon first means you can mark off the mortise from it, possibly getting a better fit. This is easier than the other way round. Either way, play safe by making the tenon a little too large (or the mortise a little too small), rather than the reverse. You can always cut off a bit more.

Marking and cutting the tenon

Begin by scoring round the tenon piece with a knife and try-square to mark the length of the tenon, using the width of the mortise piece as a guide. A through tenon should be a little bit over-long to allow for planing it flush to give a neat finish; a stub tenon should go about halfway through, and be about 3mm (⅛in) shorter than the mortise to leave room for any excess adhesive.

A mortise gauge is very useful for the next stage. Choose a mortise chisel which has a blade about one third the thickness of the tenon piece (under rather than over, though you can use a wider one if the tenon piece is

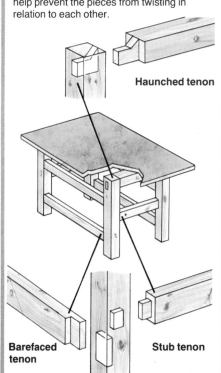
65

MARKING THE TENON

1 Lay the mortise piece on the tenon piece and mark where the tenon starts. Leave a through tenon over-long, as shown, for later trimming.

2 If you're making a stub tenon, it'll be easier to mark the tenon length if you lay the tenon piece on top of the mortise.

3 Square the mark round all four sides of the tenon piece by scoring across them with your marking knife against a try-square.

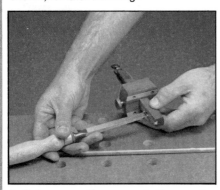

4 Set your mortise gauge to the exact blade width of your mortise chisel, or to the diameter of your drill auger bit if you have one available.

5 Use the gauge to score out the tenon width down the sides and across the end of the piece, stopping at the length marks you have already made.

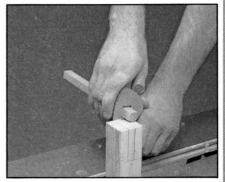

6 If you are cutting edge shoulders as well, use an ordinary marking gauge to score lines the other way for each of the shoulders in turn.

much thinner than the mortise piece), and set the gauge's twin spurs that distance apart. Then set the stock so as to place the resulting 'tramlines' in the centre of the timber thickness – unless you're deliberately off-setting the tenon – and try it from both sides, adjusting the position of the stock till the two sets of tramlines coincide.

Now you can score the edges and end of the tenon piece to mark where the tenon will be cut. If you don't have a mortise gauge, use an ordinary single-spur marking gauge and mark the tramlines separately.

For a straight tenon, that's all the marking-up you need. If you're cutting shoulders in the width as well, set a marking gauge to one sixth the width of the tenon piece and mark down both faces and across the tramlines on the end.

If you're including a haunch, use the gauge to mark its width across the end and down the faces; then mark its depth with a knife and try-square. For maximum strength, the haunch should be not more than one third the tenon's width, and its depth not

more than one quarter the length (or 12mm/½in long, whichever is smaller). We will be dealing with these joints in more detail in another section.

To cut a tenon you need, not surprisingly, a tenon saw. All you have to do is grip the piece upright in a vice and saw down each side of the tenon; then lay the wood flat and saw off the shoulders. The vital thing is always to keep your saw-cuts on the waste side of the lines.

Marking and cutting the mortise
At this stage, you can lay the tenon on the mortise piece and mark the mortise length on it. Then score its width with the gauge.

To cut the mortise, cramp the timber in position. If working near the end of a piece, leave extra length – a 'horn' which you saw off later – to prevent the wood from splitting as you chisel into it. If you have a carpenter's brace or a power drill, you can start by drilling holes close together along the length of the mortise. Make quite sure you keep the drill vertical – a drill stand will help.

Then chop and lever out the waste with the mortise chisel, and cut the recess for any haunch. Lastly, clean off the sides and ends with a bevel-edged chisel.

If you have no drill, use a mortise chisel by itself, keeping the bevel away from you and working from the centre of the mortise towards the ends – stopping just short of them so as not to bruise them when you lever out the waste before going deeper. On a through mortise, chisel halfway and then work from the other side. Clean up with a bevel-edged chisel.

Assembling the joint
Now you can fit the pieces together. Don't be tempted to force them, or you may split the wood; if the joint is impossibly tight, carefully shave the tenon with a chisel and glass-paper checking all the time. When it's a neat, close fit, glue it, cramp it and leave it to set.

Ideally, you need sash cramps – long steel bars with one fixed head and another which you tighten – plus some pieces of scrap wood to protect the work.

CUTTING THE TENON

1 *After marking off the waste areas, clamp the piece upright and start to cut the tenon. Be sure to keep the saw on the waste side of the lines.*

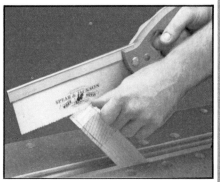

2 *You may find it easier to work accurately if you clamp the piece in the vice at an angle of about 45° while you saw down for the next few strokes.*

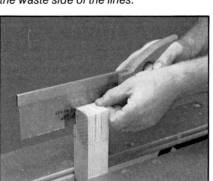

3 *Finish off the cut with the piece upright again. It's easy to overshoot when sawing along the grain, so be careful as you approach the depth marks.*

4 *Make identical cuts along the grain, down to the same depth marks, for each of the edge shoulders if you have marked any.*

5 *Firmly hold or clamp the piece down flat on the workbench as you cut away each of the tenon's face shoulders by sawing across the grain.*

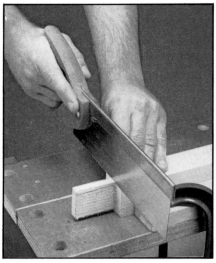

6 *Lastly, turn the piece over on to its side and make similar cross-cuts to remove the edge shoulders, if any are included. This completes the tenon.*

Ready Reference

STRENGTHENING THE JOINT

For extra strength and decorative possibilities, consider wedging or pegging the joint once it's fitted. Hardwood wedges go either into previously made saw-cuts in the end of a through tenon (A), or into the mortise above and below it (B). The mortise needs to be slightly tapered. Pegging is done with one or more dowels inserted into holes drilled sideways through the joint.

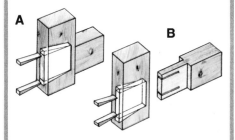

TIPS FOR BETTER JOINTS

● a through tenon should be cut too long, and made flush once the joint is assembled
● some people find it easier to start cutting the tenon while holding the piece upright, then to re-position the wood and saw at 45°, and to finish off with it upright again
● set your mortise gauge from the exact width of your mortise chisel
● if mortising near the end of your timber, leave it over-long to prevent splitting, and cut off the extra bit later
● to keep drill or chisel vertical, stand a try-square on end beside the tool as you're working

● leave it till last to pare down the mortise ends, so as not to risk bruising them while levering out the bulk of the waste
● to stop yourself drilling too deep when starting a mortise, fit a depth stop (an item you can buy) or wrap masking tape round the bit as a depth indicator.

MARKING AND DRILLING THE MORTISE

1 If you're working near the end of the mortise piece, mark off a short length or 'horn' as waste, for removal once the joint is assembled.

2 Lay the tenon on the mortise piece, allowing for any horn, and mark there the tenon's width.

3 Square these two length marks across the inner side of the mortise piece.

4 With the gauge at its existing setting, score down the mortise piece, between the last two marks, to give the mortise's width.

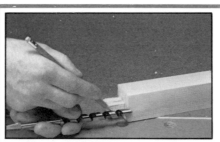

5 For a stub mortise-and-tenon joint, mark out the tenon length on your drill bit, if you have a bit of the right diameter.

6 Drill holes to remove the bulk of the mortise. For a stub joint the tape at the mark on the bit warns of the depth.

CHISELLING OUT THE MORTISE

1 Instead of drilling, you can chop and lever out the waste with a mortise chisel, starting halfway down the length of the mortise.

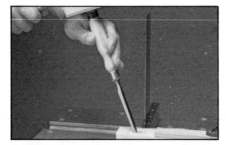

2 Work along to its ends as you chisel deeper. For a through mortise, chop halfway through, then work from the other side of the piece.

3 For a stub mortise and tenon joint it pays to mark off the length of the tenon on the chisel as a depth guide, just as you would for a drill bit.

4 Then you can wind sticky tape round it next to the mark, again as a depth indicator, for use when you chisel out the bottom of the mortise.

5 After removing most of the waste, use a bevel-edged chisel to pare down each end of the mortise, shaving off any irregularities.

6 Work on the sides likewise. As you're cutting along the grain, you'll need greater care, to avoid splitting out more wood than you want.

ASSEMBLING THE JOINT

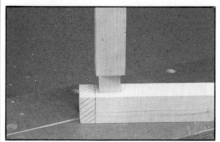

1 Try the pieces together to see if they fit – but without forcing the tenon all the way in. Carefully sand or pare away as needed.

2 A through joint can be strengthened with small wedges cut from scrap hardwood and inserted in or next to the tenon after assembly.

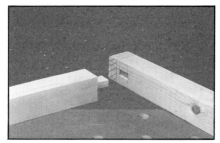

3 A stub joint will need to be glued, and cramped. If working at a corner, leave the horn on until this is done.

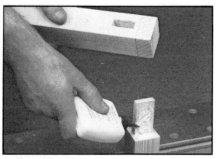

4 For either type, start by spreading adhesive all over the tenon and shoulders. Use a wet rag to wipe off any excess after assembly.

5 Once the through tenon is fully home, insert any wedges you are using and drive them carefully into place with a wooden mallet.

6 To get wedges tight, you'll probably need a piece of scrap wood to help drive them fully home past the projecting end of the tenon.

7 Saw off the excess length of the tenon and any wedges so that they're almost flush with the surface of the mortise piece.

8 Lastly, turn the assembly round and complete the operation by planing across the end of the joint to give it a smooth finish.

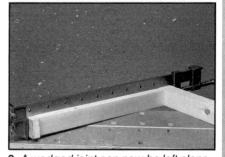

9 A wedged joint can now be left alone while it sets, but any other (whether it's through or stub) will need cramping during this stage.

10 After the adhesive has set, saw off any horn that you may have been leaving at the end of the mortise piece while making the joint.

11 Now plane the end you've just sawn, to get it smooth. Work inwards, as shown, to avoid splitting from the mortise piece.

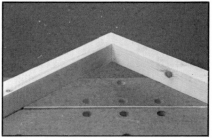

12 The finished mortise-and-tenon joint is both strong and neat. A corner version is shown here, but a T shape is equally possible.

USING A ROUTER : 1

The router is the ultimate portable power tool. Almost all the jobs it tackles are difficult or impossible with any other machine. We begin with one of the simpler tasks – making grooves.

The power router is both beautifully simple and outstandingly versatile. As on all power tools, its heart is an electric motor which turns a spindle. Its most important feature, however, is the motor's very high speed – between 18,000 and 27,000 rpm, compared with the maximum of 4000 rpm given by power drills. This is what allows it to handle such an enormous variety of grooving, rebating, shaping and other cutting jobs in wood, plastic and even soft metals.

A router's power is from 300 to 2000W. Naturally, the more powerful models are meant for professionals and are more expensive. The power sets strict limits on the amount of material you can cut away without overloading the motor. A 300W model will make a groove 6mm (¼in) square in one go, whereas a 600W motor allows a 10x6mm (⅜x¼in) groove.

This means that some jobs take a bit longer with a low-powered machine, because you need to make two or three passes (adjusting it for a deeper cut each time) instead of just one or two.

At the end of the spindle is a 'collet chuck', into which you fit the bit (also called a cutter), very much as you fit a drill bit into a drill chuck. A collet chuck, however, is tightened with a spanner – while you hold the spindle steady with a tommy bar, another spanner, or a locking switch. Collets are made in three main sizes, to accept bits whose shank diameter is ¼, ⅜ or ½in.

The 'overhead router' used in industry is a fixed machine, suspended in a large stand – like an enormous drill stand, but fastened to the floor – and lowered onto the workpiece with a lever. On the portable router, however, the motor (complete with spindle) is mounted in a frame or 'carriage' with handles, in which it moves up and down as you adjust it. This frame has a flat base, through which the bit projects to make the cut. In operation you generally rest the base on the workpiece, and move the machine along bodily – though you can fix the machine and move the workpiece instead.

The general principle is the same as when using shaping cutters in a power drill to form profiled edges on timber and man-made boards. But the router is far easier to handle (though larger models can be quite heavy), and it's capable of harder and more efficient work because it's purpose-built.

The plunging router

Portable routers are either fixed-base or plunging models. A fixed-base router is lowered into the material with the bit already protruding from the base, after you've got it to project the required amount by adjusting the height of the motor in the carriage.

With a plunging router, on the other hand, the motor is on sprung mountings, and this means you set the projection (ie, the depth of cut) in two stages. First you lower the motor until the bit just touches the workpiece, and you rotate one of the handles to lock it in position. Then, on most models, you simply adjust the height of the depth bar – a sliding or threaded vertical rod fixed to the side of the motor – so that, when you 'plunge' the motor right down to cut, the lower end of the rod will meet the base of the carriage and prevent your going any deeper than you want. Lastly, you turn the handle the other way to release the motor so that it springs right up, back to its original position.

That done, you're ready to start cutting. This is a straightforward matter of positioning the router where you want it, switching on, and pressing down fully on the handles to plunge the rotating bit into the workpiece.

Then you turn the handle again to lock it there, before running the tool along to do the actual job. When you've finished, you just use the handle to unlock it, allow it to spring back up, and switch off.

The plunging router's sprung action makes it safer than the fixed-base type, and also ensures that the bit always enters the work at exactly 90°.

Using a router

If the sound of a router motor drops from a high-pitched whine during a cut, you're probably trying to work too fast – or cut too deeply. The harder the material and the wider the bit, the slower and shallower each cut will have to be to avoid straining the motor. The general rule is to cut no deeper than the diameter of the bit.

A smell of burning, on the other hand, may mean you're cutting too slowly. The important thing is to acquire a feeling for the tool's natural cutting rate. It shouldn't take long.

But either of these symptoms may denote a blunt bit instead. So may a 'furry' finish (although that's common on moist wood anyway), or difficulty in pushing the router along. And remember that, as with any other tool, the texture of your material matters. In solid timber, the grain may dictate the direction in which you have to move the machine for a clean cut.

As for safety, remember that a power router runs at a tremendous speed. Treat it with respect. Wear goggles to protect your eyes from whirling dust. On a plunging router, always release the lock after a cut to let the bit spring up out of the way. Unplug the machine whenever you're not using it – and keep it in a cupboard. If stored on a shelf, it could fall off; and, if you leave it on the floor, wood chips and other debris may get into the air intake.

Router bits

Router bits come in an extremely wide range of shapes – from straight bits, which are for grooving, to angled and curved patterns, plus a number of others. Not only knowledge but also imagination is required to exploit them to the full, for just about all can be used in several different ways; and of course you can use more than one in succession for creating compound shapes – see below.

It's also important to know what they're made from. Although special drilling bits have been designed for use with plunging routers, no bit or cutter of ordinary steel should ever be used in a power router, because the high speed will very likely smash it to pieces. Proper router bits are made, instead, of high-speed steel (HSS) and tungsten carbide (TC).

HSS bits are cheaper, and fine for working softwoods and fairly soft plastics. Their draw-

SETTING UP FOR A CUT

1 *With the machine unplugged and the motor removed from its carriage if possible, steady the spindle with the tommy bar.*

2 *Insert the shank of the bit into the collet, tighten the nut as far as you can by hand, and then finish securing it with a spanner.*

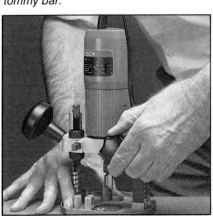

3 *If you've removed the motor, fit it back into the carriage now, and tighten it up firmly with the knob or other fastening provided.*

4 *'Plunge' the motor down in its carriage till the bit meets the surface on which the machine is standing, and lock it there with the handle.*

5 *Adjust the depth bar until the gap below it roughly equals the depth of cut you want – ie, the amount the bit should project. Release the lock.*

6 *Plunge the bit below the surface through a convenient hole, use the gauge to check the depth, and let the motor spring back up.*

ROUTING GROOVES

1 Set the fence attachment so that, with the fence against the edge, the groove will be in the position you want. Mark the groove out first if you like.

2 Switch on, plunge into the workpiece some way along the groove, and lock the handle when you've reached the full pre-set depth.

3 Move the router along, still holding the fence firmly against the edge – especially at the end. Then return across the piece to complete the groove.

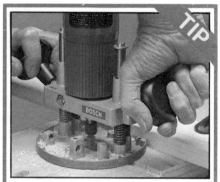

5 If grooving across the middle of a piece, you may have to abandon the fence attachment and instead cramp on a straight batten as a guide.

6 A router will cut through knots and other blemishes without difficulty – provided you keep its cutting speed up, without dawdling.

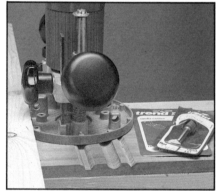

7 Grooves needn't have square bottoms. Different-shaped bits produce a whole variety of profiles, many of which are extremely decorative.

back is a tendency to blunt quickly, which is greatly accelerated if they're used on harder and/or more abrasive materials. However, by the same token, they're soft enough to sharpen at home – if you know how. Not only must the front of each cutting edge be dead flat and smooth; there must also be a 'clearance angle' of at least 15° between its back and the circle made by the bit as it rotates.

For chipboard, plywood and blockboard (all of which contain synthetic resins), as well as for plastic laminates and glass-reinforced plastics, you need TC bits. They're even a good idea for use on hardboard and hardwoods. Their higher initial cost – and they can be very expensive – is often outweighed by their much longer life. Usually they consist of TC tips (cutting edges) brazed onto steel bits – but you can get bits made from solid TC. For eventual sharpening, TC and TC-tipped (TCT) bits must go back to the manufacturer or another specialist firm.

Remember that a router is only as good as its bit. If you find you have a blunt one, don't just go on using it and hoping for the best – see that it's sharpened. What's more, bit shanks should be kept smooth and undamaged to avoid damaging the collet when you insert them.

Routing grooves

Cutting grooves across the face of timber or boards is a fine example of a task which is as trouble-free with a router as it's demanding by hand.

Even the marking-out process (see pages 40-43 for details) is simpler, because you need only indicate where one side of the groove is to go. In some cases you can even omit marking-out altogether, because the essential thing in all routing work (except for a very few truly freehand applications) is to make sure the tool is properly guided anyway: see *Ready Reference*.

The simplest method of doing this is to use a fence attachment. This is very similar to the rip fence on a circular saw: in other words, it's a removable metal fitting which locates against the edge of the workpiece, and thus keeps the router on a parallel course. It's important that the edge should be reasonably straight in the first place – in other words, that there should be no bumps or hollows which are pronounced, and/or which run for any distance. However, if there are only small unevennesses, the fence attachment will actually bridge the defects and allow a straight groove despite a less-than-perfect edge.

You can extend the fence attachment, too, by screwing to it a piece of timber or board about double its length. This is very useful when the groove runs right out at one side of the material, because you can 'follow through' with it, still keeping it pressed against the edge as the cut finishes – thereby preventing

4 Repeat the procedure after doubling the depth of cut. Sometimes a cut takes three passes, depending on the machine, the material and the bit.

8 Grooving with a shaped bit can produce a panelled effect. Sharp corners will always occur where the grooves cross each other.

the tool from suddenly slipping, as it can easily do with an ordinary fence.

Better still, you can also cramp a straight-edged piece of scrap material (an 'overcut board') beyond the workpiece and level with it, and simply continue the cut into that. This will not only prevent a ragged end to the cut, especially when working across the grain, but also provide additional support for the fence and so help to ensure an absolutely parallel groove.

Some manufacturers supply a special guide roller or extra fence plates, to enable the router to follow edges which have fairly gentle curves. These are screwed to the main fence attachment. However, edges which have sharp concave curves, or are otherwise too elaborate, will rule out such devices.

Even if you want a straight groove, the fence attachment itself will be no use if the edge is curved or angled, or if you're working

too far in from the nearest parallel straight edge. In either of these cases your best plan is to cramp on a straight, solid guide batten parallel to your intended groove, and run the machine against that. The batten must, of course, be at such a distance that the bit will run along your mark. That means the distance from the edge of the router base to the centre of the bit, minus half the bit diameter.

It also helps if the batten overhangs at both ends, so you can keep the router pressed against it when entering and leaving the cut. The idea is, once again, to avoid swinging off course.

If you're cutting a whole set of housings, you can even add a T-piece to the end of the batten. Apart from forming an overcut board, this will enable you, without effort, to locate the batten squarely every time. Moreover, when you've continued a groove through into the T-piece, you'll be able to use it as a guide mark for aligning subsequent cuts (see *Ready Reference*).

If possible, fit your router with a straight bit whose diameter equals the width of the groove you want. In the case of a housing, this will be the thickness of the piece being housed (usually a shelf).

With a light-duty router, start by setting the depth of cut at about 2 to 3mm (1/16 to 1/8in), and remove that much again with each subsequent pass; in other words, double the setting for the second pass and treble it for the third. That way, three passes will cut a housing 6 to 9mm (1/4 to 3/8in) deep. In chipboard, don't go deeper than half the board's thickness, in case you weaken it too much.

Some routers have a 'rotary turret stop', which is simply a means of pre-setting the depth bar for three different heights. This allows you to change the depth of cut for the second and third passes merely by rotating the device to the next setting, without having to stop and adjust the tool.

Rotating bits mean that all routed internal corners will be rounded, however slightly (the radius depends, of course, on the bit diameter). The ends of stopped housings are no exception; you'll either have to chisel them square, or round the edges of the housed pieces to match. The latter operation, however (see pages 75-79), is simply another straightforward cut in the router's repertoire.

Shaped grooves
A groove needn't be square-bottomed. There are a number of graceful shapes for decorative work. You can create panelled effects, too (although grooving in man-made boards will, of course, expose the core).

Moreover, even simple combined cuts – for example, a rounded groove 15mm (5/8in) wide superimposed on a deeper square groove 10mm (3/8in) wide – can look very good.

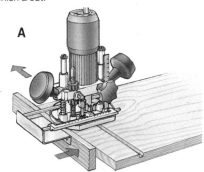
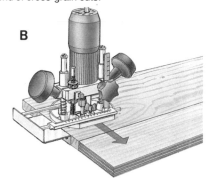
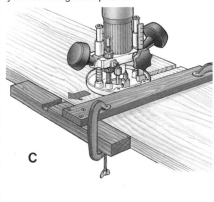

KNOW YOUR ROUTER

To get the best from a power router, you need to know how to set it up for the cut you want. This is a typical 'plunge' model – so called because of the sprung mountings, which make for safety and accuracy. You position the router before pushing down to start the cut – and let the motor spring up again as soon as you've finished.

All these router bits (cutters) will make grooves – and shape edges (see pages 75-79). Some, like 10, give varied profiles.

KEY

1 Straight: one-flute (veining)
2 Straight: two-flute
3 Groove and chamfer
4 Radius (veining)
5 Core box, radius or half-round
6 V-carving or V-groove (veining)
7 V-groove and chamfer
8 Panel raising
9 Chamfer
10 Ovolo
11 Pointed round or quarter-round
12 Pointed ogee
13 Ogee (end cutting)
14 Panelling
15 Classic

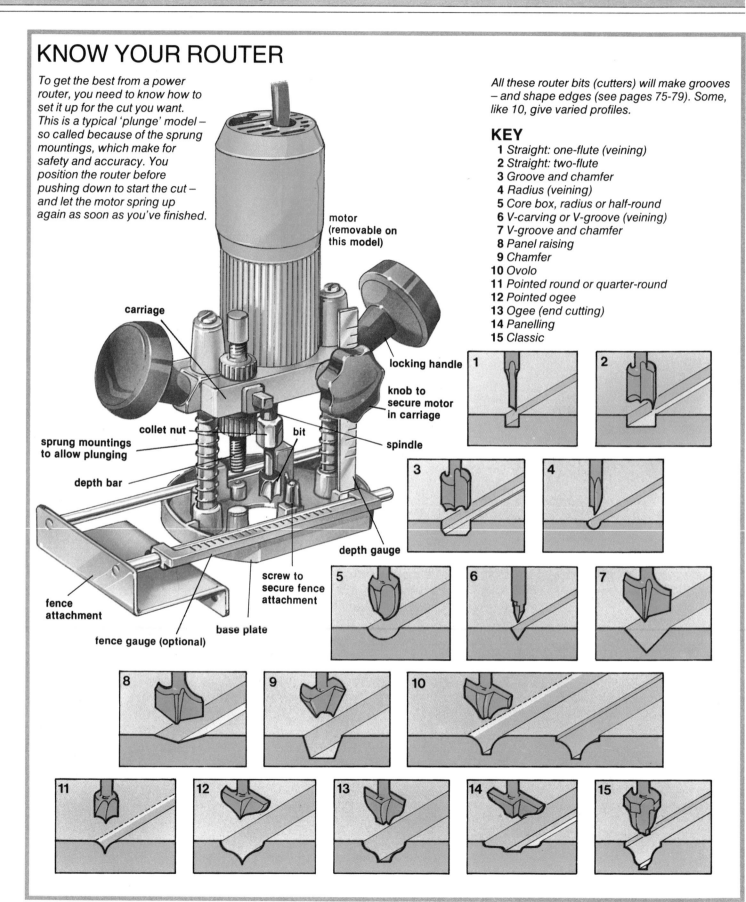

motor (removable on this model)

carriage

locking handle

knob to secure motor in carriage

collet nut

bit

spindle

sprung mountings to allow plunging

depth bar

depth gauge

fence attachment

screw to secure fence attachment

fence gauge (optional)

base plate

USING A ROUTER : 2

Once you've grasped the power router's basic workings, you can move on from making simple grooving cuts to the vast possibilities of edge profiling, box jointing and other techniques.

After cutting housings and other square or shaped grooves (see pages 70-74), the use of the router that next springs to mind is usually shaping edges.

That may sound unimportant, but it covers a tremendous range of jobs, both functional and decorative. The router will cut any number of ornamental mouldings (eg, ovolo, ogee) along the edges of tabletops, shelves, skirting-boards and the like – and indeed make lengths of moulding, such as architrave or staff bead, to your own design from the timber of your choice, as an alternative to buying them off the shelf. It will also produce straightforward rebates, plus bevels and chamfers at various angles; trim off overhanging edges of plastic laminate after it's been glued down; and, very importantly, make a whole variety of joints which involve grooved, tongued and rebated edges.

Bits for edging

The first step, of course, is to choose the right shape from the range of bits available. All grooving bits (see opposite) can be used for edging, and there are also several for edging alone. Rebates, for example, can be cut either with an ordinary two-flute bit, or a special wide rebating bit. Other edging bits include rounding-over, coving, ogee and a number of others. Any router supplier should be able to give you further details, or tell you where to find them.

Each individual router bit will produce cuts of different shapes, depending not only on its profile and size but also on your depth setting. In the case of edging, you can also vary the shape according to the width of cut – ie, whether the bit just skims the edge or bites deeply into it.

Guiding the cut

There are two main ways of profiling edges with a router. One is to use the fence attachment – if necessary with accessories for following curves. The other is to fit a 'self-guiding' bit.

As when grooving, working with the fence attachment is a simple matter of keeping it pressed firmly against the edge of the material. In this case, that's the self-same edge in which you're making the cut – therefore the fence must be right underneath the router base, on or near its centre line.

A self-guiding bit has its own built-in guide, in the form of a pin – like a small extra shank, but at the opposite end – or else a roller bearing. This guide is in addition to the cutting edges and almost always below them. You keep it pressed against the workpiece (whether straight or curved) in exactly the same manner as a fence attachment, thus ensuring a uniform cut all the way.

Self-guiding bits involve no cumbersome setting up, unlike the various types of fence. They will also follow the tightest curves, and even go round corners. Their corresponding snag is that they reproduce any bumps or hollows in the original edge, to a greater extent than fence attachments do. On blockboard, for instance, the guide will wander into any exposed voids between the core battens. So, if you can't get your edge absolutely true and smooth, it's best to stick with the fence attachment – or, still better, a guide batten clamped across the work. A template which the router can follow is another possibility.

A guide batten (or template) is also needed if for any reason you have to cut away the whole of an edge, rather than just part of it, since there will be nothing for a guide pin or bearing to run against when using less than the bit's maximum width of cut.

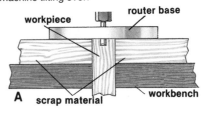
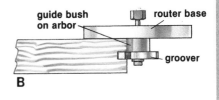
75

ROUTER BITS FOR EDGING

Some bits (1-5) must be used with a fence attachment, guide batten or template.
1 *Dovetailing*
2 *Edge-rounding*
3 *Double edge-rounding*
4 *Staff bead*
5 *Tongueing for staff bead*

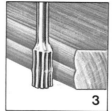
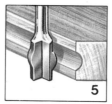

also cuts groove

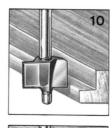

Others have a guide pin or bearing, whose size (6-9) varies the cut.
6 *Rounding-over (large pin)*
7 *Ovolo or corner round (small pin)*
8 *Ovolo or corner round (small bearing)*

9 *Rounding-over (large bearing)*
10 *Rebating (pin)*
11 *Chamfering (pin)*
12 *Coving (pin)*
13 *Roman ogee (pin)*

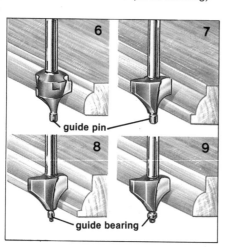
guide pin

guide bearing

There are also special bits for trimming plastic laminates.
14 *Pierce and trim*
15 *90° trimmer (self-guiding)*
16 *90° trimmer*
17 *90° trimmer with guide bearing*
18 *Bevel trimmer*

The pierce and trim bit (14) drills through the laminate, then cuts it away cleanly. This is useful if you've laminated over an internal cut-out, for a sink in a kitchen worktop, for example.

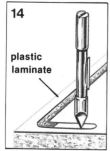

plastic laminate

cutting edge

guide

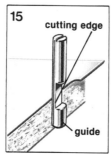

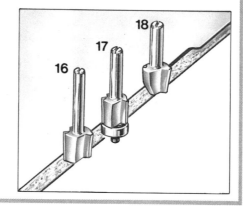

PROFILING EDGES

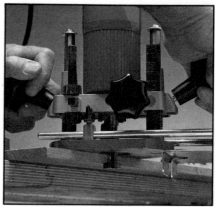

1 *Set the depth for the exact edge profile you require (see page 71). The bit shown inserted here is known as a staff bead cutter.*

5 *When cutting, keep the guide pin pressed against the edge. That way, the bit will follow the edge even if it's curved or has corners.*

Bits with roller bearings, as opposed to pins, are very expensive, and so only worth getting if you'll be using them a great deal. Their advantages are that the bearing, unlike a pin, won't burn or mark the edge, and that you have only to change the bearing in order to vary the width of the cut (and thus its shape).

In all edging work it's important to remember that routers can usually only do their job properly if they're fed (moved along the workpiece) against the rotation of the bit — ie, so that the bit's cutting edges are always travelling into the cut rather than away from it. Remember that the bit rotates clockwise if you're looking from above at a router pointing downwards. The same principle applies if the router is fixed in position to a router table.

You can in fact work the other way, eg, for a clean cut in difficult grain. But care is needed in order to prevent the bit from 'snatching' uncontrollably.

2 *If you're not using a self-guiding bit – see below – slide the fence attachment in and adjust it for the precise width of cut.*

3 *With the router plunged and locked at the pre-set depth, switch it on and make the cut. Always 'feed' it so the bit rotates into the work.*

4 *A self-guiding bit lets you do without a fence, because it has its own guide pin (like the one shown here) or roller-bearing guide.*

6 *A rounding-over bit like this will also give a 'stepped' moulding: you just have to set it for a deeper cut (see no. 10, page 74).*

7 *A coving bit gives yet another edge profile. Simply stopping a cut short always produces a nicely rounded end like the one shown here.*

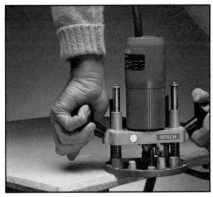

8 *A chamfer bit puts a neat angle on the edge. A guide pin, like a guide bearing, enables you to follow corners as well as curved edges.*

Routing joints

When you make box furniture (see pages 60-63 for details), one of your prime considerations must naturally be how to joint it. In the ordinary way, this isn't an easy decision. Butt joints are weak, and almost any form of strengthening (nails, screws, timber strips or even assembly fittings) is bound to show – inside the cabinet, if not outside.

The professional answer is to use a joint which doesn't need reinforcement, and it's here that power tools come into their own. The router, in particular, is ideal when you want a rebate in one or both pieces. You can match a rebate in one piece with a groove in the other, to form a barefaced housing joint – see pages 40-43 for details. And one of the strongest joints available (though it's not for corners, and not for chipboard) is the dovetail housing. This is very easily made by using a dovetail bit – set to a uniform depth –

to cut both the groove and the sides of the matching tongue. You'll need the fence attachment, and maybe a guide batten for the groove. For a tongue of exactly the right width to fit the groove, careful alignment is required. Remember, too, that the 'undercut' dovetail shape means you can't plunge into the work.

Any kind of tongue-and-groove joint, in fact, is a natural for the router. If you're grooving an edge, make sure that the machine is properly supported so it can't tilt while cutting. This may mean clamping additional pieces on either side of the work. It's better, however, if you're doing a lot of edge grooving, to use an arbor with a groover fixed over it. An arbor is a separate shank, often with a guide bush or bearing, that fits into the collet. A groover is like a circular-saw blade but smaller, and with fewer and thicker teeth. The advantage of this arrangement is that you can run the router base over the

face of the work, as with most edging jobs, and thereby gain stability.

A matching tongue can usually best be formed by cutting two rebates.

Trimming plastic laminates

Before fixing a sheet of plastic laminate to a timber or board base, you'll naturally try to cut it to approximately the right size, aiming to trim the slight overhang once the sheet is stuck down in position.

Laminates are exceptionally hard, and therefore not really suitable for shaving with a hand plane. A router, however, makes light work of the job. You'll need a tungsten carbide (TC) bit, solid or tipped, to avoid rapid blunting. Special trimming bits are available; some make right-angled cuts, some make bevelled cuts at various slopes, and some provide a choice between the two. Several are self-guiding – and, to make the work even easier, there are bits which will trim

ROUTING BOX JOINTS

1 *For a dovetail housing, start by cutting the groove. Use a dovetail bit – and don't plunge into the material, or you'll spoil the job.*

2 *Clamp the other piece on end, with scrap wood either side. Without changing the depth of cut, set the fence and mould one side of the tongue.*

3 *Re-adjust the fence to cut the other side. Keep the scrap edge on your left – ie, against the direction in which the bit rotates.*

6 *Clamp the other piece on end and make an identical cut; if using a fence, don't change the setting. Use scrap timber to steady the router as you work.*

7 *When you fit the pieces together, the cuts should match exactly. You may need to fix lipping to conceal the exposed core of a man-made board.*

8 *For edge grooving, a slotter on an arbor makes it easier to keep the tool steady, since it still rests on the face. The guide bearing follows the edge.*

laminate from both faces of a panel at once.

Even when using a TC bit, make sure the laminate doesn't overhang by more than about one-third of the bit diameter, otherwise you'll cause unnecessary wear. Varying the depth setting, too, will spread the wear more evenly along the cutting edges.

Unless you're using a self-guiding bit, you'll need to set up the fence attachment for the job. What's known as a 'fine screw feed' – available on some machines – is very useful here, as for many other tasks. It's a mechanism that adjusts the fence attachment more precisely than you can manage when you just slide it over and tighten the screws.

If the panel's edge is lipped with laminate too, it's best to trim that before laminating the top surface – so that any marks left by the bit will only mar the top of the base board, to which the laminate has still to be fixed, rather than the plastic finish itself. Marks on the edge lipping will be much less obvious.

You needn't turn the router on its side for this, as long as you're using a bit with a 'bottom cut' – namely cutting edges at the bottom as well as on each side. At least one router manufacturer supplies a special 'sub-base' accessory to act as a guide for this particular operation

Occasionally, you may have already cut holes in the base board (eg, for an inset sink and taps) before laminating it. If you fit a 'pierce and trim' bit, you can then drill through the laminate – and trim it exactly to follow the shape of the cut-out, because the bit is self-guiding, with the pin being aligned for this purpose.

Cutting circles

A unique feature of the router is the ease with which it will make a perfect circle. Most models come with an accessory which acts like the point of a pair of compasses. You use it as a pivot while you swing the machine round.

This way you can employ the various grooving bits to make any number of patterns which depend on circles or parts of circles. If you take enough passes at successively greater depths, you can even cut right through the material – producing, for example, a perfectly circular table-top or bread-board. Such a job is almost impossible with hand tools alone.

Freehand routing

It's also possible to use a router completely freehand, without any sort of fence or other guide at all. This happens mainly when you're 'carving' or 'engraving' lettering or other patterns on a flat surface, and it needs a bit of practice. A light machine is easiest to handle on this type of job. The usual bits for the purpose are 'veining' bits (see USING A ROUTER 1, page 70), which have very small diameters and square, V-shaped or rounded ends.

4 *The tongue should be a tight push-fit in the groove. Cut it too thick, if anything: you can always re-set the fence and make it thinner.*

5 *For a double rebate joint, set a two-flute or rebating bit to a depth of half the board thickness before cutting. The bit used here is self-guiding.*

9 *A loose tongue, usually of thin plywood, is often useful. If necessary, widen the groove by making a second cut, slightly higher or lower.*

10 *When grooving the second piece, be sure to keep it the same way up, for perfect alignment when you glue the tongue into position.*

Ready Reference

ROUTED JOINTS

Because a router cuts grooves and rebates very easily, it lets you make several strong yet inconspicuous board joints. The plain housing (A) requires no edge work – just a groove. The barefaced housing (B) needs a rebate as well. Rebate (C) and double rebate joints (D) are also simple; while the dovetail housing (E, and see photographs) repays in strength what it demands in precision. Tongued-and-grooved joints can have a moulded tongue (F) or a loose tongue in paired grooves (G).

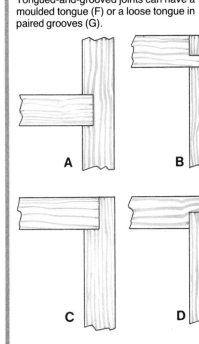

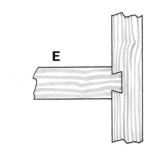

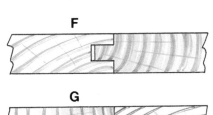

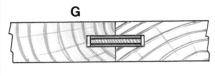

As with all other routing techniques, your best plan is simply to make a few test runs on scrap timber and board to see what effects you can obtain, before applying your ideas to an actual project.

Setting up a job

As a matter of fact, the use of a 'test piece' is absolutely standard practice in professional woodworking shops. In general, power tools are capable of very fine adjustment, and among do-it-yourself models this is especially true of the router. An alteration of even a millimetre or so in the setting – up, down or sideways – will usually have a noticeable effect when you come to do the actual machining.

Indeed, in the timber trades 'setting up' a tool quite often takes longer than the job itself. This preparation time isn't wasted; on the contrary, it's essential for a trouble-free result. The care you invest in choosing the right bit,

setting the depth, adjusting the fence, and so on, will always be repaid with better finished work.

Router safety

Despite its extremely high speed, the portable router in normal use is probably less dangerous than a circular saw. Plunge routers score in this respect because the bit retracts.

However, you need to get into the habit of only plunging immediately before cutting, and always letting the motor spring back immediately afterwards. Don't lay the machine down, either upright or on its side, while it's still plunged – and certainly never, ever, if it's switched on too. That would mean either a hole in your workbench, or a horribly dangerous exposed bit.

While cutting, keep both hands on the tool, and feed it in the right direction when doing edging jobs. Lastly, when changing bits, pull the plug out.

USING A ROUTER: 3

Earlier articles on using a router have dealt with basic techniques. To exploit your machine to the full, it's also well worth knowing some of the methods professionals use for speed and accuracy.

The advanced uses of the router fall under three main headings. You can use special jigs and templates; you can mount it for use as a 'spindle'; and you can mount it in a stand.

Using a jig

What marks out a good wood machinist is largely his inventiveness in using jigs and templates – devices for guiding the cutter or blade accurately through, into, along or round the workpiece and vice versa. The clamped-on batten, which guides the router to cut a straight groove (see pages 70-74) is a very simple jig, but the same principle is used for all others.

Suppose, for a start, that you want a wide groove, but have no bit large enough. You merely clamp battens on both sides, instead of just one, and move the router from side to side as well as forwards.

You can extend the batten principle to cut joints, too. If you want a number of identical halvings, it's usually a simple matter to clamp all the pieces side by side, fix battens across them, and move the router between these as if making a groove – cutting all the halvings at once. This ensures speed, plus (if you've set the job up correctly) total accuracy.

Similarly, suppose you want a recess – eg, for a flush handle in a sliding door. Trying to make this freehand is most unwise, because you're unlikely to cut accurately all the way round. Even if you manage it once, you'll never repeat the trick – as you might need to if you were fitting a pair of handles.

The solution is, of course, a jig: in this case, a 'box guide', the equivalent of four straight battens to guide the tool round the four sides of the recess. These pieces should be positioned and joined so that, when the router base is run against them, the bit will cut round the line you require. The box guide must therefore be bigger than the recess you want, so the base fits inside with room to manoeuvre.

You'll also need a means of locating any jig firmly and accurately. For small jobs, cramps are probably most efficient. In general, too, jigs and templates should be fairly heavy and substantial. That way there's less risk of slipping and harming the work or yourself.

A BEDSIDE CABINET

Almost all the joints in this unit are cut with the router, like the shapes at the bottom – see photographs. The groove in each front leg stops above the mortise.

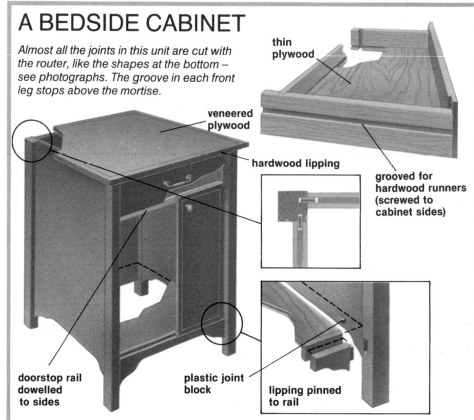

thin plywood

veneered plywood

hardwood lipping

grooved for hardwood runners (screwed to cabinet sides)

doorstop rail dowelled to sides

plastic joint block

lipping pinned to rail

A ROUTER TABLE

Made of chipboard, plywood or blockboard, and jointed with screws and/or plastic blocks, this table serves for a spindle (below) or for an 'overarm router' set-up (see Ready Reference).

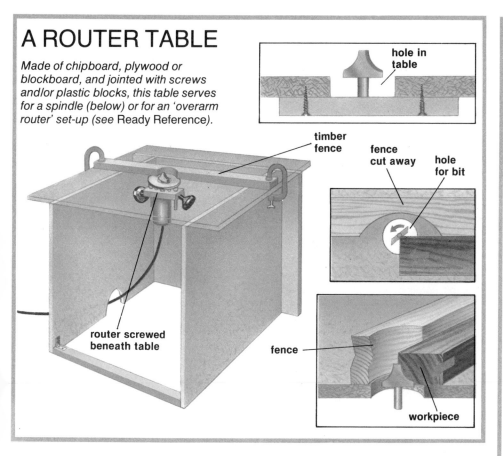

hole in table

timber fence

fence cut away

hole for bit

router screwed beneath table

fence

workpiece

THE OVERARM ROUTER

One way of making a router table is to fit the machine into a drill stand. Lower it, and push the work under the bit – usually against a fence.

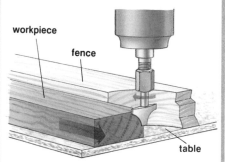

workpiece

fence

table

USING TEMPLATES

With a hand-held router, you fit a template guide to follow a jig or template which will produce the required shape. The template needs to be a different size from the workpiece. To find out by how much (A), subtract the bit diameter (B) from the outside diameter of the guide (C). Make the template thicker than the amount the guide protrudes from the router base to allow the guide to slide easily.

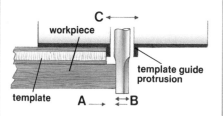

C

workpiece

template guide protrusion

template

A

B

On the overarm router, templates are used with a guide pin, centred under the bit. A pin and bit of the same diameter (1) let you make the template the same size as the workpiece. Otherwise make the template smaller (2) or larger. The pin can be made of hardwood or steel. A hardwood pin lets you do without a packing piece, allowing the bit right down to meet the pin.

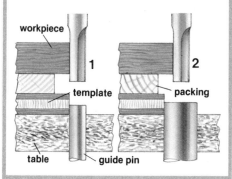

workpiece

1

2

template

packing

table

guide pin

The template guide

When the router is guided by its base, you have to allow for as much as half the base diameter when making the jig or positioning your guide battens. This is no good for fine work, especially where curves are involved. The answer there is a 'template guide'. This is a small metal plate with a sort of funnel in the middle. The plate is screwed across the hole in the router base, so that the funnel fits over the bit like a sleeve and projects in the same way as the bit does.

You can then guide the router by running the side of the funnel along the edge of a jig, which is often a flat pattern or 'template' of plywood (or a harder material) cut to the desired profile. The workpiece – often cut roughly to shape already – is fixed under the template with cramps, pins or double-sided adhesive tape, so that the bit cuts into or through it as the router is guided along. The template must be thicker than the funnel is long, so the guide will slide easily.

When making a template (see *Ready Reference*) for use with the hand-held router, you have to allow for the difference between the diameter of the bit and the outside diameter of the funnel. If you subtract the former from the latter and divide by two, you'll know how much smaller (or larger) the template should be than the piece you want to end up with.

Templates are useful whenever you want to repeat a special shape. You'll get perfect copies – provided the template doesn't include any concave curves whose radius is smaller than that of the funnel, because the template guide won't follow them. The results, of course, depend on the accuracy of the template. To make it, use shaping tools to cut out and create exactly the profile you require for the job.

Self-guiding trimming bits (shown on pages 75-79) are also useful for template work. While the ball-bearing guide runs along the template, the cutter cuts the workpiece. The template goes on top of or underneath the piece, depending on the position of the bearing.

Such bits do away with the template guide, and – provided the bearing is the same size as the cutter – they let you make the template the same size as the final shape. In fact, you don't need a template as such. You just make the first piece the right shape by hand, and use that instead.

The template guide itself has other uses than for making repeated shapes. It can be used for recessing, if you make a jig on the lines described, and for mortising, because a mortise is simply a deep, narrow recess.

Lastly, it can be used for dovetailing – in conjunction with a dovetail bit, plus a dovetailing jig which you clamp over the

USING A SPINDLE

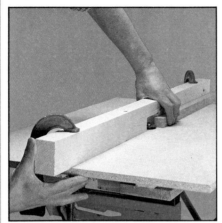

1 *With the bit poking up through the table, move the cutaway fence over it, and cramp it tightly in position to give the width of cut you need for the job.*

2 *Switch on and push a test piece into the bit, holding it against the fence. Then check the depth and width of cut, adjusting either or both if necessary.*

3 *For stopped cuts (those which don't continue right along the piece) cramp a block of timber to the fence as a buffer in the position you want.*

4 *When you're sure the setting is right, switch the router on again and push each workpiece carefully past the bit with both hands to make the cut.*

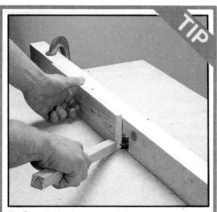

5 *Good design may let you re-use a setting for several cuts. This is a drawer side. When ending a cut, it's often safest to use a push stick.*

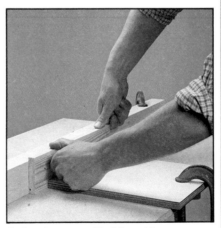

6 *Another way of holding thin workpieces safely against the bit is with a straight board, cramped to the table so the pieces can just be pushed past it.*

workpieces. The procedure is very like dovetailing with a power drill.

And you can use the same jig with a straight bit (in a router or drill) to cut finger joints.

The spindle

As already hinted, you can turn the portable router into a fixed machine. This is especially convenient for small workpieces – or long, narrow ones such as lengths of moulding – where it's hard to support the tool properly.

In a 'router table', as the fixed set-up is called, the machine may point upwards or downwards. Some manufacturers supply mountings in which it points sideways. The first arrangement is known as a spindle. You can buy a ready-made table for this, or make one from timber and boards – see illustration on page 81. The essentials are solid construction, and a flat top. The router is secured to the underside of the top, with its bit sticking up through a hole. Use wood or chipboard screws – or, better still, machine screws in threaded bushes.

You'll also require a timber or plywood 'fence' along which to slide the work past the bit. Ideally this should itself be mounted to slide back and forwards, so you can vary the width of cut more easily, but it can be clamped on. It should be cut away, in width or thickness, at the point where the bit emerges through the table. You can adjust the depth of cut (ie, the amount the bit protrudes) on the machine as usual.

When using a spindle, safety should never leave your mind. Don't switch the router on until you're sure that both it and the fence are firmly fixed in position. Make sure you feed the workpiece against the rotation of the bit – ie, from right to left – or it may kick back at you. Always hold it firmly on course; this is important for accuracy as well as safety. And **keep your hands clear of the rotating bit at all times.** At the end of a cut, it's often better to push the workpiece through with a stick, while still holding the already machined end with your other hand.

The 'overarm' router

The alternative to a spindle is to mount the router in a stand, just like a power drill (removing it from the carriage first if necessary). This makes an 'overarm' router. Here too you'll need a table; the photographs show a ready-made pattern, but again, you can improvise if you prefer. You'll also require a removable fence.

Apart from all everyday jobs, the overarm router will tackle mortising, like a drill mounted in a shaping table. Tenoning is possible on either type of table (though it's usually more accurate on a spindle). You just fit a large straight bit and run the workpiece over (or under) it, end-on to the fence; then

MORTISING AND TENONING

1 For mortising with a hand-held router, first screw the metal 'template guide' into position in the router base. Its 'bush' projects below the base plate.

2 Allowing for the size of the guide, make a jig for it to follow when cutting. This should locate over the workpiece to give the cut you want.

3 Cramp the workpiece and jig together. Fit a straight bit (ideally one which is the same width as the mortise) and place the router on the jig.

4 With the template guide against the side of the jig, switch on, plunge and cut – still keeping the guide pressed against the jig's side and ends.

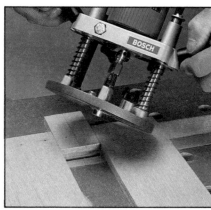

5 You'll end up with a round-ended mortise. A bit which was smaller than the mortise width would need a jig with four sides for an accurate groove.

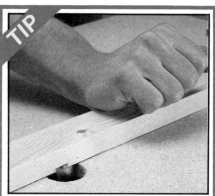

6 Use a spindle for routing tenons. Fit a wide straight bit, adjust it for the tenon shoulder depth and push the timber fence gently over it.

7 Clamp the fence at the right width of cut. Short tenons need only one cut on each side. Use a broad push block to keep the piece square to the fence.

8 Re-adjust the depth of cut (but not the fence). Then turn the piece on edge and cut each of the edge shoulders in turn in the same way.

9 Round the corners of the tenon with a chisel, and try it in the mortise for fit. If necessary, re-adjust the spindle slightly and re-cut the tenon.

turn the piece over to cut the other side – plus any edge shoulders. If the diameter of your bit is smaller than the length of the tenon, you'll need two or more passes. Set the fence so that you'll have cut the full length of the tenon by the time you're holding the piece up against it.

On any router table, you can make repeat shapes by removing the fence and using a template (you don't need a template guide). Again, you can use a self-guiding trimming bit. On the overarm router, however, there's an alternative – namely, to fit a guide pin. The guide pin is simply a cylindrical length of steel or even hardwood – or maybe a round-headed screw – driven into the table top with its centre exactly beneath the cutter's centre. It sticks up so you can run the template against it, lowering the router to cut the workpiece at the same time. A packing piece between workpiece and template helps ensure that the bit doesn't meet the guide pin.

In all template work (except on the spindle), you can cut internal as well as external shapes. You can shape, for example, the inside of a frame as well as the outside. The guide pin will do nicely for this. What's more, you can use the pin for recessing. Suppose you want to make a small box from a piece of solid hardwood, by recessing out the inside. You just make a template to the same size and shape as the recess, fasten the wood on top of it, and place it over the pin. Then you switch on, lower the router into the piece, and move the template and workpiece to and fro until the recess is hollowed out. The sides of the template will come up against the pin and stop you cutting too far.

If the template matches the shape you want, and the guide pin's diameter matches that of the bit, you'll get exact copies. If you vary the size of the pin (see *Ready Reference*) or bit, you'll get a shape that's larger or smaller – just as if you vary the size of the template instead.

The possibilities don't end there. For example, if you nail a board to the table and rotate it, you can cut a circle whose radius is the distance between the nail and the outside edge of the bit. It's simple enough – if you've got the imagination!

The router lathe
Perhaps the most ingenious appliance for routing is the router lathe. A do-it-yourself version of the automatic lathes now used in industry, this lets you make and shape cylindrical pieces.

You secure your length of timber – initially square in section – between the 'stocks' at each end, and fit your router to the carriage which slides on rails above it. You turn the work with a hand crank while the bit, often shaped, makes the cut. The router can also move along simultaneously at a pre-set rate, giving spiral cuts.

USING TEMPLATES

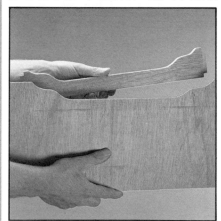

1 Template work is one use of the overarm router. Shape the workpiece roughly, then fix it over the template – eg, with double-sided adhesive tape.

2 When cutting, hold the template against the guide pin. If the pin is wooden, lower the bit into it – you need no packing between template and workpiece.

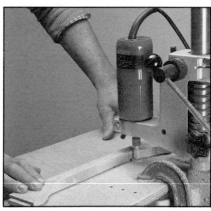

3 Hold the work firmly and feed it against the bit's rotation. Note that a larger guide pin means a smaller template (and vice versa).

4 With larger pieces, it's easier to fix the template on top, and cut with a hand-held router – plus a template guide with which to follow the shape.

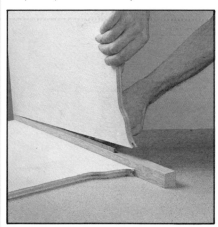

5 The cabinet's legs are joined to the sides and back with plywood tongues in routed grooves. The shaped template is used for sides, back and lower rail.

6 Routed grooves also take the drawer runners and bottom, and join its sides and back. Rebates are routed in the front to accept the sides.

USING CIRCULAR SAWS

The circular saw cuts natural timber and man-made boards accurately. It's an indispensable tool for all types of woodwork – as long as you know how to get the most out of it.

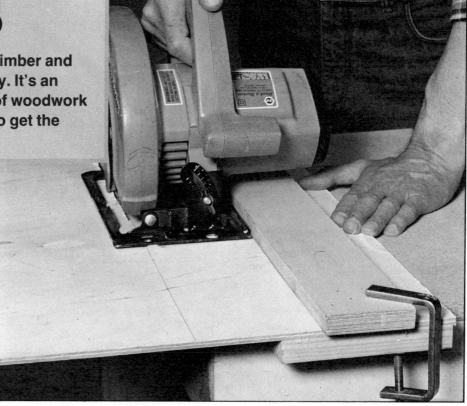

Circular saws do nothing that hand tools can't do, but they do the job much more quickly. This eliminates much tiring work – which in many cases also means greater accuracy, especially for the beginner. They're particularly useful for cutting man-made boards, because of the long cuts involved.

The one thing of which you must be constantly aware is the need to work safely. But that, of course, is a matter of developing good habits.

Choosing a saw

Circular saws are available either as integral units on their own, or as attachments for power drills; each type has its advantages. There's also a range of sizes and power outputs which demands careful consideration before buying. And there's a special blade for every purpose from coarse to fine cutting, in timber or man-made boards.

Circular saw drill attachments are often satisfactory for general use, and fairly cheap. Naturally, however, this depends on the power of the drill itself – and that's unlikely to be enough if you do a great deal of sawing, or if you frequently use hardwoods. There's also the fact that the attachment has to be removed if you want to do any drilling, and must then be replaced afterwards.

If you do get a saw attachment for your drill, remember one thing. Unlike integral circular saws, most drills can be locked in the 'on' position so that the drill is rotating even if it is unattended – in a saw bench, for example. Never do this while the saw attachment is fitted. You *must* always be able to stop a saw in an emergency by simply lifting your finger from the trigger.

Integral saws (those with their own motors) are rated according to size and power in a quite complex way. The lowest-powered, with a motor of 300-450W, will generally accept blades 125mm (5in) in diameter and will be capable of making cuts up to 30mm (1³⁄₁₆in) deep. The highest-powered saws have motors around 1000W, use 180mm (7in) blades, and can make cuts to a depth of 60mm (2³⁄₈in).

What you should check before you choose a saw is whether its vital statistics suit your likely use of it. Saws vary considerably in their maximum and minimum cutting depths – and these will be reduced if you're cutting with the blade at an angle.

The larger and more powerful the saw, the faster it will cut. This may not be all that important unless you make constant use of it. You may get good value from a cheaper saw, and some people find the larger ones daunting. But there's always the risk of burning out the motor on a low-powered saw by overloading it (ie, trying to cut too fast, or through material that's too tough).

The anatomy of a saw

On almost all types of circular saw, the blade cuts on the up-stroke. It's attached to the drive shaft or 'arbor' with a bolt fitted with a washer.

The top of the blade is protected by a permanent safety guard; the bottom (protruding) part has a spring-loaded guard which recedes automatically as the cut progresses, and springs back as you finish. This sprung guard may be made of either metal or plastic. If at any time you intend to cut metal or masonry, choose a saw with metal guards, which can't come to any harm from flying fragments, etc; plastic ones may crack or chip.

The depth of cut (ie, the amount by which the blade protrudes through the bottom of the saw) is adjusted by a calibrated knob on the side of the machine, raising and lowering

KNOW YOUR SAW

A circular saw is an indispensable tool, especially for cutting up man-made boards quickly and easily. You'll find it's not at all complicated to use, once you know your way round it. Very useful features are the depth adjustment, which regulates how far the blade protrudes downwards, and the angle adjustment, which enables you to cut with the blade at a slope (eg, for mitres).

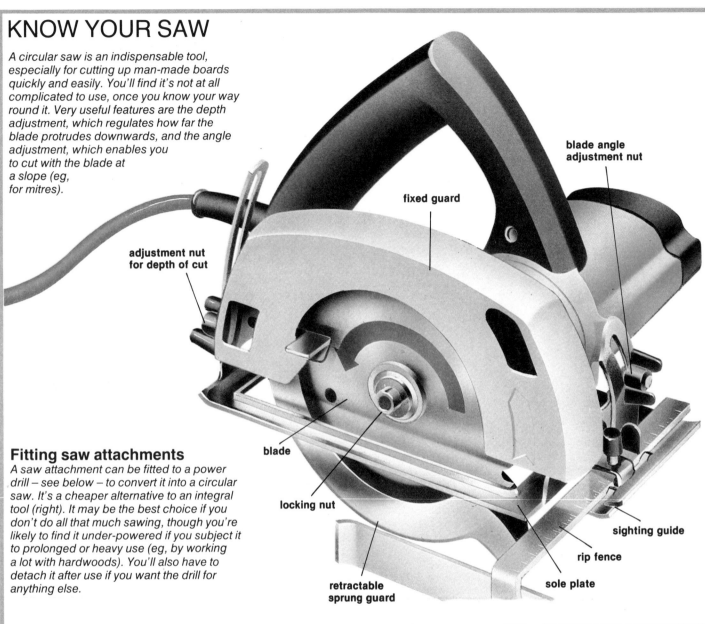

blade angle
adjustment nut

fixed guard

adjustment nut
for depth of cut

blade

locking nut

retractable
sprung guard

sole plate

rip fence

sighting guide

Fitting saw attachments

A saw attachment can be fitted to a power drill – see below – to convert it into a circular saw. It's a cheaper alternative to an integral tool (right). It may be the best choice if you don't do all that much sawing, though you're likely to find it under-powered if you subject it to prolonged or heavy use (eg, by working a lot with hardwoods). You'll also have to detach it after use if you want the drill for anything else.

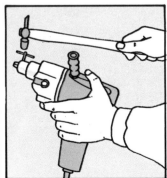

1 *Remove the chuck from the front of the drill, inserting the chuck key and tapping it with a hammer if necessary.*

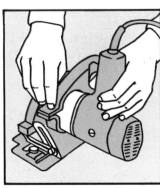

2 *Locate the saw attachment over the front of the drill, and tighten any fixing nuts which are provided.*

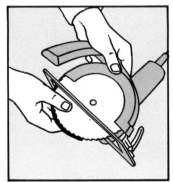

3 *Fit the blade, together with the retractable lower guard, into position over the shaft of the drill.*

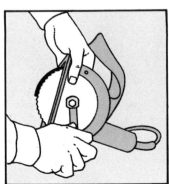

4 *Add the nut which holds the blade in place, get it finger-tight by hand, and finish tightening it up with a spanner.*

the body of the saw in relation to the sole plate (the saw's flat base). This depth should be slightly greater, by a millimetre or two, than the thickness of the material to be cut; if the blade protrudes too much, it will cause splintering.

There's also a second knob for angling the blade, usually adjustable in 5° steps – but you'll need to double-check with a protractor to guarantee accuracy, and make test cuts in scrap wood. Bear in mind that you'll also need to increase the cutting depth to allow for the cut being at an angle.

Circular saws use a detachable rip fence to guide the saw when making long, straight cuts parallel to the edge of the workpiece (eg, when 'ripping' – that is, cutting solid timber lengthwise). This is a T-shaped piece of metal; the 'leg' is fitted to the sole plate so that it sticks out to one side, while the cross of the T locates over the edge of the material you're cutting.

Some saws are also fitted with a 'riving knife' behind the blade, which keeps the cut open to prevent the saw from sticking.

Fitting the blade

Using a circular saw is extremely simple once you know your way around it and have practised a bit and gained confidence.

Fit the blade with the power off and the saw resting safely on the workbench. Be sure that the blade is the right way round and is properly centred on the spindle. Then jam it in place. Most blades have holes in them through which you can put a screwdriver blade for this purpose; otherwise, insert a piece of wood between the teeth. Start the fixing bolt on the thread with the utmost care – you want it to be a tight accurate fit to avoid accidents. Don't forget the washer, either.

Making a cut

Before you switch the mains power on, check that the retractable safety guard is working smoothly.

Always make sure, too, that the piece of wood you're cutting is securely clamped, either in a vice or with G-cramps. Don't work along long unsupported runs of material; clamp the other end as well, if necessary, to stop the piece wobbling about. And check that there's nothing beneath the work to get in the way of the saw. In a situation like this, it's all too easy to cut through your workbench by mistake, so beware.

Don't start the saw and then present it to the workpiece. It could jump back at you. Instead, rest the sole plate of the saw flat on the work and line the blade up, but keep it just a few millimetres back from the actual start of the cut. Then press the trigger and wait for a moment for the saw to reach full speed. Holding it firmly, advance it to the start of the cut.

SETTING UP AND BASIC CUTTING

1 Fit the blade and jam a piece of wood between the teeth to stop it moving. Some blades have holes for you to insert a screwdriver instead.

2 Tighten the blade nut very firmly indeed with a spanner. It's absolutely vital that it shouldn't come loose while you're cutting.

3 Adjust the height of the saw's body in relation to its sole plate, so the blade just protrudes through what you're cutting.

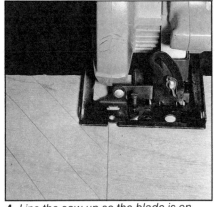
4 Line the saw up so the blade is on the waste side of your cutting line. A mark or cut-out on the front of the sole plate will guide you.

5 Draw the saw back, still keeping its sole plate flat on the surface. Press the trigger and let it reach full speed before starting to cut.

6 As you move the saw forward, the guard is pushed up from the back. It springs back down to cover the blade when the cut is finished.

USING A RIP FENCE

1 To cut timber lengthwise, or remove any narrow strip parallel to an edge, fit the fence the required distance from the blade and tighten the screw.

2 While cutting, make sure the fence stays flat against the edge of the material so you end up with a straight, parallel cut.

3 Where a rip fence is too short, use a batten instead. First measure from the side of the saw teeth to the edge of the sole plate.

The motion of the blade itself will help to draw the saw forward: don't force it, because that will strain the motor and may snag the blade, causing kickback – though most modern saws do have a slip clutch to prevent this kind of trouble.

At the end of the cut, switch off the saw and let the blade stop before removing it. Otherwise you'll cause splintering (always a problem with circular saws).

Using a guide batten

There will often be times when you want more accuracy than you can get from cutting freehand, yet the rip fence is no use, because your intended cut is either too far from the edge or not parallel to it.

In such cases the answer is to cramp a batten across the surface of the material you're cutting, so that you can keep the sole plate of the saw against it while sawing, thus maintaining a straight line. If you fix it to the part you want to keep, rather than on the waste side, you'll make it impossible for the saw to wander into the wrong area; the worst than can happen is for it to deviate onto the waste side, so that the workpiece will require trimming afterwards.

The batten needs to be thin enough for the body of the saw to pass over it. Also ensure that you position it accurately so that the blade cuts exactly down the waste side of the cutting line you've marked otherwise you'll simply be making more work for yourself.

Cutting joints

Jointing boards (for example, when you're making box furniture) always demands thought and care. The circular saw is a great help here, because it can cut three types of joint: mitre, rebate and housing.

Cutting a mitre (ie, a mitre in the thickness of a board, rather than across it – see photograph 2 on page 89) is simply a matter of setting the blade accurately to an angle of 45° from the vertical. The great thing about the mitre is that it hides the end grain of both pieces, and this makes it very useful in furniture construction, especially where man-made boards are used. However, in freestanding structures it needs some reinforcement, such as plastic jointing blocks.

CUTTING REBATES AND HOUSINGS

1 Using the rip fence, cut along the inside of the marked rebate first. Set the depth of cut to less than the material's thickness.

2 Make parallel cuts to remove the rest, moving the fence in each time, and clean up the finished rebate with a chisel if necessary.

3 Make a housing in a similar way. Cut its sides first, then remove waste from the middle of the housing with successive parallel cuts.

4 *Align a straight piece of timber or plywood parallel to the cutting line, distancing it from the line by the amount you've just measured.*

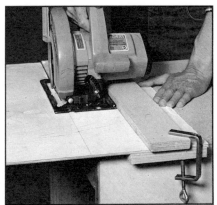

5 *Cramp the batten on and hold the saw against it as you cut. If it's fixed to the workpiece, not the waste, you can't cut too much off.*

A rebate can be cut by using the rip fence, set very close in and adjusted for successive parallel cuts until you've made the required 'ledge' across the edge of the piece.

Parallel saw cuts also make housings and grooves (for example, to take the ends of shelves). The rip fence may be too short for use here, so you may need a batten instead; re-locate it for each individual cut.

Using a saw table
So far we've dealt with using a portable circular saw freehand. However, professional woodworking shops possess larger circular saws ('bench saws') which are mounted in fixed units. The advantage of fixed saws is that you have both hands free to guide the work into the blade. That, plus a flat surface on which to rest the work, means greater convenience and accuracy.

While full-scale purpose-built home bench saws for the keen do-it-yourselfer are available, there's a cheaper alternative. You can mount your portable circular saw in a bench – basically a table with a hole in it. The saw is fixed underneath the bench so that the blade sticks up through the hole. The bench can be either bought or home-made from timber and man-made boards.

All saw benches are fitted with adjustable fences for accurate cutting, whether parallel to an edge or at an angle. Perhaps their only drawback is that the exposed blade makes them more dangerous than portable saws.

MAKING ANGLED CUTS

1 *To cut at other than 90°, adjust the angle of the sole plate in relation to the blade. Degree markings are calibrated on the fitting.*

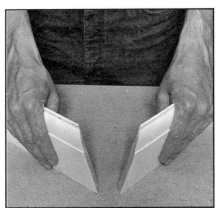

2 *A circular saw with the blade set at 45° is ideal for cutting mitres in skirting boards where they join at external corners.*

Ready Reference

WHAT BLADE TO USE
There are a number of blades available for cutting a variety of materials. These are some of the more common:

General purpose blade
Sometimes known as a **combination blade** (A). This is good for softwood and chipboard. You can buy blades for rip (B) or cross-cuts (C).

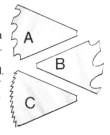

Planer blade
This gives a neat cut in timber hardboard and plywood.

Compo or wallboard blade
Used for cutting wallboards. It has fine teeth to prevent fraying.

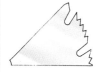

Flooring blade
You should use this blade for old wood that might conceal nails.

Masonry cutting disc
Cuts ceramics and other tough materials. It's hard going using one of these without a powerful saw.

Metal cutting blade
This is used for soft metals.

Metal cutting wheel
You'll have to use one of these when cutting hard metal or plastics.

CUTTING LAMINATES
Circular saws are not ideal for cutting laminates, but you can cut them with a tungsten carbide blade. For coated boarding cut with the decorative side down. Otherwise use a hand tenon saw or a fine toothed jig saw.

BASIC VENEERING

Veneering offers effects of spectacular beauty which you can't obtain in any other way. It's a specialised procedure, but you can soon master the basic techniques and produce highly acceptable results on almost every kind of furniture.

The word 'veneering' smacks slightly of deceit and camouflage. This is unfair. For centuries, sticking down a thin sheet or veneer of especially attractive and often exotic timber to a 'ground' of cheaper and commoner material has been a means of displaying its beauty where cost, rarity (and often available sizes) would prevent its use in any other way.

Veneering was extensively used throughout the golden age of cabinet-making, and nowadays veneers of even the highest quality are mass-produced. The invention of artificial boards has been another stage of progress – closely related, in that plywood is made entirely of veneers, and blockboard includes them on both faces. The two developments have combined in the veneered boards which go into a huge proportion of all modern furniture.

A companion skill is that of marquetry – the creating of patterns, often incredibly beautiful and complex, from small pieces of veneer arranged side-by-side. Though within the scope of the skilled do-it-yourselfer, this demands a lot of time and practice, so consult a specialist book first.

Types of veneer

Veneers are produced in three main ways:
● sawing, the traditional method, which is now only used for hard and difficult woods
● rotary cutting, which has revolutionised veneer production and made plywood possible. It involves steaming the log and rotating it against a knife to peel the veneer off in a continuous sheet. This is why a large piece of plywood often displays a repeated pattern. Such veneers are usually cut from cheap, plentiful and featureless timbers, eg birch, pine, gaboon and lauan. They can be anything from 0.25mm (1/100in) to 10mm (3/8in) thick
● knife cutting, which has solved the problem of mass-producing veneers that display fine timbers at their best, unlike most examples of rotary cutting. In this process, standard for decorative face veneers, the log (again usually steamed) is slid repeatedly against a fixed knife. The resulting thickness is generally 0.7mm.

Basic considerations

Although even the nearest equivalent to industrial veneering gear would require a huge outlay, you still have at your disposal two time-honoured if much less sophisticated methods – hot veneering and caul veneering.

But what advantage is there in veneering? It enables you to make furniture and fittings with natural decorative effects which are exactly tailored to your own requirements. You can put the uniformity of factory pieces behind you. Even simple white-painted units, if they incorporate your own veneered doors and drawers, give an air of quality to any room.

How do you obtain veneers? If you don't live within easy reach of a veneer merchant, you can order them by post. Addresses can be found in woodworking magazines, and a wide range of timber species is on sale.

Veneer merchants are helpful people who will give you advice on comparative costs, size, availability, quality, matching, suitability, etc. As a general guide, remember that there's little point in using common African hardwoods which are widely available already laid on boards, nor in taking a lot of trouble with bland, characterless veneers such as beech. But don't go to the other extreme. Exotic and expensive veneers such as Rio rosewood and macassar ebony should be left alone until you've had some experience; they can be difficult to work with, and you don't want to waste your money.

You need not only the decorative facing

Ready Reference

USING ANIMAL GLUE

Animal glue comes as jelly and liquid, but more often in 'pearls' or slabs which you soak 2:1 with water in a plastic container (breakable if the contents solidify) and heated over a gas or electric ring. It must be used hot, but never boiled or it won't stick. Dried scraps and crusts can be put back in the pot and melted down.

USING LIPPING

Lipping is often best applied (A) before flushing off and veneering over (B). On doors, it's not needed below eye level – but make it thicker to take hinges.

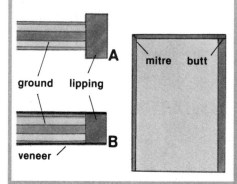

ground   lipping   **A**   mitre   butt

veneer   **B**

HOT VENEERING

1 *Clear your work area, and make ready a fresh pot of glue, a warm iron, hot water and rags. Put your veneer hammer in the water to warm.*

2 *Check the glue is very hot and free of lumps, then quickly spread it all over your 'ground' (the board on which you're laying the veneer).*

3 *Slightly dampen the veneer (trimmed just oversize), lay it on the ground, spread a little glue on top as a lubricant, and push hard with the hammer.*

4 *Squeeze out as much of the glue as you can. When it gels as it cools, fold a wet cloth and iron the veneer through it. Don't let it steam too much.*

5 *Then use your hammer again to force out the rest of the glue and ensure suction all over. You can hold it by the handle instead of the head.*

6 *Trim edges by placing a scrap block on top and tilting it to press the overhang downwards; then cut through the underside with a sharp knife.*

veneer but also a 'balancer' veneer for the reverse side – even if, for example, it's the underside of a table top that will never be seen. If only one side of a board is veneered, it will quickly bow. A balancer equalises the stresses and thus removes this tendency. Naturally, a cheaper wood – commonly African mahogany – is used for this purpose.

You can veneer on solid timber or man-made board. However, chipboard is too porous for hot veneering. If used for caul work, it must have a 'furniture finish' – a surface of small particles.

Whatever ground you use will require edge treatment ('lipping') if the edges are to be visible. This can be a strip of veneer, but the way edge veneers chip and come unstuck gives veneering a bad name. Instead, use a solid wood lipping (see page 320) – especially if the edges are likely to come in for a lot of wear. This will never chip, and bruises can eventually be planed off.

If you first lip and then veneer the board, the veneer covers the edges of the lipping. It will never be seen, and the result will look like solid timber. Use the same wood for the lipping as for the face veneer.

Make your lipping about 4mm wider than the board is thick, because it's impossible to cramp in position with absolute accuracy: plane off the excess afterwards. Tongued-and-grooved lipping should locate more precisely. Thin lippings are best cramped with 'softening' battens to distribute the pressure evenly right along them.

Hot veneering

Success in all veneering depends on leaving nothing to chance. Begin by giving your panel a good sanding, for smoothness and so the adhesive will stick. Don't use glasspaper in case you cause scratches or leave lumps of glass in it: both may show through the veneer.

The adhesive must be animal ('Scotch') glue – not an impact type. This has the tremendous advantage of quick setting coupled with equally fast melting under heat. It's prepared by soaking or heating; it mustn't be burnt or boiled.

First 'size' your prepared panel with thin glue from a fresh pot and leave it to dry. Meanwhile, trim your veneer to size by making repeated gentle cuts with a very sharp knife. Leave about 12mm (½in) overhang on all sides in case the veneer slips; don't leave too much or you'll find it tends to lift from the edges.

Before going any further make sure you have at hand a veneer hammer (see *Ready Reference*), a supply of clean rags and clean hot water, a hot iron and some more fresh glue. Your bench top should be cleared of all other tools and equipment, and free of dirt and shavings. When you're hot veneering,

POSITIONING VENEERS

Decorative veneers, if not bought singly, come in bundles or 'packs' sliced from the log and stacked like rashers of bacon. These leaves can be cut and arranged in numerous patterns (A).

On solid wood, the veneer grain should run parallel to that of the ground (B), to allow shrinkage and swelling in tandem. If veneering only one side, make it the 'heart' side, to equalise natural bowing or 'cupping' (C). On artificial boards, the grain of the decorative veneer you're laying should be at right angles to that of the existing face veneer (D).

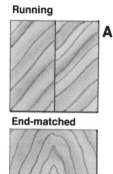

Running **A**

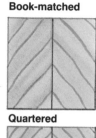

Book-matched

End-matched

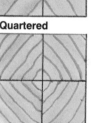

Quartered

B

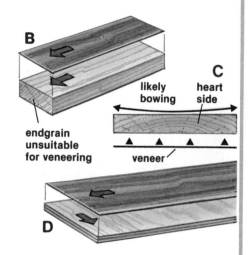

endgrain unsuitable for veneering

C

likely bowing — heart side

veneer

D

CROSSBANDING AND JOINTING

1 A crossband is a strip of veneer cut across the grain, glued along the margin next to the main veneer, hammered towards it and trimmed.

2 To join two sheets when hot veneering, first lay one in the usual way, ensuring it overlaps a centre line marked on the edge of the ground.

3 Lay the second piece likewise, again overlapping the centre line. If you're matching the grain (see illustration above), the overlaps must be equal.

4 Position (and ideally cramp) a straight edge along the line, and cut through both pieces at once. Avoid rust by taping its underside.

5 Remove the offcut of the second piece; then prise that up to remove the offcut of the first. Add more glue and/or iron the joint if needed, then hammer it.

6 Tape across and then along the joint to counteract shrinkage as the veneers dry out. As the surface is damp, gummed paper tape will stick best.

the glue gets everywhere, so you may want to cover the whole surface with newspaper – but you may also find that its tendency to get stuck to the work makes this more trouble than it's worth. Animal glue is water-soluble; you can wipe any surplus off with a damp cloth when you've finished.

Damp (without soaking) both surfaces of the veneer to stop them curling up with the glue. Spread it quickly and evenly on the ground and position the veneer. Some craftsmen advocate gluing the veneer too (perhaps temporarily securing it to the bench with four dabs of glue first); but this may not be necessary. Still working very fast, press the veneer down with your hammer. You may well find it helpful to spread glue on top of the veneer first as a lubricant, because you'll be applying a lot of pressure. Start from the middle and make zig-zag strokes to squeeze out every bit of excess glue; it should ripple ahead of the hammer. Always push along the grain, never across it.

However quickly you work, you're unlikely to finish before the glue has cooled enough to form intractable jellified lumps under the veneer. Fold a piece of cloth and iron the veneer through it. Keep the iron moving, and ensure that it's not so hot as to make steam: like soaking, this will expand the veneer, causing trouble when it shrinks as it dries after laying. An aluminium-soled iron, incidentally, avoids rust and consequent stains

Use your hammer again as before. When you think the veneer is well and truly down (held by suction as well as by the glue), tap the surface to detect any unglued parts.

Correct these by either of two methods. One is to slit the veneer with the grain, ease it up, add a little more glue, squeeze the surplus out and then cover the slit with adhesive paper – to be removed with water when the glue is properly set. It won't show. The other is to push some glue towards the loose patch, let it cool, force it away again, and then iron the veneer to get rid of the glue with a hammer before bursting the blister with a pin and finally sticking it down.

A sharp-edged piece of wood makes a safe and effective scraper for excess glue. Lay the balancer veneer in exactly the same way, and leave the board to dry for a day or two before sanding.

Many exotic veneers are only available in narrow widths (because they come from thin trees) and will require jointing – a technique also used to form decorative patterns. You do this by laying the pieces so they overlap, and cutting through both.

Traditionally, veneered work was cleaned up with a cabinet scraper and fine glass-paper or garnet paper. Nowadays these have been largely replaced by the orbital sander. Don't use a coarse abrasive: you can soon go through a thin veneer.

Caul veneering

Hot veneering, though fascinating, may sound too risky and too much like hard work. Caul veneering is a different story. It's a straightforward technique which produces excellent results even for beginners. And it lets you do a dry run first.

You need a board at least 18mm (¾in) and preferably 25 to 32mm (1 to 1¼in) thick – slightly larger than the panel to be veneered. This 'caul' is laid on top of the veneer, which in turn is laid on top of the glued panel, and pressure is applied to it – usually by means of cramps.

Obviously, even large G-cramps don't reach to the middle of a wide panel, so battens are enlisted to help. These need to be strong – at least 50x25mm (2x1in) and, for larger jobs, preferably 75x50mm (3x2in). Both caul and battens can be used for any number of jobs.

Prepare and lip the ground just as for hot veneering, and select your veneers likewise. If using more than one leaf, match the pieces as necessary and cut them to length, adding about 6mm (¼in) at either end. Don't cut them to width, because your next job is to plane their edges to make a perfect joint – an apparently impossible task that is, in reality, quite easy. All you do is to cramp the veneers between two lengths of wood which act as a guide for the plane.

Now tape them together. A transparent adhesive tape is probably best, though some people still prefer sticky paper. Then trim the veneers to width on the outer edges, leaving an overhang here too.

Place your panel on the bench, or another suitable base if you don't want your bench out of action. Nearby, position your caul and battens, plus cramps which have been opened at the correct distance (base + panel + caul + battens + 12mm/½in).

Veneer both sides at once (in fact, you can even veneer several panels at once, stacking them up before cramping). A PVA adhesive is best here; cover the panel, and allow it to get just a little tacky (but only a little) to prevent slippage. Then position the panel on the backing veneer – itself laid on a sheet of plastic to prevent it sticking to the base. Position the face veneer (or veneers) on top, followed by the caul. Position the battens and tighten the cramps as shown in *Ready Reference*.

Leave the job until the adhesive has set. At that stage, remove the cramps, batten and caul, and trim the veneer – but resist the temptation to pull off the tape. The veneer may come with it. Instead, test a short length first. If the tape doesn't come away cleanly, gently sand it off.

Glue that's come through to the face interferes with some finishes, so a good final cleaning-up is essential.

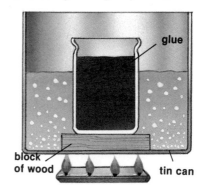
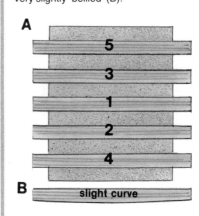

CAUL VENEERING

1 To join two pieces for caul work, cut them roughly straight with a knife, then stack and cramp them between battens so 2-3mm (1/8in) protrudes.

2 Plane the twin edges flush with the battens. You may find it easiest to start by planing the far end, and then work back towards you.

3 Join these pieces – or the sections of any pattern – tightly across and along with transparent adhesive tape (which is also easy to remove).

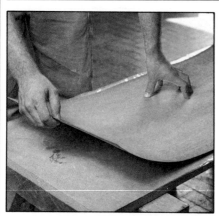

4 Preferably on trestles, lay a stiff board larger than the panel to be veneered, followed by plastic (not newspaper) and backing veneer – also slightly oversize.

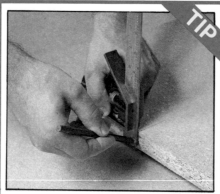

5 Mark on the panel edge where you want to position any joint between veneers (eg, on the centre line). This is the only way to align the pattern.

6 Spread PVA adhesive thinly but evenly and thoroughly over one side of the panel (especially edges), reverse it, and lay it on the backing veneer.

7 Spread PVA on top of the panel, and carefully position the face veneer. Be sure to align any joint with the appropriate mark on the panel edge.

8 Gently lay another sheet of plastic on the face veneer, and position a thick, oversized board (the caul) squarely on top of the stack.

9 Squeeze the 'sandwich' with stout battens (Ready Reference) and lots of cramps, hired if necessary. An extra-thick caul and weights might work too.

MAKING DOVETAIL JOINTS

Dovetail joints are not only beautiful, they're very strong. Once you know the right way to cut them, it only takes practice to get a good fit every time.

Most pieces of wooden furniture are built as either frames or boxes. The mortise and tenon, as the principal framing joint, is common in chairs and tables. But in box construction the dovetail has traditionally reigned supreme.

True, modern storage furniture often uses screws, dowels, assembly fittings, and edge joints cut with power tools. But you only have to look at a set of dovetails to see that they make the perfect corner joint between flat timbers such as box sides – including the top and side panels of furniture 'carcases'.

In fact, dovetails are impossible to pull apart. That's why they're found joining drawer sides to drawer fronts and sometimes backs. Every time you open a drawer, you're trying to pull the front off – and the dovetail joint withstands this tendency as no other joint can. Note, however, that it only locks in one direction. If you use it the wrong way round where its strength matters, its unique properties are wasted.

There's one other major point to remember. Chipboard is far too weak a material in which to cut dovetails – although, at a pinch, they'll work in plywood and good-quality blockboard.

The dovetail joint is always admired and even respected. But there's really no mystery about it. While no one could pretend that well-fitting dovetails are easy for a beginner to cut, the only secret of success is practice; and you'll find things go a lot more smoothly if you stick closely to the time-tested procedure described here.

Anatomy of a dovetail joint
Dovetails themselves are fan-shaped cutouts in the end of one of the pieces being joined – fan-shaped, that is, when you look at the face of the piece.

The sides of each tail slope along the grain at an angle of between 1 in 5 (for a 'coarse' but strong joint, suitable for softwood and man-made boards) and 1 in 8 (generally considered the best-looking, and usually used with hardwoods). If you make them any coarser, they may break; any finer, and they may tend to slip out under strain.

Between the tails, when the joint is assembled, you can see the 'pins' cut in the other piece. These, of course, follow exactly the same slope or 'rake' as the tails – but across the endgrain, so you can only see their true shape when looking at them end-on. Note that there's always a pin at either end; this helps to secure both pieces against curling up.

The spacing of the tails is another factor in the joint's appearance. In general, the wider they are (and therefore the further apart the pins are) the better – but this too affects the strength if you overdo it.

Marking out the tails
The first step in making a dovetail joint is to get the ends of both pieces square (they needn't be the same thickness). Particularly if it's your first attempt, you may find it wise to leave a little extra length as well – say a millimetre or two.

After that, it's customary to start with the tail piece (which is the side, not the front, in the case of a drawer). First decide on the slope of your dovetails – say 1 in 6 – and mark it out on a scrap of wood or paper. That's just a matter of drawing two lines at right angles to each other, then making a mark six units along one, and another mark one unit up the other. Join up the marks with a diagonal, and set a sliding bevel to the same slope.

Now you need to work out where each tail should come. However, there's no need for fiddly calculations. First decide the width of

Ready Reference

WHAT IS A DOVETAIL JOINT?
A dovetail joint consists of 'tails' on one piece and 'pins' on the other. When they're fitted together, the joint is completely inseparable in one direction (shown by an arrow). It's very strong the other way too.

The contrast between endgrain and face grain (especially if the two pieces are of different woods) can also make an attractive decorative feature.

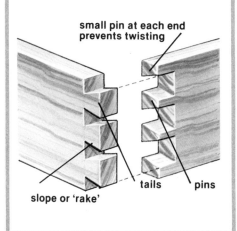

small pin at each end prevents twisting

slope or 'rake'

tails

pins

95

MARKING OUT THE TAILS

1 Plane both pieces to exactly the same width, and check that the ends are dead square. Correct with a block plane if necessary.

2 Square the end pins' width along the tail piece, then slant a measure between the lines to give handy divisions for the pin centres.

3 Use a gauge to extend these centre marks from the slanting line down to the end of the piece, where the tails will be cut.

4 Make another mark 3mm (¹⁄₈in) either side of each centre mark. This will give you the widths of the tails at their widest.

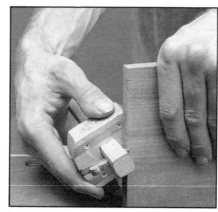

5 Set a sharp marking gauge, or preferably a cutting gauge, to the exact thickness of the pin piece or a bit more – but no less.

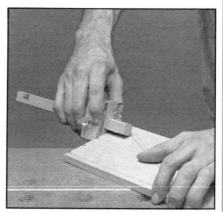

6 Score a neat line all round the end of the tail piece with the gauge. It's usual to leave this visible in the finished joint.

7 Set a sliding bevel (or make a card template) to a slope of 1 in 6 – ie, six units in one direction and one unit in the other direction.

8 Use the bevel or template to mark out the slope of the tails, working inwards from the marks which denote the tail widths.

9 Square the width marks across the end of the piece, then mark the slope again on the far side with the bevel or template.

TYPES OF DOVETAIL JOINT

Coarse and fine dovetails
For general work, tails and pins are equally spaced and steeply raked (below left) – unlike fine work (below right).

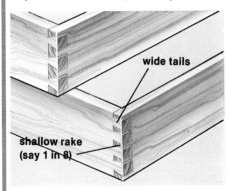

Lap dovetails
Concealed by an overlap, unlike through dovetails (shown in Ready Reference*), these are traditional in drawers.*

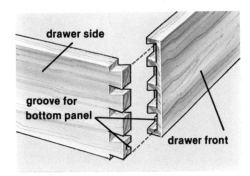

Dovetail housings
The dovetail housing is the odd man out – it's not a corner joint. The tail runs across the width.

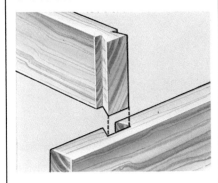

Cut like other housing joints (see pages 40-43), it can be plain (above) or barefaced (below). The latter will usually do.

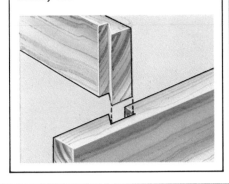

Carcase dovetails
A coarse dovetail joint traditionally joins sides to top on solid timber cabinets. An added top panel hides it.

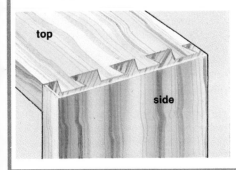

Framing dovetails
A large dovetail can provide useful strength in a frame where its locking properties are especially vital.

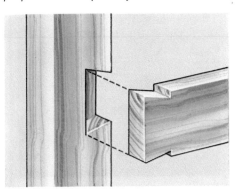

---

the pin at each end, and square that along the grain. Then place a tape measure diagonally between the squared lines, and swing it round to give a figure easily divisible into equal parts. Mark off these equal divisions, and square them along to the end of the piece. These are the centres of the gaps between your tails.

Then make a mark 3mm (1/8in) either side of each centre mark, and draw a line sloping inwards from it along the face – using the sliding bevel as your guide. Square these marks across the end, and then repeat them on the other face.

Lastly, set a marking or cutting gauge to the exact thickness of the pin piece, and scribe a line all round the end of the tail piece. If you've been allowing for extra length, add that to the scribed thickness. This will make the tails slightly too long; when the joint is complete, trim them flush with a block plane.

At this stage, a very wise precaution is to hatch in – or mark with an X – all the bits you're going to cut out.

Cutting the tails and pins
The next essential is to have the right saw. An ordinary tenon saw is too heavy; you need the lighter version actually known as a dovetail saw, or the still finer gent's saw. But even one of these, especially if new, will have too much 'set' – the teeth will project too far sideways, giving too wide and inaccurate a cut. You can remedy this by placing the blade on an oilstone, flat on its side, and very lightly rubbing it along. Do this once or twice for each side.

To make your cuts, cramp the tail piece in a vice. (If making, say, two identical sides for a box, you can cut more than one piece at the same time.) Align the timber so that one set of sloping marked lines is vertical. Cut along all these, one after the other, before tilting the piece the other way and cutting those on the opposite slope.

Saw immediately on the outside of each marked line, and begin each cut with the saw angled backwards, steadying its blade with your thumbnail. Once you've got the cut

established, tilt the saw forwards to make sure you're keeping to the line on the other side. Lastly, level the saw up as you finish the cut. Whatever you do, don't cut down past the gauged line!

The next step is to use your gauge to mark the thickness of the tail piece in turn on the pin piece.

A neat trick follows. Hold the pin piece in a vice, and cramp the tail piece over its end in exactly the intended position. Then, inserting the saw in the cuts you've just made, use it to score corresponding marks on the endgrain of the pin piece. Square these across its faces.

At this point you can remove the waste from between the tails. Begin by sawing out the little piece next to each of the two outer tails; then use a chisel. (Some people like to get the bulk of the waste out with a coping saw first.) Drive the chisel down into the face each time, keeping well in front of the gauge line, then tap the blade into the endgrain to get the chips up and out. Turn the piece over and do the same on the other side.

COMPLETING THE JOINT

1 With your gauge at the exact thickness of the tail piece or a little more, scribe a line all round the end of the pin piece.

2 Square along from this gauged line, on each side, to the ends of the slanting lines you've scored across the endgrain with the saw.

3 Make all the saw cuts at one angle first, then those at the other – their edges exactly on the outsides of the lines, as before.

4 After chiselling out the waste between the pins as for the tails, pare down the inside edge of each tail a little, for a smooth fit.

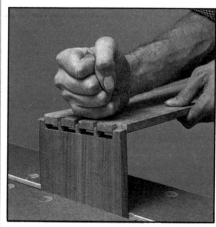

5 Fit the joint together halfway (but no further), keeping the pieces square to each other. Note any places where it sticks.

6 Holding the chisel blade, carefully shave where needed. Glue and cramp the joint, and plane the endgrain flush if necessary.

Lastly, place the chisel against (not over) the gauge line and pare away the rest. It's sensible to angle the tool inwards from each side, so that you actually 'undercut' – ie, cut beyond the line, but only inside the timber where it won't be seen. This helps to ensure the joint goes all the way home.

Saw out the pins as you did the tails. Again, the crucial thing is to cut immediately on the waste side – so that the outer edge of the saw teeth touches the line. If anything this is even more important now, at the pin stage, because you won't be able to make any further adjustments if the pins are loose between the tails.

Lastly, chisel out the gaps between the pins. Here too the procedure is similar to that for the tails.

Putting it together

Before you try assembling the joint, pare away any remaining unevenness which might make things difficult – being quite sure not to overdo it. You can even carefully shave the inside edge off both sides of each tail (especially the outer ones). This will be hidden after assembly.

Now comes the nerve-racking part: fitting the pieces together. At first, don't attempt to force them more than halfway, because dovetails fitted more than once become slack. See how well they go home, separate them, and make further adjustments with a chisel.

Then put some adhesive between the pins, and tap the tails right in. That's it. If it's a good joint, congratulations. If not, your next will be better, and the one after that better still – as long as you rely on sharp tools and gentle, accurate cutting. Hurry and force will only cause imprecision and heartbreak.

Lap dovetails

'Through dovetails', described above, can be seen from both sides. They look fine in most circumstances – especially since the modern tendency is to make a feature of them, using them in preference to hidden versions.

However, there is one variant worth knowing. In 'lap dovetails', only part of the endgrain on the pin piece is cut away to form pins; the rest (say one-third of the thickness) is left to overlap and thus hide the endgrain of the tails. For this reason, lap dovetails are traditional in fitting drawer-fronts.

When marking them out, you have to remember not to score a gauge line round the outside of the pin piece, and to allow for the lap thickness when gauging for the tails and pins. Cutting the pins is likewise a bit more difficult. However, mastery of through dovetails will give you the confidence to tackle lap dovetails, and thus expand your range of techniques still further.

LAMINATING WOOD

Laminating is a first-class way of making strong curved shapes. In its simplest forms it's ideal for several types of do-it-yourself job – so it's well worth adding to your range of skills. Here's how (and why) it's done.

For all its advantages, timber has one crucial limitation as a structural material – its strength is directional.

A square piece cut off a 150mm (6in) wide floorboard will be almost impossible to break across its width. Lengthwise, however, you can probably snap it in half by hand. The reason is fairly obvious. Almost all the timber's toughness is in the fibres themselves. There's relatively little strength in the bonds which hold them together, side-by-side.

This has important consequences. If you take a more or less straight-grained length of wood and cut from it a piece which has more than a very slight curve, you're liable to get areas of 'short grain': in other words, areas which measure less along the grain than across it. Such areas are very weak.

This problem becomes worse as the curve becomes more pronounced. It can be avoided by assembling the piece in several sections, each with its grain running at an angle which makes the best use of it. But this, though sometimes the only answer, is always a compromise.

Curved grain, bent wood and boards
The ideal answer is to use wood which is already the shape you want. But this could be difficult to find, and, in any case, many timbers are straight-grained.

Alternatively, you can bend pieces into shape. Components for Windsor chairs (page 184) were at first made by bending saplings. In the case of mature timber, however, all but the thinnest pieces will first need steaming to make them more pliable. This is perfectly practicable, even at home; but it does demand a bit of enthusiasm in setting-up, because you need to make a steam box.

The third possibility is to cut your shapes from man-made boards. In this case there's no short grain, since man-made boards either have no grain (as in the cases of chipboard, hardboard and the like) or have grain directions which alternate between layers (as with plywood and blockboard). However, it's usually very wasteful for the do-it-yourselfer to cut relatively small components from large sheets of board – and there are often finishing problems, especially on edges.

Why laminating?
Mention of plywood brings us to perhaps the most convenient method of all: laminating.

A laminate (or lamina) is a thin sheet of any material, intended for glueing to one or more further layers. The familiar plastic laminates, for example, are often glued to sheets of board material: the result is a 'laminated' structure, such as a worktop. Plywood and blockboard are themselves laminated.

The great thing about laminating wood is that it allows you to produce curves with the greatest of ease. Laminates, being very thin, will bend readily without any steaming: so you just glue together any number of them to make a curved piece of the thickness you want. In effect, it's purpose-built timber.

While laminating isn't a technique you need every day, it's a skill worth acquiring because of the added scope it gives you when designing a special item. It can simplify structures which would otherwise demand complex jointing, and it can often look very good into the bargain.

In addition, the slight flexibility of most laminated pieces gives them resilience; this adds to their strength, which is greater than that of solid timber anyway. 25mm (1in) is usually thick enough.

Materials for laminating
Some timbers are much better for laminating than others. Top of the league come beech, ash and elm, which are very pliable. Tropical

Ready Reference

LONG AND SHORT GRAIN
Experienced woodworkers automatically take into account the fact that timber is stronger along than across the grain. In most situations, a short-grained piece (A) will break far more easily than a long-grained piece (B).

Ways round this are shown on page 101. They include
● careful positioning of components in relation to one another
● selection of pieces for their grain pattern
● steam-bending
● the use of man-made boards
● laminating.

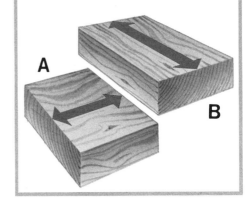

PREPARING THE FORMER AND LAMINATES

1 Start by drawing out the exact shape you want on a piece of card or stiff board. To begin with, it's best to steer clear of sharp curves.

2 Make a 'former' from softwood blocks glued and screwed to one another and to a base board. It must be strong and rigid to avoid distortion.

3 Use a Surform or rasp, plus a file if necessary, to remove any unevenness on the outside of the shape. It should match the inside curve on your drawing.

4 Wax the outside of the shape well with ordinary furniture wax, to ensure the laminates won't stick to it. It will help if you first apply a coat of paint.

5 Measure the distance along the outside of the shape you've drawn, in sections if necessary. Then cut all your laminates to a little over this length.

6 Stack the laminates neatly, flush along one edge. If they're of solid timber, the grain should run lengthwise along each one.

7 Very thin plywood is another excellent material for laminates. In this case, they should be cut across the grain of the face veneers.

8 Position the stack of laminates where it can be easily cut to width (eg, overhanging the edge of a bench), and cramp it there with a suitable batten.

9 Cut along the laminates, allowing a margin of about 6mm (¼in) extra in the overall width. A jigsaw is probably the best tool for this operation.

MAKING CURVES

In woodwork, curves pose interesting problems.
1 *This table looks simple. But how can the leg structures be made strong enough – especially if fixed to the top without rails or other framing?*
2 *Cutting each from a single piece (or two glued side-by-side) is no good. The short grain means almost certain breakage.*
3 *Assembly in jointed sections is fine. But it takes time – and there may be snags (A) unless you can find a piece with suitably curved grain (B).*
4 *Bending makes an even stronger piece, but needs special equipment.*
5 *Using a man-made board also eliminates short grain, but may mean ragged edges. Obviously, the shape must be cut out in the flat.*
6 *For this job, laminating is ideal. It gets the most strength from the material, and makes a piece you can easily fix to the top.*
7 *The principle is simple; see also photographs.*

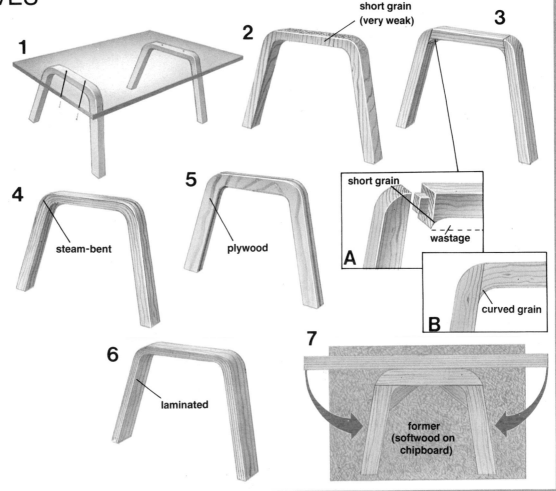

hardwoods such as mahogany aren't ruled out, but should only be used for gentle curves.

Softwoods are generally no good, because when bent they usually fracture at knots and other points of weakness.

Where do you buy laminates? They're really a type of veneer (see pages 90-94 for details) – sometimes, in fact, they're called 'constructional veneers'. So your most likely supplier is a veneer merchant. Even if he doesn't stock them, he'll be able to advise you. You won't find them on sale in a DIY shop, or even the average timber yard.

Laminates are usually sold by the sheet. They don't come in regular sizes and they vary considerably in length and width. In thickness, however, there's a degree of uniformity: most are available 1, 2 or 3mm (up to ⅛in) thick.

What thickness should you use? The general rule is: the tighter the curve, the thinner the laminates you need. So why not always use thin laminates – or even veneers? The only trouble is that you use more glue, and need more time to put them together.

The range of timbers available to you as laminates may be limited. You might, for instance, want to make a laminated coffee table in teak to match your existing furniture, yet be unable to find teak laminates. Do you give up and make for the nearest furniture shop? By no means. It's quite usual (and often cheaper) to use one timber for the basic lamination and add another in the form of a decorative veneer which goes on top. The only snag occurs if the sides of the piece must match its surface.

If you have your own circular saw table set up in your workshop, you can produce your own laminates. Unfortunately, this tends to be expensive, because for every laminate produced one disappears in sawdust. However, the technique may come in handy for special pieces of work, or to produce single laminates for decorative facings. You needn't plane saw-cut laminates, as their surfaces glue quite well.

The grain of solid timber laminates should always run lengthwise, or the finished piece will be short-grained and therefore weak.

But very thin plywood (0.8, 1.5 or 3mm thick) will, of course, bend very easily (like hardboard); better, in fact, than solid timber of the same thickness. It's therefore highly suitable for use as a laminate. In this case each piece should be cut so that the grain of its two outer veneers runs across it; this will make for easier bending, while the long grain of the middle veneer provides ample strength.

Which adhesive?
Not all adhesives are suitable for laminating. A word or two about adhesives in general is useful here.

A 'thermosetting' adhesive, such as a urea-formaldehyde type, can never be softened or reconstituted. Once set, it's set for good. 'Thermoplastic' adhesives, on the other hand (PVA and contact types), will soften if heat is applied. They also 'creep': surfaces glued with them will gradually come apart under stress. So, as laminated structures are always in tension, a thermosetting adhesive is absolutely essential for bonding the surfaces.

Because the adhesive is so important, do make sure that you follow the manufacturer's instructions precisely. Too much liquid and too much powder in the mix are equally likely to cause trouble.

Preparing the job

Simple laminating requires next to no special tools or equipment.

For each component you make, you'll need to build a 'former' on which you can bend and cramp the laminates. This can be used many hundreds of times; it's generally made of solid timber, screwed and glued to a stiff piece of board. Purely functional, it can incorporate scrap material; but it must be sturdy. In addition, the shape round which you'll be cramping the work must be exactly the one you want; and it should be longer (by 75-100mm/3-4in) and wider (by 6mm/¼in) than the finished size.

If you're looking for really tight curvature, only trial and error will tell you what can be achieved with particular laminates. Soaking them, and then cramping them without adhesive, may help – as long as you let them dry out thoroughly before final assembly; otherwise you'll weaken the glue. This is all part of the design process which gives you the former's final shape.

When the former is ready, mark your laminates and cut them to size, allowing the same margins as with the former itself. Many people say you need an odd number of layers, but in practice it makes no difference. The thickness of the adhesive, moreover, can be left out of your calculations when working out how many laminates to include.

The only specialised accessory you may need is a 'strap'. The same length and width as the shape on the former, this should ideally be of stainless steel, but can be of any thin metal – or even plywood, again cut across the face grain. Its purpose is twofold. Firstly, it prevents the outer laminate from fracturing as you bend it round the former. On gentle curves this probably wouldn't happen anyway; if the radius is small, however, it almost certainly would. Secondly, the strap is the best means of applying pressure to curves. Under tension it not only replaces cramps, but produces a smoother curve by distributing the force more evenly.

As with all glueing operations, the secret of success lies in the preparation. Clear your work surface, place the laminates next to the former, and wax the former thoroughly so the laminates can't stick to it; nothing is more frustrating than to find you can't get the work out of the former when the job is done. Any proprietary brand of furniture polish will do. It's also a good idea to apply a film of wax to the metal strap while you're about it.

Next, having mustered as many G-cramps as you can, set them to the correct opening.

GLUEING, CRAMPING AND FINISHING

1 *Mix the adhesive to a smooth paste, and coat both faces of all except the outer laminate. Work your way methodically through the stack.*

2 *Place the glued stack against the former, add a waxed steel or thin plywood 'strap', and cramp up – usually starting in the middle of the shape.*

5 *Now bend the strap and laminates round the curve. On well-rounded shapes, it helps if you G-cramp them together – loosely, to allow sliding.*

6 *When you're past the apex of the bend, remove the sliding cramp (if you've used one) and hold the stack in position close to the shape on the former.*

9 *Remove the lamination from the former and clean it off to leave neat, square edges. A Surform is ideal for this, as the adhesive will blunt a plane iron.*

10 *Sand the edges for a perfect finish: the result can be quite decorative. Remove any blemishes from the faces, too, and smooth them down.*

This is 12mm (½in) plus the combined thickness of the former, laminates and 'softening' timber. This last is needed because the strap only applies pressure to bends. You cramp any flat surface in the usual way, with G-cramps and a batten or wedges. The batten goes on the outside of the strap.

You can also use shaped softening blocks which follow the curves. These must be accurately cut – but they can do away with the strap entirely if you leave no gaps between them on the curves, or if such gaps are negligible.

Apply adhesive (not too little and not too much) to both surfaces of each laminate – apart from the two outer ones, which only require glue on one side. Use a brush; an old 25mm (1in) paintbrush will do, but don't use anything smaller, as you need to work quickly. Stack the laminates neatly in order.

Cramping up

Place your bundle of laminates against the former, with the strap over the bundle.

If your shape is a single smooth curve, cramp the whole lot together at one end. If not, it may be easier to start in the centre, with the addition of a softening batten.

Now you need to pull the laminates round the curve, keeping them pressed against each other and against the former. You can often do this by hand, but it's a good idea to place a cramp over the bundle and strap (not over the former) and leave it a fraction loose, so that the laminates are free to slide as they bend. Remove it when they've done so.

Then cramp the bent laminates to the former, and repeat the procedure elsewhere on the shape as needed. Tap the laminates down before finally tightening each cramp, so that all their lower edges are in contact with the base board.

Finally, wash off the surplus adhesive. Don't be too generous with the water, or you'll dilute the adhesive between the laminates. Put the job on one side and leave it to set. The time needed will depend on the room temperature.

When the cramps and metal strap are released, you'll find that your previously springy laminates are permanently set in their new shape.

It only remains to clean the piece up. The 6mm (¼in) margin – 3mm at both sides – allows for this. Often it's most convenient to cramp the piece back onto the former first. Since resin glues are ruinous to plane irons, it's best to do the job with a Surform or similar tool. After this, sand it smooth.

Now, at last, you'll be able to admire the interesting effect produced by the laminates' edges. This can often be used as a decorative feature. Either way, go ahead and treat the finished piece exactly as you would any other prepared timber.

3 Shaped wooden blocks (female formers) can be an adjunct to the strap. They can even replace it altogether if they extend far enough round the curves.

4 It's an idea to tap the laminates down so they all meet the base board. Ensure, too, that the cramp – like all subsequent ones – is fitted square.

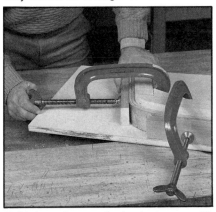

7 Make quite sure the laminates are still stacked tightly together, hugging the desired shape, and cramp them in place, using another batten.

8 Repeat the procedure for the rest of the shape. Straight sections can be cramped with wedges instead. Leave everything to set.

11 Returning to your drawing, mark where the ends of the piece need cutting off. Note how the laminates have become 'staggered' by the bending.

12 Square the mark round the piece and cut off the end. Remember that an angled component, like this one, will probably need an angled cut.

CHAPTER 5

HANDYMAN PROJECTS

Making things from wood is one of the most satisfying hobbies,
and there is literally no limit to what you can create with the skills
you have acquired from earlier chapters.

BUILDING CUPBOARDS IN ALCOVES

Built-in cupboards save you money because you use your walls instead of side, back and top panels. Fitting them neatly and snugly is just a matter of knowing the right methods.

Making freestanding storage furniture that's rigid and stable – even fairly simple box-type pieces – calls for accuracy, plus a certain amount of basic woodworking ability and design sense. It's certainly worth taking the trouble to acquire these. But you may be unsure of your skills, especially when it comes to large items – or perhaps you just don't want to take chances.

The answer is built-in units. These are almost sure to be structurally sound, because they're anchored to the walls – and often to the floor and ceiling too. They don't usually require any joints more complex than halvings (see pages 32-35 for details). And, of course, fitting storage facilities into alcoves and odd corners is an excellent way to make the most of available space.

But any built-in cupboard does face a disadvantage. The walls of your room will probably not be flat or true. Although (at least in modern homes) the masonry itself will be vertical, and walls will be square with one another, it's impossible to apply plaster to a uniform thickness over an entire wall, so there will be variations. This means you'll have to take some trouble to make your cupboard fit.

Working in an alcove

Let's suppose you're building a cupboard in an alcove – the most obvious place, and a very sensible one. What you need to know first is the alcove's width at its narrowest.

This is very hard to find accurately with a tape measure, because it's flexible and the casing gets in the way. Instead you can use 'pinch rods'. Improvise these from a couple of pieces of square-sectioned timber – say 25x25mm (1x1in) or 38x38mm (1½x1½in). Each should be longer than half the width of the alcove. Hold them together horizontally inside the alcove, and slide them until the end of each one meets a side wall.

Now move them up and down the alcove until you've found its narrowest part, and tilt them till you're sure they're level – that is, when they show the shortest width yet still have both ends touching the walls.

Then, grasping them tightly, draw a pencil line across both, so that you can re-assemble them in the correct position. Take them down from the wall and measure their combined length.

Making a frame

Your next job is to make a simple rectangular frame, to the overall width you've just measured. This consists of two cross pieces, plus two uprights which can be any height you choose – possibly dictated by the height of ready-made doors (such as louvre doors) if you plan to fit them.

You can use square or rectangular timber for the frame, making the corners with halving joints, glued together and then screwed from the inside. Keep checking the frame for squareness as you assemble it. To ensure it stays square during the rest of the job, tack battens of thin timber diagonally across two opposite corners.

Place the frame in the alcove where you want it, and fix it by drilling and screwing through the frame sides into wall plugs. Alternatively, if the frame is made of rectangular timber such as 50x25mm (2x1in), you can screw vertical battens to the wall at either side and fix the frame to them, with timber strips or plastic jointing blocks. Use a spirit level to make quite sure it's upright. If it leans forward, the doors will always tend to fall open; if it slopes backwards, they'll be

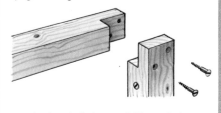
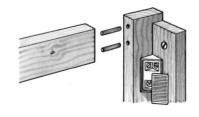

inclined to stay shut. And of course, the frame needs to be set truly horizontal too.

The frame probably won't fit exactly. If it's too wide, you can plane it down; take an equal amount off both sides. On the other hand, there may be gaps. Don't attempt to make the timber follow the contours of the wall if this is so.

If the gaps are narrower than about 5mm (³⁄₁₆in), you can stop them up with filler, which will be disguised with paint. A length of foam plastic draught strip, inset about 3mm (⅛in) back from the front, and inserted before you screw the frame to the wall, makes an excellent backing for the filler.

If you don't want a painted finish, glue and pin moulding (eg, quadrant) to the front of the frame so it hides the gaps. Hold it in position, mark it as best you can and shape it with a file; then re-position, re-mark and re-shape it till it hugs the wall tightly.

Wider gaps call for the insertion of packing strips of thin timber, plywood or hardboard before adding the moulding.

Supporting the top

If the cupboard doesn't reach to the ceiling, it will need a top. This can be of blockboard or plywood – painted, veneered or covered with plastic laminate if you wish. But, as always, proprietary veneered or laminated chipboard is a cheap and attractive alternative. If you decide on this, bear in mind that it comes in standard widths, with each long edge ready-finished. So, unless you're lipping the front edge yourself in any way, you need to fix the frame at a distance from the back wall that allows you to make use of one of these widths.

Think about the details beforehand: do you want the top to overhang the cupboard doors, or to project even further? The treatment of the front edge is one of the small points which make all the difference to the final appearance of the unit, so it's worth making sure you've got it right from the start. A few of the possibilities are shown in *Ready Reference*. Small strips of decorative mouldings such as astragal, ogee, scotia and even glass bead may come in handy as ways of giving the edge a slightly softer and more interesting look, and getting away from the functional effect of straight lines everywhere.

In any case, allow enough extra width for trimming the top panel to fit the contours of the back wall.

Supported on the frame at the front, the top rests at the back on a corresponding horizontal batten screwed to the wall. This must be at exactly the same height as the top of the frame. You can use a spirit level to achieve this. If your level is too small, place it on top of a straight length of wood.

For a cupboard that rises above eye level,

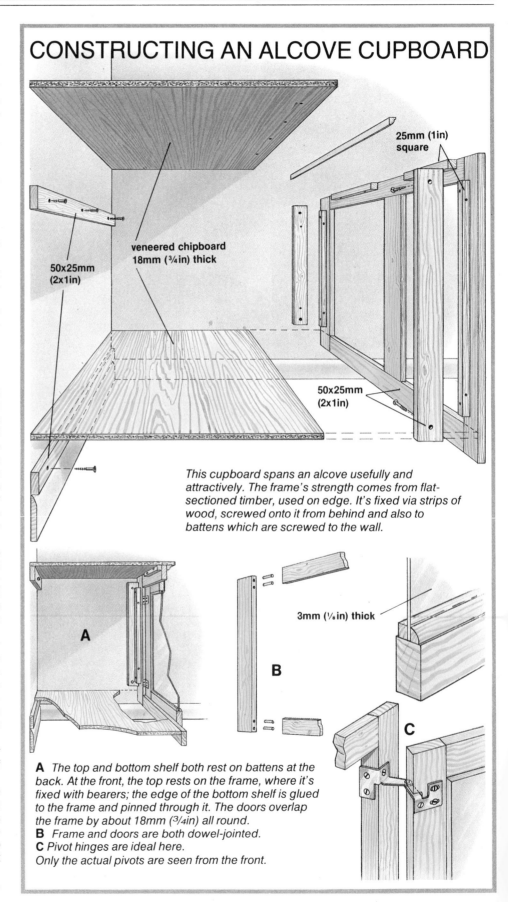

CONSTRUCTING AN ALCOVE CUPBOARD

25mm (1in) square

veneered chipboard 18mm (³⁄₄in) thick

50x25mm (2x1in)

50x25mm (2x1in)

This cupboard spans an alcove usefully and attractively. The frame's strength comes from flat-sectioned timber, used on edge. It's fixed via strips of wood, screwed onto it from behind and also to battens which are screwed to the wall.

3mm (⅛in) thick

A

B

C

A *The top and bottom shelf both rest on battens at the back. At the front, the top rests on the frame, where it's fixed with bearers; the edge of the bottom shelf is glued to the frame and pinned through it. The doors overlap the frame by about 18mm (³⁄₄in) all round.*
B *Frame and doors are both dowel-jointed.*
C *Pivot hinges are ideal here.*
Only the actual pivots are seen from the front.

MAKING THE FRAME

1 Cut 'pinch rods' to find the alcove width. Slide them apart till each meets a wall, mark across both, and measure their combined length.

2 Make up a front frame for the cupboard to this width. Use dowels or halving joints; glue them and if possible cramp the frame together.

3 If the side uprights overlap the cross members, not the other way round, they'll be easier to plane down later if necessary.

4 Cut two battens, and hold one vertically where you want it on the wall, allowing for frame and door thickness. Mark its position.

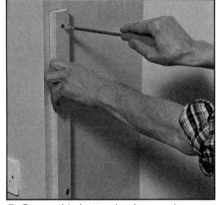

5 Screw this batten in place, using wall plugs, after making sure that it's not long enough to get in the way of the bottom shelf.

6 Measure its distance from the back wall, so you can position and fix another batten the same distance from the wall at the other side.

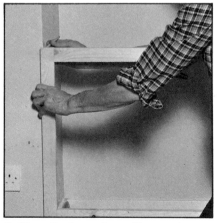

7 Place the frame in position, and mark it if it's too wide. Alternatively, it may need packing out with timber or thin board.

8 If the frame is too wide, plane a bit from both ends. Bevelling each edge inwards across the thickness will give an even easier fit.

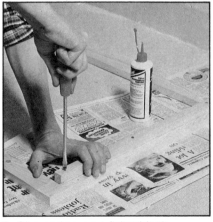

9 Glue and screw a fixing block down each side of the frame, insetting it by the thickness of the battens you've fastened to the wall.

COMPLETING THE UNIT

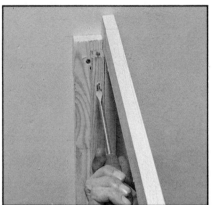

1 Re-position the frame, and glue and screw in the other direction through each fixing block, attaching it to the batten.

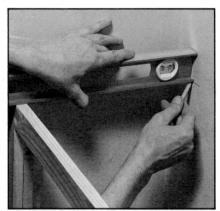

2 Use a level to mark on the back wall, in at least two places, the position of the bearer which will support the cupboard's top.

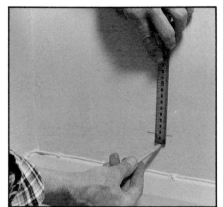

3 After making similar marks for the bottom shelf, add a second mark below each one, to indicate the shelf thickness accurately.

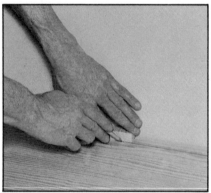

5 After checking the side walls and cutting each shelf to fit at either end, scribe the contours of the wall along its back edge.

6 Fit the top shelf into position. Fasten it to the cross-bearers with plastic jointing blocks, or more strips of wood glued and screwed.

7 After positioning the bottom shelf, glue and pin into its front edge through the front cross-bearer, to give it extra rigidity.

you needn't even use chipboard for the top. Thin plywood or hardboard will do. However, hardboard should never span a greater distance than 450mm (18in) without support. This is bound to mean fitting an extra bearer or two from front to back, halved across the front cross piece and rear batten.

Fitting the top

Next, you need to make the top. First, use pinch rods to see if the alcove is the same width at front and back. If the angles are more or less square and the walls straight, go ahead and cut the top to size. Whatever you do, don't make it any smaller than the space; rather leave it a bit too big, then trim the back edge and one end with a plane, filing or Surforming where necessary to ensure that you have a perfect fit.

If, on the other hand, the end walls are well out of true, you'll have to make angled cuts at either end. Cut pieces of cardboard to fit by trial and error, then use them as templates to mark out the top panel before you saw it.

Lastly, note where the top needs trimming at the back. If the back wall is very bumpy, it's best to scribe the top to fit. That means holding it a bit less than 25mm (1in) from the wall, and placing a small block of 25mm (1in) thick timber there, with one face against the wall. Hold a pencil against it, and move both block and pencil along the top. This will give you a line on the board which follows the contours of the wall, so you can cut along it for a perfect fit.

The top can be held in place by screws driven up through the battens and frame if the timber is square in section, or otherwise through small strips of timber screwed to the inside faces of the frame and battens.

Fitting a bottom panel

A cupboard that stops short of the floor will need a bottom shelf panel, which should be measured and prepared in just the same way as the top. It rests on a batten screwed to the wall at the back, also like the top.

You can position this level with the top of the bottom cross piece in the frame, notching the panel at the front corners so it fits round the uprights and rests on the bottom cross piece. In that case it can act as a doorstop if you cut it short of the front. Or, cutting it even shorter, you can let it rest on a small additional bearer (say 25mm/1in square). This can be screwed to the inside of the cross piece, and positioned so that the panel is flush with the top of the cross piece. For the same result, you can simply glue and pin the front edge of the panel through the cross piece. Either way, you'll need to adjust the height of the rear batten accordingly.

Further possibilities

If you want shelves inside the cupboard, they too can rest on bearers screwed to the

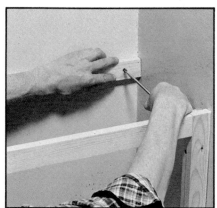

4 *Screw the top bearer to the wall, keeping its upper edge against the pencil marks. Screw the bottom bearer against the lower set of marks there.*

8 *A small moulding (eg, a glass bead), glued and pinned below the top overhang, improves its looks. Now add doors to the unit.*

walls at the back and sides. Alternatively, you can make them adjustable, in case your storage requirements change. Just use one of the proprietary systems described on pages 52-55.

If your cupboard reaches to the floor, you'll have to take account of the skirting board. One option is to take it off (for replacement or re-use), complete your cupboard, saw the skirting to length, and re-fix it to any stretches of wall that are visible outside the cupboard – and inside it, too, if you wish. The other possibility, where the skirting isn't too thick, is to scribe and cut away the frame of the cupboard to fit.

Full-height cupboards

An alcove cupboard that reaches to the ceiling as well as the floor presents its own problems. In theory you could build a frame to the correct size, slide it into position, and fix it in the way already described. But, since

it would be the same height as the room itself, it would be difficult to manoeuvre into position. You'd do far better to assemble it all in place.

It pays, however, to be wary. Filling or packing gaps isn't really satisfactory for such a large structure. Place a spirit level vertically against each wall. If either of them is out of true by more than, say, 20mm (¾in) along its length, or if any curves in it are deeper than that, cut the upright member of the frame to a length equal to the height of the alcove at its lowest and scribe it to fit the wall – using a pencil and block of wood while holding the timber precisely vertical. Then cut halving joints in each end.

A bottom frame cross piece is also needed to act as a doorstop, if nothing else. Cut it to length (ie, as long as the alcove's narrowest width), and screw it to the floor, making sure it's truly level. (Incidentally, before driving screws or nails into a floor, you should always try to make sure there are no water or gas pipes underneath. If in doubt, choose screws too short to pass through floorboards.)

Then glue the joints, and screw both uprights to the wall. Cut the top cross piece to the same length as the one on the floor. Joint it to the tops of the uprights, screwing it to a ceiling joist if possible. If you've worked accurately, it will be horizontal, and square to the rest – but do check!

Lastly, fit any intermediate cross pieces. You may need one to help support a shelf, and perhaps act as a doorstop, if you plan to create a small cupboard at the top.

Bottom and top panels aren't necessary in floor-to-ceiling units, but it doesn't cost much – and it makes a neat-looking touch – to fit a cupboard floor of plywood or hardboard.

Adding doors

Doors, or course, are what complete the cupboard. They can be sliding or hinged, and in construction they can be flush – perhaps consisting of single pieces of board – or else panelled. They can even be glazed; louvres are also a popular feature.

All these types can easily be installed in the front frame of the cupboard. For sliding doors, you fit tracks or channels; others can be hinged to the timber uprights, either overlapping them or inset between them. On a wide cupboard, you can always add extra uprights.

Whatever plan you decide on, it's always sensible to sort out the details before you buy any materials or begin work on the project. In both construction and design you'll find it pays dividends to think of the doors as an integral part of the unit.

You'll find more information given on pages 110-113.

You'll find more information given on pages 110-113.

Ready Reference

FITTED CUPBOARD POSSIBILITIES
At the top
Details 1 to 4 use 'lay-on' doors (ie, doors which overlap the front frame).

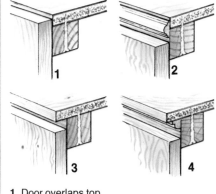

1 Door overlaps top
2 Using decorative edging
3 Top overhangs door
4 Overhanging top and moulding
5 Inset door with timber strip as doorstop, glued and pinned to the underside of the top frame member.

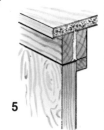

At the bottom
The bottom panel rests on a timber strip, and a lay-on door is fitted.

An inset door uses the bottom panel as a doorstop.

ADDING DOORS TO BASIC BOXES

Doors for furniture should be much more than an afterthought. In usefulness and appearance, they make all the difference – so it's vital that they look good and work smoothly.

When you're building cabinet furniture or fitted units, it's worth considering from the outset how you're going to make and fit the doors.

The first decision you have to take is whether they'll be hinged or sliding.

Sliding doors

Sliding doors don't create any obstruction in the room when open – you're never likely to bang yourself on them. What's more, if they're small and light they can be extremely easy to fit. But they have the big disadvantage that only half the cupboard is accessible at one time (a third, if you fit three doors). This can be a real irritant.

Folding doors, of course, are a variant which avoids that particular problem. However, for all folding doors, and for large and heavy sliding doors such as those on a wardrobe, you'll need special mechanical fittings, which come with their own detailed instructions. To make sure you buy the right pattern, get the overall construction of the cupboard clear in your mind first – but don't buy any materials or begin construction, because some types of sliding and folding gear require a minimum door thickness, and all affect the doors' other dimensions. So you'll have to finalise these details after buying the fittings, rather than before.

For smaller items (eg, wall-hung bathroom cabinets), it's quite enough to have doors of thin plywood or hardboard which slide in simple channels glued and/or screwed to the inside of the cabinet at top and bottom. These channels can be wooden or plastic; in either case, top channelling is slightly deeper than bottom channelling. This enables you to push each door up into the top channel first, before positioning it over the bottom channel and dropping it into place without its falling out at the top.

Sliding doors should, of course, be of such a width that they overlap each other when they're all closed. Lightweight ones will slide more easily in their channels if their width is greater than their height. Rubbing the doors' bottom edges with soap or candle wax will make for an even easier ride – and plastic channelling is smoother than wood.

Hinged doors

Hinged doors can be fitted in either of two ways: inset or lay-on. An inset door fits inside the cabinet. A lay-on door overlaps its front, either wholly or partly. Each type gives quite a different look, so think carefully about the effect you want before deciding which to choose.

Inset doors are a bit harder to fit, because you have to achieve a more or less accurate and consistent clearance all round – variations will be noticeable, and the door may stick if it sags even slightly on its hinges after fitting.

If you've decided on a natural varnished timber finish for an inset door, try to make it an exact push fit in the opening. Subsequent cleaning-up and sanding, before you apply the finish, will make it just the right size. If you're going to paint it, aim to leave 3mm (⅛in) all round, after sanding, so that the various coats of paint do not cause it to bind.

Another thing an inset door needs is some kind of doorstop to close against. This could be a strip or strips of timber, fixed inside the cabinet, or the bottom and top panels of the cabinet itself – or, perhaps most commonly, a catch (see below). Remember that you can place the doorstop so the door closes flush with the front of the cabinet, or slightly inside it. Again, your choice is dictated by looks.

Fitting hinges

Your choice of hinges for hanging the doors on the cabinet must of course be made at the same time. Some hinges are suitable for inset doors, some for lay-on doors, and some for both.

The traditional butt hinge, for example, can be used for either arrangement. With an inset door, it's screwed to the edge of the door and the inner face of the cabinet side. With a lay-on door you just reverse the process, screwing the hinge to the inner face of the door and the front edge of the cabinet, so that its knuckle projects at the side.

Either way, you have to mark out the hinge positions with a pencil, try-square and marking gauge, then cut recesses for them in the door or cabinet or (more usually) both.

A modern alternative is the concealed hinge. This is a much more complex mechanism which actually lifts the door out from the frame rather than simply letting it swing. While its primary purpose is to allow lay-on doors to open to 90° within the overall width of the cabinet (which a butt hinge cannot achieve), some kinds of concealed hinge can also be used for inset doors.

Cranked hinges do a similar job – though only on lay-on doors – and their shape makes them especially easy to locate in position. However, they're only partly concealed

FITTING SLIDING DOORS

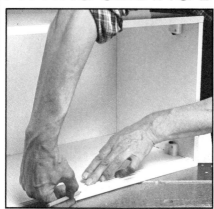

1 Cut the top and bottom channelling to length; align it where you want it in the cabinet, and mark out its position in pencil.

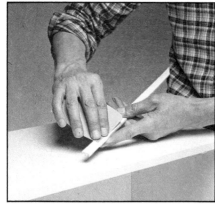

2 Roughen the bottom of the plastic channelling to provide a 'key', then fix it back on with contact adhesive (the type you spread on both surfaces).

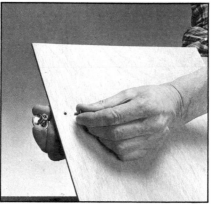

3 After measuring for the doors and cutting them to size from thin plywood or hardboard, drill for and fit handles in matching positions.

4 Fit each door by pushing it up into the top channel, then swinging it into position and letting it drop into the bottom channel.

Ready Reference

WAYS OF FITTING DOORS

An inset door (A) closes inside the cabinet. A lay-on door (B) closes against its front edges.

inset door   lay-on door

CHOOSING A CATCH

Magnetic catches are useful because the plate doesn't have to be lined up perfectly. (A), a light model, fits in a drilled hole. (B) and (C) screw onto the surface; the double version (C) deals with two doors at once.

Ball catches are neat. The cylinder fits into a drilled hole; its faceplate (if any) into a chiselled recess. The striking plate's lip guides the ball into a small countersunk socket, preventing damage to the cabinet edge. The double type (C) has a screw for strength adjustment.

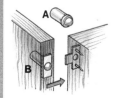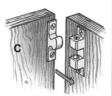

Roller catches work by sprung rollers. Both parts (like many furniture fittings) have elongated holes, for adjustment after inserting the screws.

Automatic latches are unique in opening, as well as closing, simply by pressure – you don't pull the door.

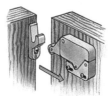

Pivot hinges are a third possibility.

What's more, you can get 'lift-off' and 'loose-pin' types of butt, cranked and pivot hinges which enable you to fix one leaf to the door and one to the cabinet separately before putting the two together – eliminating the need to hold or prop an unwieldy door in position as you screw the hinges to the cabinet.

If you're not using one of these types, the rule is to fix the hinges to the door first, then to the cabinet.

Plain doors

You can make doors for furniture in two main ways. The simpler type is made from a single slab of man-made board. You can, of course, use veneered or plastic-faced chipboard, two parallel edges of which will be ready-finished. To take advantage of that, you'll want to design your cupboard so that its doors can simply be cut to length (ie, height) from a standard width of board. This is easier with lay-on doors, since their dimensions – unlike those of an inset door – aren't dictated by the exact size of the opening. On the latter you may find yourself having to shave the ready-finished edges with a plane to make the door fit properly, which would be a pity.

Blockboard and plywood don't present these problems, since they don't come ready-edged, and their bare edges are in any case more acceptable. When using them, you can simply saw the door to size (making it slightly too big rather than too small), offer it up and plane off bits where necessary.

You can give a plain one-piece door a professional look by using hockey stick moulding round the edge, taking the moulding's thickness into account all round as you prepare the door to fit the opening. You can also use other mouldings to decorate its face if you wish.

USING BUTT HINGES

An inset one piece door with plain butt hinges

1 Mark on the door edge the distance of each hinge from the top and bottom, and square these marks across with a knife and try-square.

2 Place a hinge against each mark, and score another mark at its other end. This will give you the length of the hinge recess.

3 Chisel out a recess, the width and depth of one hinge leaf. If this recess is as wide as the door edge, you can make saw cuts for it first.

4 After screwing each hinge to the door so the knuckle just protrudes in front, align the door and mark each hinge length in the cabinet.

5 Mark the width of each hinge position in the cabinet. A marking gauge, set to the width of a single hinge leaf, is ideal here.

TIP

6 Screw the hinge to the cabinet. In veneered chipboard, don't cut a recess; instead, make the recess in the door twice the usual depth.

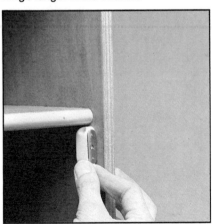

7 If you're using a magnetic catch, screw it in place after ensuring the door fits. Inset it by the thickness of the door and plate combined. Then position the plate on the catch.

8 Close the door firmly, in such a way that the little bumps on the back of the plate make dents on the inside face of the door. If necessary, loosen the screws and adjust the catch.

9 Remove the plate from the catch, use the dents to position the plate on the door, make a hole with a bradawl in the appropriate position and screw it in place.

MAKING A FRAMED DOOR

A lay-on framed door with cranked lift-off hinges

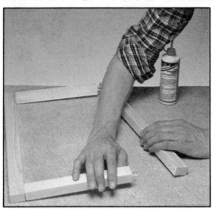

1 *The frame is easily assembled with glued dowel joints. Cramp it to a flat surface to stop it twisting while the adhesive sets.*

2 *Cut the hinge recesses for a lay-on door in its inner face, instead of in the edge. Mark them out carefully with a marking gauge first.*

3 *Screw one half of a lift-off hinge to the cabinet, the other separately to the door. The cranked type locates over the door edge.*

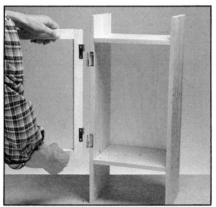

4 *The spindle half of the hinge goes on the cabinet, spindle upwards. Place the door on these spindles to check its alignment.*

5 *Mitre a small quadrant moulding or glass bead neatly and tightly, then glue and pin it round the inside of the frame at the front.*

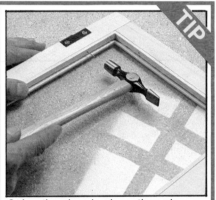

6 *Lay the glass in place, then pin strips of wood all round at the back. Don't glue them in case you ever need to remove the glass.*

Framed doors

The other type of door consists of a frame with some kind of panel fitted inside it. This has a rather more traditional look, and an attractiveness all of its own. You can easily make the frame from four pieces of plain rectangular-sectioned timber – a typical size would be 50x25mm (2x1in); use dowels for the corners, or mortise-and-tenon joints. (Plain mitre joints aren't strong enough.)

Make sure that you cramp all the components during assembly. Twisting is a common problem when assembling a frame, so it's wise to cramp the whole thing to a flat surface while the adhesive sets.

Then glue and pin a quadrant moulding or glass bead round the inside of the frame and just inside its front edge. Lay in a sheet of thin plywood or 3mm thick glass, marked and cut to fit, and hold that in place with a thin strip of timber, say 6mm (¼in) square,

pinned round at the back.

You can buy ready-made frame-and-panel doors, in which the frame is specially shaped – a tricky job for the inexperienced woodworker. Louvred doors are another attractive variation on this theme which it would be most unwise to tackle yourself – and unnecessary, since they're so widely available.

Choosing a catch

A catch is a vital piece of hardware for most cupboards with hinged doors – though some concealed hinges have a spring that holds the door closed without one.

The best catch for the do-it-yourselfer is undoubtedly the magnetic type, since it will still work even if its magnet doesn't exactly face the striking plate. So it remains unaffected even if the door drops out of alignment over a period of time.

Other types of catch include friction, roller, double roller, ball, double ball and peglock. None of them share the advantage of magnetic catches, though the single ball catch has the virtue of being unobtrusive.

However, one very clever and useful device is the automatic latch, which – though hidden from outside the cabinet – springs open, as well as closed, simply by hand pressure.

If you're fitting only a single catch, it's wise to place it behind the spot where the door handle will be, to avoid uneven tension on the door, catch mountings and handle.

Choosing a handle

Handles, perhaps more than anything else, make or mar furniture. Here, as so often, the best plan is to go to a good hardware store. Most types of handle either screw into or bolt through the surface of the door.

IILDING E : the basics

Building your own bed – single or double – isn't difficult. You'll save a lot of money and get something which is not only attractive but custom-built to suit your needs exactly.

Constructing a bed may sound a big task, but there are occasions when it can definitely be worth tackling yourself.

Your home-made bed may not be as luxuriously comfortable, or give you quite so many years of service as the ones you buy in the shops (remember that a bed is usually occupied for at least eight hours a day – much longer than any other piece of furniture). But it will be a lot less expensive; and often this consideration can be of prime importance.

For example a home-made bed might be the ideal solution for a young couple setting up their first home on a tight budget, or for a guest room that's not often used. Likewise, when a child grows out of sleeping in a cot, its first bed could easily be one you make yourself. Children don't demand the same standards of comfort as adults and, since they weigh much less, they impose less strain on a bed.

The basic box

There's more than one way of building a bed, but this one is straightforward and economical.

Although you can do the initial carpentry anywhere that's convenient, the final assembly should be carried out in the room the bed will occupy. Hauling it up or downstairs and through doorways is no joke.

But your first job is to buy the mattress, so you can be sure it will fit on the bed. Even if you're making your own mattress by buying foam and covering it, you should still do that first. When completed, the bed should be slightly wider and longer than the mattress, so that there's enough room to tuck the bedclothes in properly. An extra 25mm (1in) all round should be ample.

The basic principle is to take four lengths of wood or man-made board and make up a big, shallow, rectangular box without a bottom. Veneered or plastic-faced chipboard is a good material, combining cheapness with an attractive range of finishes. It comes in standard lengths of 2440mm (8ft) and 1830mm (6ft). You could make a single bed from three pieces of 2440mm (8ft) – cutting one in half to form the head and foot – and a double bed from two pieces of 2440mm (8ft)

and two of 1830mm (6ft). There's a good range of widths, so you'd be able to make the box any depth you wanted.

Chipboard of this kind is veneered or plastic-faced on both sides and on the two long edges. The raw ends and other cut edges can be disguised with iron-on edging strip or timber lipping (see pages 14-16).

Just as convenient to use, yet even stronger, is 25mm (1in) thick natural timber. And of course you don't have to hide its edges. However, it's difficult to obtain in widths over 225mm (9in), which somewhat restricts your design possibilities.

You could also use 12mm (½in) thick plywood – with or without a decorative wood veneer or plastic facing. This will involve you in extra work if you have to cut the pieces to size (it doesn't usually come in sheets less than 1220mm/4ft wide), but it gives a strong, attractive result, without any restriction on width. Many people find bare plywood edges quite acceptable. If you have a circular saw, it might be economical to buy a standard 2440x1220mm (8x4ft) sheet, and cut it into four pieces yourself.

Putting it together

When joining the corners of the box, you must carefully consider whether you are going to have legs on the bed.

You can, of course, do without them, and simply put your basic box directly onto the floor. But most people prefer to fit beds with

legs as it looks better, and gives a more convenient height for bedmaking. A good overall height from the floor to the top of the box is 450mm (18in). For a single bed, two legs on each side is enough, but three is safer on a double.

A good method of adding legs is to cut four pieces of 50mm (2in) square planed timber, and fix them to the inside of the box so that they project below it. In this way you can also form corner joints for the box – tackling both details in one go. If you use screws, they should enter from the outside, for a secure hold. Brass screws in brass cups will turn this into a decorative feature.

Adding glue on only one side of each leg (while screwing into two sides) ensures that all the joints can be dismantled at least once by simply removing the screws through the unglued parts. Bolts here will make an even stronger fixing, and enable you to take the bed apart any number of times without loss of strength.

Other options are dowels, with or without the ends on view from the outside, and nails. These, of course, can't be removed; but you could use nails or dowels through one piece and screws or bolts through the other.

Another idea is to make up legs which are L-shaped in section. (These cannot of course number more than four). Each one consists of two lengths of planed softwood 38mm (1½in) thick, fixed to the outside of the box at each corner – one to the side, the

114

PUTTING THE BED TOGETHER

These details show all the parts of the bed, including the joints you'll need to cut in the

bearers – plus two other ways of making legs: one L-shaped and one notched.

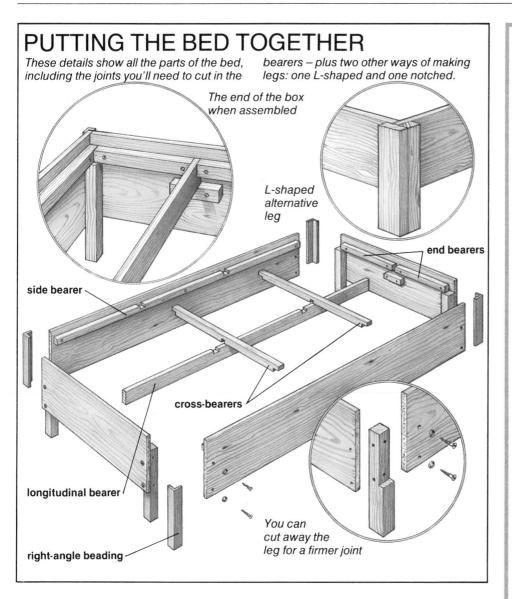

The end of the box when assembled

L-shaped alternative leg

end bearers

side bearer

cross-bearers

longitudinal bearer

right-angle beading

You can cut away the leg for a firmer joint

Ready Reference

BED DIMENSIONS

Height: it's best to choose a height at which you can sit down comfortably – that is, unless you prefer an 'on-the-floor' bed. Usual heights are
● 100-300mm (4-12in) without legs
● 300-450mm (12-18in) including legs.

Width: standard widths are
● narrow single bed 750mm (2ft 6in)
● standard single 900mm (3ft)
● twin 975mm (3ft 3in)
● double 1350mm (4ft 6in)
● large double 1500mm (5ft)
● extra large double 1900mm (6ft 4in).

Length: ideally a bed should be 75mm (3in) longer than its occupant's standing height. The common lengths are:
● standard 1875mm (6ft 3in)
● large 2100mm (7ft).

FITTING CASTORS

The socket-fixing castor has a spindle which fits into a metal or plastic sleeve. You drill a hole in the timber, insert the sleeve and then push in the spindle. Provided you drill the hole accurately, this makes a secure mounting even in end grain, eg on the bottom of a leg.

The plate castor is screwed directly onto the timber. Often a special block will be needed to mount it. For a box-type bed, your best plan is to cut out a triangular block from timber which is at least 25mm (1in) thick, and screw it inside the corner of the box at the appropriate height. Then just screw the plate to that. You cannot do this, however, if your bed has legs.

other to the foot or head – so that they overlap. To get both sides of the L of equal width, you'll need to buy one piece 75mm (3in) wide and one 100mm (4in) wide, and plane down the narrower one.

The two pieces can then be glued, and screwed or nailed in place, while the corner joint itself is made with any of the methods described in detail on pages 60-63. If a screwed-on reinforcement is used, the whole thing can still be dismantled, provided you haven't glued the halves of the L where they overlap.

It's a good idea to fit castors to the legs, so you can move the bed around easily. But this is difficult with L-shaped legs, which may make you decide on plain ones. Use a socket-fixing type castor – for which you bore a hole in the legs, then insert a metal or plastic sleeve before pushing home the spindle of the castor. The other kind, mounted on a plate, isn't suitable for legs,

because to fix it you'd need to drive screws into end grain – something to avoid wherever possible. However, it is the one to use if you're omitting legs; just mount it on a triangular block screwed inside each corner of the box.

Supporting the mattress

The next consideration is how to support the mattress. Any mattress, but especially a foam one, must be able to 'breathe'. So a good material is perforated hardboard, or pegboard, as it's more commonly called. This is strong enough, provided that it's well supported in its turn.

The pegboard rests on pieces of 38mm (1½in) square planed softwood, screwed horizontally inside the head, foot and sides of the box. Position them with their upper faces 38 to 50mm (1½ to 2in) below the top of the box. This will ensure not only that the top of the mattress stands well clear of the

THE BASIC BOX

1 *Square a mark across the legs to indicate how much will protrude below the main box. For speed and accuracy, mark them all out at once.*

2 *Align the mark on each leg carefully with the lower edge of the box head or foot, cramp both pieces together and drill them.*

1 *Mark out and cut two halvings in each of the bearers which will be screwed to the sides of the box. Work on both pieces at once.*

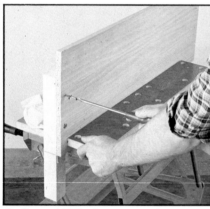

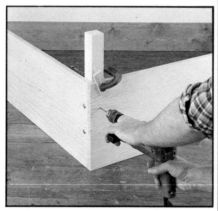

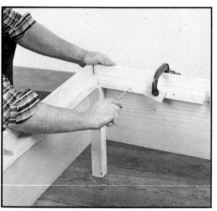

3 *Spread PVA glue on one piece, then fix the joint with 50mm (2in) No 10 screws. Keep a wet rag handy to wipe off excess adhesive.*

4 *Cramp the box side over the joint, drill it and screw it to the leg. Then repeat the same procedure for the other three corners of the box.*

5 *Cut two pieces from each end bearer, cramp them against this pencil line and screw them on, leaving a gap for the longitudinal bearer.*

bed – so you don't bang yourself on the sides when you sit down on the bed or get in and out of it – but also that you can tuck the bedclothes in without bruising your knuckles on the box. These bearers, as they are called, can fit at each end on top of the legs.

You'll also need two cross-bearers, which should be fitted over the side bearers with some halving joints (see pages 32-35 for details), plus a longitudinal bearer (two or three on a double bed). The latter should be made of 75x25mm (3x1in) planed timber, used on edge; it can be slotted into gaps between the pairs of bearers screwed to head and foot, and rest on another short piece of 38mm (1½in) square timber also screwed in place. None of these pieces needs to be glued, or even screwed or nailed. This too makes for easy dismantling if you ever want to move the bed.

An alternative to pegboard is a series of slats running across the width. They should be of 50x25mm (2x1in) or 75x19mm (3x¾in) planed timber, spaced at most 75mm (3in) apart, and screwed on top of the bearers at either side. To protect the bedclothes, countersink the screw heads. In this instance, there's no need for cross-bearers, and the longitudinal bearer can fit at each end between three short pieces of 38mm (1½in) square timber which are screwed vertically to the head and foot, forming a U-shaped bracket.

Finishing the bed

For a smooth finish on veneer or solid timber, your first step is to sand it down with a fine-grade glass- or garnet-paper. Then you can stain it to a different colour and apply varnish or wax finish. Alternatively paint it.

9 *Position the longitudinal bearer, re-position each cross-bearer over it, and mark out on both pieces the halving joint where they overlap.*

SUPPORTING THE MATTRESS

2 Screw a bearer to each side with 50mm (2in) No 8 chipboard screws, making sure it's quite straight and doesn't rise or dip along its length.

3 Mark and cut all the other bearers to length. Position one at each end. Halfway along mark the thickness of the longitudinal bearer.

4 Still resting the end bearer in position, use it as a straight edge to mark where its upper edge comes on the inside face of the box.

6 With the box on its side, position the longitudinal bearer (its top edge flush with the side bearers) and mark its bottom edge.

7 Screw a short length of wood, the same size as the bearers, centrally to each end of the box, with its upper face against the mark you've made.

8 Position each cross-bearer in the halvings you've cut in the side bearers, and mark out on it the other half of the joint.

10 Once all the halvings are cut, you can fit the longitudinal and cross-bearers into place without glue or any other fixing.

11 If the box sides are made of chipboard or blockboard, hide their cut ends with right-angle beading, glued and fixed with moulding pins.

12 Lastly, cut the pegboard to size and simply lay it on top of the bearers. The bed is now ready for finishing, and to receive its mattress.

BUILDING BUNKS: THE BASICS

Bunk beds save space. What's more, children love them, so it's easier to persuade them that bedtime has arrived! Bunks must be strong – but that doesn't mean they aren't straightforward to make.

Here's a way to build a set of very simple freestanding bunks. Like any furniture design, it's only one of many possible variations, and you can regard it as a basis for adding your own ideas. In particular, you can vary the dimensions to suit your needs.

However, a word of warning is necessary before going into the details of the construction. When you build bunks, you're making something which rises well above the floor, and which will be used by active, boisterous children. Your paramount consideration must be that of safety. Be quite sure that everything is firmly fixed, that the whole thing is rigid and stable, and that there's no danger to either the child in the top bunk or the one below.

As when constructing any other type of bed, you should begin with the mattresses: everything must fit round them. If making or buying new ones, go for the smallest single bed size. Children don't need that much sleeping space – and the larger the mattresses, the more cumbersome the structure you'll have to build.

Of course, if you're using mattresses you already own, they must both be exactly the same length and width. The thickness isn't so important.

Using box construction

The basic idea is the same as for the bed design described earlier on pages 114-117. Solid pine is the ideal material throughout for the construction – none of the flat sections are wide enough for veneered boards to be useful.

Each bunk is a box frame, with bearers inside it for the mattress base. A sensible size for the four sides of the frame, not too wide and not too weak, is 100x25mm (4x1in). For easy bedmaking, build the frame's slightly larger than the mattresses – say 25mm (1in) extra all round. Screw bearers of 50x25mm (2x1in) timber to the

sides and 25mm (1in) square timber to the ends, about 25mm (1in) below the top edge. Leave a gap in each end bearer and screw on an extra bearer below it (see photograph 10 on page 117).

Then join the corners of the frame together. Bear in mind that you shouldn't screw or nail into end grain. And the frame sides won't be wide enough to include a strip of wood or plastic jointing blocks as an internal reinforcement. This leaves three possibilities: see *Ready Reference*. One is dowels, and the second is a barefaced housing joint (see pages 40-43 for details). If you arrange things so that the shorter pieces (the head and foot) overlap the sides, you'll end up with an especially neat finish: the end grain, which is less attractive, will be hidden by the bedposts. The third possibility is a halving joint in the width. This is probably the strongest of the three.

You will in any case need to glue the joint well with PVA adhesive. Rough usage by children means you'll have to forget the idea of making each bunk capable of being dismantled. Instead, for real strength, it pays to glue every joint, even when it's screwed or nailed as well. (But you can make bunks that turn into separate beds – see below.)

Adding the bedposts

The four bedposts – one at each corner – are 75x50mm (3x2in). When deciding on their length, take into account the distance from the bottom of the lower bunk to the floor (say 300mm/1ft); the height of the lower bunk and its mattress; the clearance between that and

Ready Reference

BUNK CORNER JOINTS
There are three suitable ways of joining frame corners without screwing or nailing into end grain, and where there's no room for a timber reinforcement or plastic jointing blocks in the internal angle.

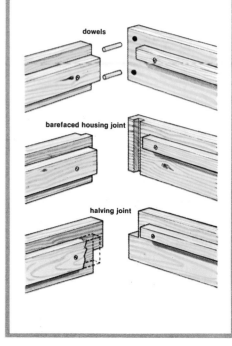

dowels

barefaced housing joint

halving joint

118

BUILDING THE STRUCTURE

1 One cut in each direction with a tenon saw is enough to make the halvings for the four corners of each bed frame.

2 After notching the side bearers to take the cross-bearers, glue and screw them inside the frame sides, 20mm (³/₄in) from the top edge.

3 Glue and screw two more bearers to each end at the same height, plus a third lower down to support the central longitudinal bearer.

4 After glueing each frame corner joint, drive in one nail each way to cramp it – checking constantly that all the joints are square.

5 Cut the bedposts to length, then glue and nail 300mm (1ft) of 75 x 25mm (3 x 1in) timber flat against the bottom of each, planing it flush.

6 Laying the posts on the floor, glue and screw the lower frame flush with their outer edges, resting it against the top of the 75 x 25mm (3 x 1in) timber.

Ready Reference

BUNK BED SIZES

These dimensions should be right for children's bunks – depending on the age and size of the occupants.

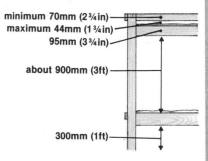

minimum 70mm (2³/₄in)
maximum 44mm (1³/₄in)
95mm (3³/₄in)
about 900mm (3ft)
300mm (1ft)

FIXED LADDERS

75 x 25mm (3 x 1in) slats, screwed at each end to the outer sides of the bedposts, and with their top edges rounded.

maximum gap 44mm (1³/₄in) to top of mattress

One upright is 50mm (2in) square, screwed to the sides of the bunks; the other is the bedpost. The rungs can be pieces of broomstick – or more pieces of 50 x 50mm, housed at both ends, their top edges rounded. This type of ladder is unsuitable for bunks which separate.

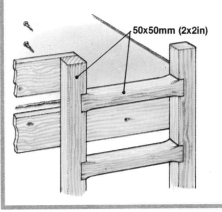

50x50mm (2x2in)

COMPLETING THE BED

1 Cut two longer pieces of 75 x 25mm, and glue and nail one along each post, so their bottom ends butt against the lower bed frame.

2 After adding the top frame and the other two posts, glue and screw a reinforcement across each end, flush with the top of the lower frame.

3 Glue and screw a guard rail above the end of the top bunk where necessary. Otherwise put another reinforcement across it.

4 Glue and screw a side guard rail, where needed, to the insides of the posts – flush with their tops, and butting against the end guard rail.

5 Insert the central bearer, after cutting notches in its top edge to take the cross-bearers, plus another notch in the bottom of each end.

6 Lastly, after inserting the two cross-bearers in the notches in the side and central bearers, fit a piece of pegboard into each bunk.

the bottom of the top bunk (say 900mm/3ft); and the height of the top bunk (including mattress and a guard rail). This will make something over 1500mm (5ft).

The two frames must be fixed to the posts very securely indeed – you don't want the disaster of the top bunk crashing down onto the occupant of the bottom one in the middle of the night. You can use glue and screws, driving the screws through the frame sides and into the bedposts. Countersink them well, so that they won't cut your hands or tear the fabric when you tuck the bedclothes in. Glue and dowels would be even better. Either way, use two per post per bunk.

You'd do well to give this fixing some support. This can take the form of lengths of 75x25mm (3x1in) planed timber glued and nailed to the inside of each post, below the bottom bunk and in between the two bunks, so the edges of the sides butt against them.

Using planed timber
Here you may well come up against a minor problem which often arises when, as is usually the case with non-structural carpentry, you buy your wood ready-planed from the timber merchant. The sizes are inconsistent, and can vary by as much as 6mm (¼in).

You'll have asked for 75x50mm (3x2in), 75x25mm (3x1in), and so on. You'll have received timber which is narrower and thinner than the size in question – the 'nominal' size – because some of it has been planed off at the mill. This, of course, is universal practice, and – provided you expect it – it should cause you no problems.

The snag is, however, that the amount that's planed off isn't always the same. It can vary by 3 or 4mm (⅛ or (³⁄₁₆in). You can often get over that by designing your work to allow for the variation. But you'll still have difficulties when it comes to matching two

pieces. Here, the 50mm (2in) side of the 75x50mm (3x2in) probably won't match the 50mm side of the 75x25mm (3x1in) although it's known by the same measurement.

The way out, of course, is to wait till the glue has set, then use your plane and trim the wider piece till it matches the narrower one exactly. That's why you need at least one bench plane in your tool kit. It saves your having to rely on what the timber merchant provides.

Bearers and guard rails
At this point you can fit the cross-bearers and the central longitudinal bearer in each bunk, plus the sheet of pegboard which forms the mattress base. Instead of pegboard you can use slats of timber, say 75 x 19mm (3 x ¾in), spaced their own width apart and screwed down onto the side bearers. If so, it's best to support the central

bearer in a different way – see page 453. Slats are especially suitable for sprung mattresses.

You also need at least one guard rail for the top bunk, to stop a child from falling out of bed while asleep. Fix a rail wherever the bunk isn't next to a wall. For each long side of the bunk, you can just extend the posts upwards and screw a further length of 75 x 25mm (3x1in) timber to their insides – horizontally, so it runs between them. But this isn't such a good method at the ends, because the rail will be too far in. Instead, screw it to the outsides of the posts, using brass screws in cups for decorative effect.

It's extremely important to leave only a small gap between the bottom edge of the guard rail and the top of the mattress, to avoid the very real danger of heads or limbs getting stuck there. The maximum gap is 44mm (1¾in).

Reinforcing the structure

The only snag with this design is that it doesn't have much strength if it's subjected to pulling or racking from side to side. It demands too much from the frame corner joints: within a few weeks or months of use energetic children may well succeed in pulling them apart!

One simple answer is to include reinforcing pieces. These too can be of 75x25mm (3x1in) timber, and each one should be glued and screwed in place across the end, exactly like an end guard rail. If you position its upper edge flush with the top of the frame, you'll neatly cover the end grain in the halving joints. And this is another case where brass screws will make an attractive feature out of a necessity, especially if used in brass cups.

Such reinforcements are needed on both ends of the bottom bunk, and on the top bunk at whichever end doesn't possess a guard rail. Of course, if you're screwing slats between the posts anyway – see below – they'll give all the strength you require.

Separating the bunks

You may find it useful to be able to make your double bunk into two separate beds.

You can arrange this without much alteration in the design – but, when you're designing and making a 'knock-down' assembly of this kind, you need to take special care that the fixing in question is solid. One method is to make each post in two parts, of which the upper rests on the lower. Do the same with the 75 x 25mm (3 x 1in) timber which is fixed to the inside of the post – but 75mm (3in) further up, so that you're left with a staggered joint. Then you should bolt the end of the thicker piece, which protrudes downwards, to the end of the thinner piece, which protrudes upwards.

You should use two bolts for each post, plus washers, and do the nuts up very tightly with a spanner. For safety's sake, it might be sensible to use two nuts on each bolt.

Alternatively, you can follow the same procedure without staggering the joint, and drill corresponding holes in the end grain of the 75x25mm – one in the top end of the bottom piece, and one in the bottom end of the top piece. Glue a piece of broomstick into the first hole, and use that as a locator.

The posts should extend 300mm (1ft) below the bottom of each bunk, to form legs, and 600mm (2ft) above the top of the bottom bunk's mattress. This will provide your 900mm (3ft) clearance between the two.

If you want to make the beds identical, extend the posts 600mm (2ft) above the top bunk as well. This will leave you with tall 'goalposts' when the beds are separated. But you can make these look good (and stabilise the structure) by screwing slats of 75 x 25mm (3 x 1in) timber to their outer faces at each end.

Installing a ladder

You'll need a ladder for access to the top bunk. Slats are one possibility here, too: run them up just far enough for the top one to serve as a guard rail. Space them about 250mm (10in) apart, and round over their top edges with a file so they'll be easier on the feet.

Alternatively, you can make a detachable ladder. Simply take two pieces of 75 x 38mm (3 x 1½in) timber to form the uprights, drill through them both at once, and glue in lengths of broomstick (which is cheaper then dowel) for the rungs. Then reinforce the fixing by nailing into the rungs through the edges of the uprights.

If you don't want the ends of the rungs to be visible, you'll have to drill stopped holes separately in each upright, which is a trickier job. Mark out the holes' positions together as far as possible, so that they match.

A reasonable overall width for the ladder is 300mm (1ft). Hang it from both bunks at once with two pairs of proprietary ladder brackets. These are just hooks which you screw into the edges of the ladder uprights.

Finishing touches

You can paint or varnish the bunks, as you wish. But, whatever finish you choose, do give the whole thing a really thorough sanding, in order to round off all the corners. There must be no sharp edges on which children can hurt themselves, and no splinters to penetrate their skin as they clamber over the bunks in their bare feet.

A bright-coloured stain followed by a clear polyurethane varnish might give a cheerful and durable, yet natural, look.

Ready Reference

DEMOUNTABLE BUNKS

Here are two ways to make bunks that can be taken apart, so that they'll form a pair of separate beds. Both involve making joints in the posts, about 300mm (1ft) below the bottom of the top bunk.

● drill corresponding holes, each say 38mm (1½in) deep, in the exposed ends of the cut posts, and simply glue a piece of broomstick into the lower one.

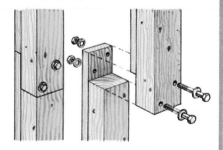

● form a staggered joint as shown, fixing it with two 6mm (¼in) diameter coach bolts, 100mm (4in) long.

If you want to make the beds similar shapes, extend the posts on the top one as well. Screw four slats of 75x25mm (3x1in) timber across the end of each.

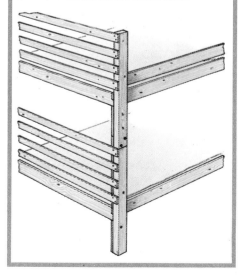

HOW TO MAKE A BUNK BED

These bunks are strong and stable. Their design is straightforward — two bed frames, fixed to four posts. Each frame is made with glued halving joints. Within it are bearers to support the pegboard on which the mattress rests. The bed has guard rails on two sides. Elsewhere, reinforcing pieces run across the ends.

Right: An easy-to-make ladder using lengths of broomstick for rungs, fitted in pieces of 75x25mm (3x1in) timber.

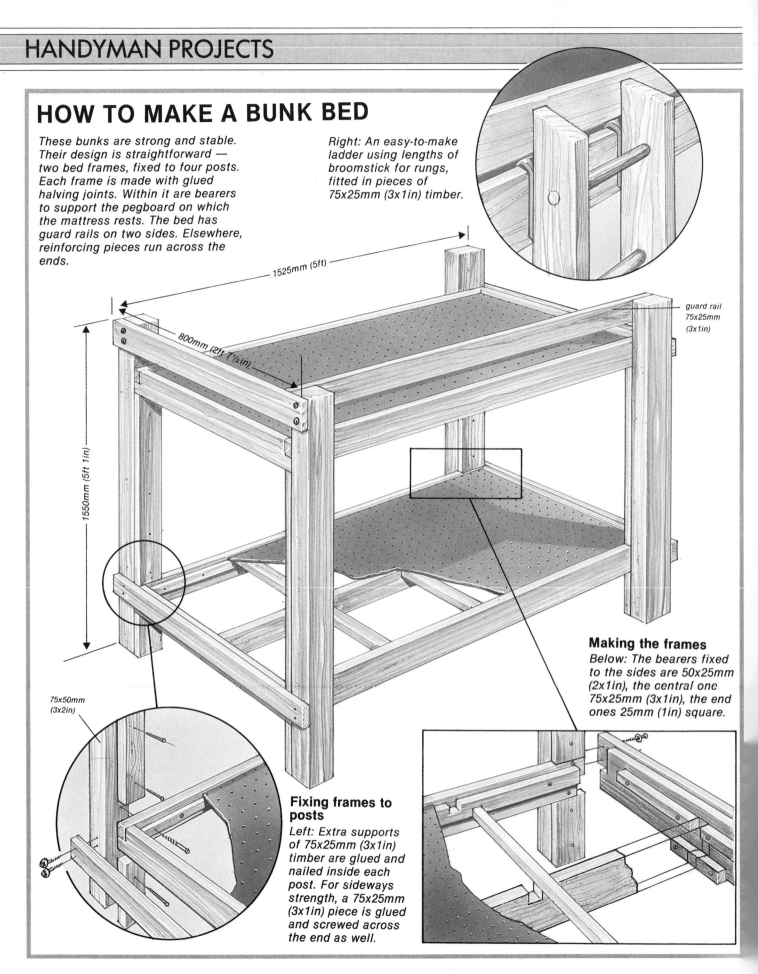

1525mm (5ft)

800mm (2ft 7½in)

1550mm (5ft 1in)

guard rail 75x25mm (3x1in)

75x50mm (3x2in)

Making the frames
Below: The bearers fixed to the sides are 50x25mm (2x1in), the central one 75x25mm (3x1in), the end ones 25mm (1in) square.

Fixing frames to posts
Left: Extra supports of 75x25mm (3x1in) timber are glued and nailed inside each post. For sideways strength, a 75x25mm (3x1in) piece is glued and screwed across the end as well.

INSTALLING SLIDING DOORS

When making the most of limited space, you don't want to waste it on giving a door room to swing. Sliding doors avoid this problem; and smooth-running, easy-to-install sliding gear is readily available.

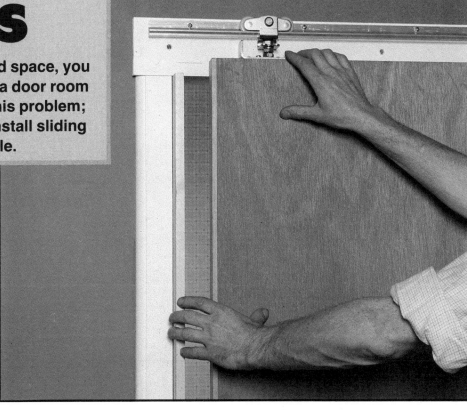

Think how much clear floor space a hinged door needs to open freely, compare it with what a sliding door needs, and you'll realise why small spaces and sliding doors make such an attractive combination. You can get in that much more in the way of furniture, fittings – and people. You can use the entire floor area, safe in the knowledge that you won't be sent flying if someone bursts into the room. And these advantages also apply to the doors of cupboards and wardrobes, for they're equally guilty of gobbling up valuable space and getting in everyone's way.

Of course, sliding doors aren't perfect. They have their drawbacks, and you need to weigh these up carefully against the benefits.

Firstly, many sliding doors leave larger gaps around them than hinged doors, and gaps tend to mean draughts. Strictly speaking, it shouldn't be necessary to draughtproof internal doors – apart from anything else, draughts play a major role in providing adequate ventilation. But if the gaps are very large, or if you live in an exceptionally draughty property, things can get uncomfortable.

Secondly, while sliding doors take up less floor space than hinged doors, they take up more wall space – because, after all, they need somewhere to slide to. So they're no good in locations where the wall space will be needed for something else (eg, to stand furniture against, or for the attachment of fittings such as shelves or washbasins).

In addition, you'll need to modify the door frame – for two reasons. One is to prevent gaps, and this needs particular thought if you're re-using the existing door (because, of course, it will be slightly smaller than the opening). The second reason is to allow the door to travel freely; existing architraves, picture rails, dado rails, skirtings, power sockets and light switches are possible sources of trouble here.

Finally, care is needed if you're to end up with an attractive result. This is partly because we're used to doors which close neatly flush with the surrounding walls; sliding doors can sometimes look a bit bulky by comparison.

More importantly, however, many homes have ornamental touches (for example, moulded skirting boards and cornices) which contrast unhappily with the often rather stark and functional look of a sliding door and its accompanying fitments. The answer is the judicious addition of mouldings to the door installation itself – and the substitution of a home-made pelmet, designed to blend in, or a ready-made one if supplied.

Choosing doors and door gear

Often the benefits offered by a sliding door outweigh the drawbacks. So how do you install one? You need two main elements: the door, and the sliding gear on which it moves.

The door itself presents no problem. A flush door will probably look best, but there's nothing to stop you using a panel door if you prefer the look of this particular type, and you can even use a plain sheet of plywood or blockboard as the door if you wish. In the case of blockboard, cut the panel so that the core battens run horizontally across the door, to enable you to make secure screw fixings into its top and bottom edges (in panel and flush doors, you must likewise avoid screwing into the end grain of the stiles). Plywood and blockboard will need hardwood lippings glued and pinned down the vertical edges to conceal them.

As for the door size, a single opening will take just about any size of single door. If the

ADAPTING THE DOORWAY

When installing a sliding door, you'll need to modify the doorway at least slightly, to make sure the door fits neatly and without gaps. A number of ways of doing this are shown here. Which you choose depends largely on the width of the door you are fitting.

Leaving the architrave

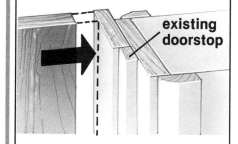

existing doorstop

The simplest plan is just to add an extra piece to narrow the opening, while leaving the existing architrave and doorstop beading in place.

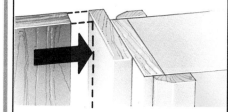

For cleaner lines, you can prise off the existing doorstop beading altogether. Fix your new piece into position after that.

Removing the architrave

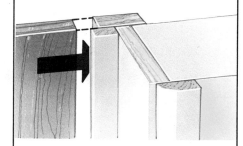

The architrave on the door side can be replaced with wider timber, planed to the width you need. Another piece covers the gap.

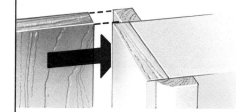

For a door that overlaps the jamb, the timber that replaces the architrave must be narrower. But the overlap eliminates the gap.

Replacing the lining

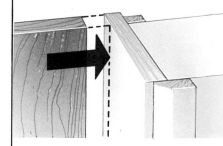

You can even remove the lining itself, fitting a new, wider lining, plus a piece on the door side to cover the exposed end of the skirting.

Finishing the rear edge

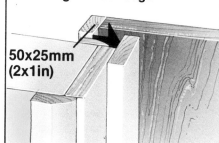

50x25mm (2x1in)

If there's a gap between the doorway and the door's rear edge, stop draughts with overlapping pieces on the door and frame.

PREPARING THE DOOR AND OPENING

1 After cutting away the architrave flush with the top of the opening, screw a batten to the wall at the same level. Paint it first.

2 Fix the guide channel to the bottom of the door, according to the manufacturer's instructions, and add the doorstop, if any.

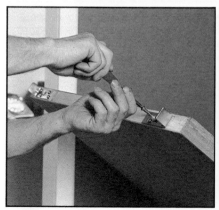

3 Screw the fixing plates to the top edge (avoiding end grain), after drilling holes for the hanger bolts to match those in the plates.

door's too wide, that's a positive advantage, for the overlap will help to avoid gaps. If it's too tall, you can saw or plane a strip off the top or bottom. And if it's too small, you can simply modify the door frame as described later.

For wider openings, much the same answers apply, except that you'll need more than one door (unless you're using a single wide sheet of board).

The door gear is a set of proprietary fittings which you buy ready-made in kit form.

When choosing the gear, forget about those types where the doors merely slide in metal, plastic or wooden channels. Such systems are no use whatever for any but the smallest, lightest cupboard doors. Try using one on anything more substantial – even a light-weight wardrobe door – and you'll be lucky if you can even get the door to move.

The fittings used on full-sized sliding doors consist, instead, of three major components. First, there's the gear itself: a set of wheels, usually nylon, which are secured by long, adjustable 'hanger bolts' to plates screwed to the top edge of the door. Next, a specially shaped track – usually aluminium but occasionally steel – is fixed to the wall above the doorway.

Tracks suitable for ceiling mounting are also available, and others can be fixed to either the wall or the ceiling – though additional brackets are sometimes needed for the latter arrangement. If the ceiling joists run parallel to the doorway, you may have to fix cross pieces between them (above the ceiling cladding) and screw the batten on those.

The wheels of the door gear hook onto the track, taking the weight of the door and allowing it to be slid from side to side. That only leaves the bottom guide, which simply holds the bottom of the door on course.

This type of gear is simple, durable, fairly cheap, and virtually the same no matter whom you buy from. The only notable variation is that certain gears designed for wall-to-wall wardrobe doors include aluminium channelling, complete with gear wheel and bottom guide; the idea is that you fit it round the edges of a piece of plywood or blockboard to form a rigid lightweight door.

However, there are a few smaller differences between models. The most important relate to strength. In some cases you can see the variations for yourself (for example, heavy-duty gears tend to have two wheels per hanger bolt, and ultra-heavy-duty types often use ball bearings instead). You'll find that each model has certain limitations regarding not only the weight but also sometimes the width, the thickness and even the height of the doors it can carry.

The correct location of the bottom guide is often the trickiest part of the installation, and also the most crucial for smooth, draught-free operation. This makes it worth looking carefully at the type of guide used. Gears intended for wardrobe doors often have a continuous channel which fits across the opening. Those for doors that people walk through use a different method: a block, wheel or revolving cam is fixed to the floor in the path of the door, and this locates in a channel. With most do-it-yourself gears you merely screw the channel to the bottom edge of the door; professional versions use a slimmer channel which is set into a groove cut in the door's bottom edge. Obviously the latter is much neater, but cutting an accurate groove isn't easy.

Various solutions are used for the problem of draughtproofing. Most involve the use of brush-type draught strips and/or specially

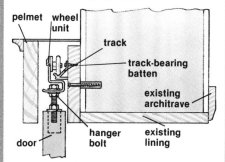
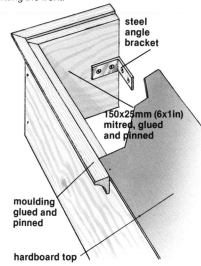
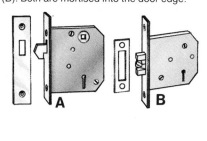
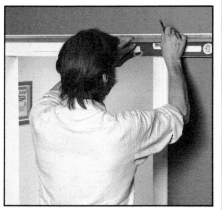

4 Stand the door up and position it so you can mark a line right along the batten, corresponding to the door's top edge.

5 Screw the track onto the batten, the recommended distance up from the line. If the line slopes, work from its highest point.

HANGING THE DOOR

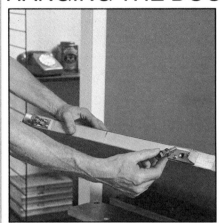

1 Screw the hanger bolts into the plates on the top edge of the door, so their ends protrude down into the holes you've drilled.

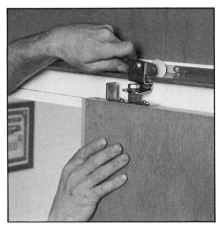

2 Slide the wheel units onto the track, and slip the hanger bolts into them – first loosening the nuts to let you do this easily.

3 Turn each bolt, so the door rides up or down on the thread, to get the door level and give a slight clearance above the floor.

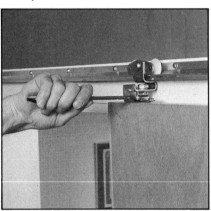

5 Tighten the bottom nut against the plate itself, so as to keep the door at the right level and to prevent vibration loosening the nuts.

6 Fit a piece of timber in position, if necessary, to narrow the opening and so eliminate gaps when the door is closed.

7 With the door hanging truly vertical and fully closed, mark exactly where the bottom corner of its opening edge comes.

9 Slide the door across so that the guide fixed to the floor engages in the channel fitted to the door's bottom edge.

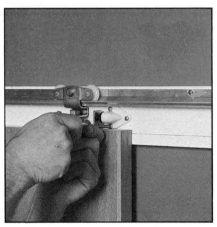

10 Move the door so the guide is just hidden, and screw a plastic doorstop (if supplied) to the batten as a buffer for the top plate.

11 Close the door, and adjust the position of the filler piece down the jamb so the door edge meets it in the way you want.

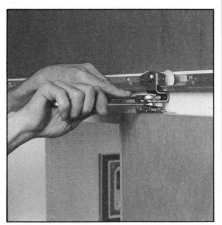

4 *Lock the bolt onto the wheel unit by holding its head with one spanner and using another to adjust the nut immediately below it.*

8 *Open the door fully, and screw the guide cam, block or wheel to the floor in accordance with the mark you've just made.*

12 *Finally, nail the filler piece in position, and complete the job by fitting a pelmet (if desired) to conceal the track and the batten.*

shaped timber strips which are attached to the back edge of the door (ie, the trailing edge as you close it). One other system, however, is worth a special mention. It uses a bottom guide channel with a kink in it, which causes the door to close hard against the door frame, thus eliminating gaps. When you open the door, the kink throws it clear again so that it can slide freely.

Special sliding doors

Although the average doorway needs only a single sliding door, wide ones usually need two or even three. This especially applies to openings, such as those in fitted wardrobes, which take up the full width of a room or alcove – because there's no wall for a single door to slide against when it's opened. For this purpose there are double tracks which enable the doors to slide past each other. These are generally suitable only for ceiling (rather than wall) mounting, but they make it easier to achieve the same net result than by using two single tracks.

There are also 'sympathetic' gears, with which one door automatically opens (or closes) when you open (or close) the other. These, however, differ in requiring sliding (ie, wall) space on both sides of the doorway.

Lastly, you can mount doors so that they slide inside a cavity. You actually build a false wall around the doorway, using plasterboard and timber studs, so that the door disappears neatly into the gap between the real and false walls as you open it. This is certainly neater than the standard arrangement which leaves the open door in plain view; and, if you line the opening in the new wall with architraves and skirting boards which match those around, it could solve the problem of making sliding doors blend with older and distinctly styled houses.

Carrying out the installation

Since the various makes of sliding door gear do differ, you'll naturally have to stick to the manufacturer's instructions to make sure you get the fixing details right. However, the basic principles of installation are common to all.

The first step is to gain a clear idea of how you want the door to fit against the frame when closed, and how the door and frame will look from all angles. There are many ways of modifying the frame to achieve various results, both functionally and in terms of appearance, several are illustrated on page 124. A lot will depend on the style of the rooms and the furniture in them, as well as the neighbouring doorways on either side, and on the width of the new door.

On the door side of the doorway, you'll always need to cut away at least the overhead section of the existing architrave – flush with the top of the opening – in order to accommo-

date the batten for the track on which the door slides.

In some cases you can leave the rest of the architrave, and simply add an extra piece or pieces of timber to the inside face of the door lining to act as a doorstop. But it's often neater to remove the architrave down the jamb against which the door closes, and substitute a thicker piece of wood as a doorstop, fixed to the face of the wall rather than inside the lining. You may even want to replace the lining of that jamb altogether with a wider piece.

When you've fitted the door, you may also need to widen or thicken the lining of the opposite jamb – by replacing it or adding a piece – to fill any gap left when the door is closed.

Once you've sorted out these major points, the remainder of the job should be straightforward, if not exactly routine. First you need to get the track-bearing batten level on the wall overhead, packing it out if the wall is crooked. Then cut the metal track itself to length (ie, slightly more than twice the door width), get that level too, and screw it to the batten.

You'll need to fit the guide channel to the bottom edge of the door before hanging it, which you do by means of plates, hanger bolts and rollers. You can make fine vertical and lateral adjustments with the appropriate nuts – both before and after screwing the guide block, wheel or cam to the floor and aligning the door with it.

Finishing off

A few other touches finish the job off. It's quite a good idea to add one or two small plastic or rubber doorstops (usually supplied as part of the kit) to prevent the door from opening too far, and make a pelmet (see *Ready Reference*). There's also the fitting of handles, plus a latch or lock if you want one, to be considered.

Your pelmet will need to be fixed to the wall invisibly for appearance's sake. Two possible answers are timber battens and metal angle brackets. In both cases, you'll probably need to screw the ends of the pelmet to the wall via these fixings first, before adding the front and top panels (otherwise you won't be able to get at the wall-fixing screws).

With imagination, a pelmet can be turned into a really impressive feature. You can look in the shops for a suitable moulding, and mitre it neatly round the upper edge of the pelmet to form a cornice. Or you can use panel mouldings of various types to make rectangular patterns right across the front.

Fitting a sliding door isn't a job you can do in a few moments – but you may well find it easier than hanging a door on hinges, and you're almost bound to end up with a smoothly gliding result.

BUILDING SHELVING UNITS

Self-supporting shelves, unlike the wall-mounted type, can be moved wherever and whenever you like – without leaving screw holes to be plugged. Here's how to make them rigid and roomy.

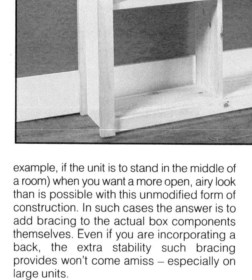

A part from their most obvious advantages over built-in units, freestanding units don't have to be tailored to fit any irregularities of walls and alcoves. But, because they aren't fixed in position, you have to devote a bit more time and thought to making them rigid.

This is often a matter of making a straight-forward box as described in detail on pages 60-63 – although frame construction is another possibility. Either way, it is important to remember that the shelves themselves won't add much stability, particularly if they're adjustable. You need additional stiffening to compensate the tendency for the whole unit to fold up sideways into a diamond shape.

The basic box
Always keep your materials in mind. The options are, of course, solid timber or man-made boards. Plywood is probably the best all-rounder, but it's quite expensive. Chipboard is cheap, and chipboard screws make a strong butt joint. In solid timber and block-board, you're restricted by the fact that you shouldn't screw or nail into end grain.

Dowels or plastic jointing blocks are good for assembling most of the structure, but dowels are less than ideal for corners, because a dowel joint isn't all that rigid. A timber strip, glued and screwed into both surfaces, can add some necessary reinforcement; but shelf units often rise above eye level, and you'll have to be careful that it's not unsightly as well.

A barefaced housing joint is one remaining possibility – that is, apart from those afforded by power tools. A circular saw or router makes it a lot easier, for example, to cut rebate joints or mitres.

An additional point is that plastic facings such as melamine laminate won't accept glue, so that some form of screw fastening is virtually your only way of fixing other components to them.

Stiffening the unit
The simplest way of making a unit rigid is to pin a back panel to the rear edges of the box and perhaps even to the back edges of the shelves as well.

However, there may be occasions (for example, if the unit is to stand in the middle of a room) when you want a more open, airy look than is possible with this unmodified form of construction. In such cases the answer is to add bracing to the actual box components themselves. Even if you are incorporating a back, the extra stability such bracing provides won't come amiss – especially on large units.

The principle works as follows. Flat boards bend under stress. You can counter this by fixing lengths of reinforcing timber along them, preferably on edge. Every board thus dealt with helps to keep the whole structure stable.

You can even stiffen the open (front) face of the cabinet, by running bracing members across it, provided these are firmly jointed to the cabinet sides – say with dowels, plastic jointing blocks or steel angle repair brackets. A recessed plinth does this job and the type of plinth that's made up separately stabilises the cabinet by stiffening its bottom.

Frequently the neatest way of stiffening the front is to place such reinforcement along the shelves – either underneath them (inset if you like) or fixed to their front edges.

Rectangular-sectioned timber such as 50x25mm (2x1in), or a metal L-section, is ideal here. The procedure has the added advantage of strengthening the shelves, and you can treat intermediate shelves in the same way – not just the top and bottom panels.

Supporting the shelves
You can fix shelves into the unit by any of the methods appropriate for box construction using hand tools. The strongest and most professional of these is to house the shelves into the uprights (for further information see pages 36-43).

A stopped housing makes the neater joint here, since it means the front edge of each upright is unbroken by the ends of the shelves, but a through housing is quite adequate. The other invisible fastening for fixed shelves is dowels. Screws will leave plastic caps showing on the outsides of the side panels.

The choice between these methods depends largely on your materials. A plastic-faced upright panel means the dowel joints can't be glued, so you rely even more than usual on the main box for strength. Timber shelves,

A STURDY SHELF UNIT

This unit's top and sides are made of plastic-faced chipboard; the softwood shelves are planed down in the width to match.

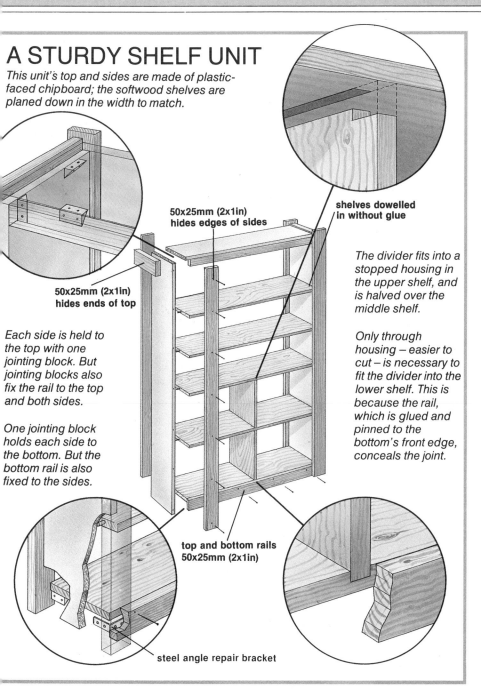

50x25mm (2x1in) hides edges of sides

50x25mm (2x1in) hides ends of top

Each side is held to the top with one jointing block. But jointing blocks also fix the rail to the top and both sides.

One jointing block holds each side to the bottom. But the bottom rail is also fixed to the sides.

shelves dowelled in without glue

The divider fits into a stopped housing in the upper shelf, and is halved over the middle shelf.

Only through housing – easier to cut – is necessary to fit the divider into the lower shelf. This is because the rail, which is glued and pinned to the bottom's front edge, conceals the joint.

top and bottom rails 50x25mm (2x1in)

steel angle repair bracket

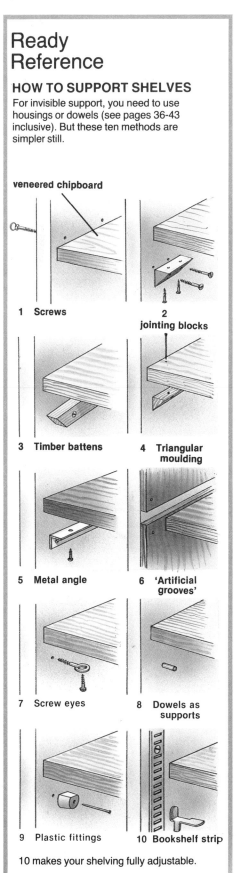

Ready Reference

HOW TO SUPPORT SHELVES

For invisible support, you need to use housings or dowels (see pages 36-43 inclusive). But these ten methods are simpler still.

veneered chipboard

1 **Screws**

2 **jointing blocks**

3 **Timber battens**

4 **Triangular moulding**

5 **Metal angle**

6 **'Artificial grooves'**

7 **Screw eyes**

8 **Dowels as supports**

9 **Plastic fittings**

10 **Bookshelf strip**

10 makes your shelving fully adjustable.

---

n the other hand, can't be screwed in directly ecause you'd be going into the end grain.

Plastic jointing blocks are an obvious and airly unobtrusive possibility. Timber battens, lued and pinned, or screwed and if possible lued, to shelves and uprights are tough; hey can also be quite neat if you chamfer heir front ends, cut them off at an angle, or ide them with a front rail. A triangular-ectioned timber 'stair rod' moulding, or an -sectioned strip of steel or aluminium, is eater still.

You can create artificial housings by using ieces of timber or board, the same width as he uprights, pinned and glued to their inside faces, and leaving just enough space for the shelves to fit between them. This means you can make the uprights themselves a bit thinner.

A rather different approach is to let the shelf ends rest on small supports sticking out of the uprights. These might be screw eyes (with screws driven up through them into the undersides of the shelves to fix them in place if necessary); they could be 6mm (¼in) diameter dowels. You can also get several sorts of plastic studs which screw in, nail in or push into drilled holes. Some are specially designed for glass shelves. And sometimes the hole is filled by a bush which

ASSEMBLING THE CARCASE

1 After cutting all the shelves to the same length, mark and cut housings for the divider halfway along the shelves above and below it.

2 Use one of the housings as a guide to mark the position of the halving to be cut in the shelf which the divider crosses.

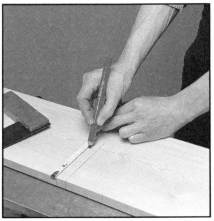

3 Measure halfway across the shelf for the depth of the halving. Then cut the divider to length, and measure and mark it out likewise.

4 Cut the matching halvings in the divider and the shelf it crosses; use a tenon saw across the grain and then a chisel to chop out the waste.

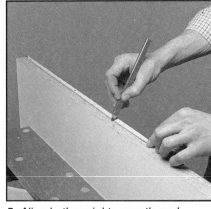

5 Align both uprights exactly and mark on them the height of each shelf (at a point which is halfway across the shelf's thickness).

6 Use a combination square at the same setting to mark the exact dowel positions on both the uprights and on all the shelf ends.

7 Drill all the dowel holes, glue the dowels into the shelf ends, and fit all but the top and bottom shelves to the uprights when the adhesive sets.

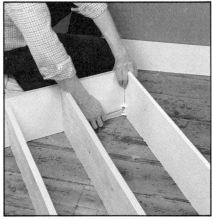

8 Screw the top and bottom shelves into position with plastic jointing blocks, or any other appropriate jointing technique.

9 Insert the divider into the unit from the back, using scrap wood to prevent damage to its rear edge as you tap it into position.

ADDING REINFORCEMENT

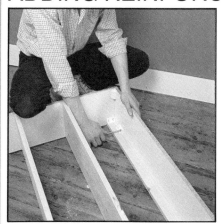

1 *Fix a stiffening rail across the top, screwing it to the uprights and the underside of the top shelf with jointing blocks.*

2 *Glue and pin the plinth rail to the front edge of the bottom shelf (which is cut narrower than the other shelves to allow for this).*

3 *Use steel angle repair brackets to hold the plinth firmly to the uprights and thus help to keep the whole unit rigid as well.*

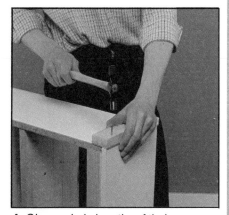

4 *Glue and pin lengths of timber, as long as the uprights are wide, to the ends of the top shelf in order to conceal them.*

5 *Glue and pin further lippings to both long edges of each upright to enhance the unit's appearance and give it extra rigidity.*

6 *Lastly, fill all nail holes with wood stopping of the appropriate shade, and varnish the timber parts to improve their looks and durability.*

will accept a number of different types of stud.

Lastly, there's a very neat way to make the shelves in a freestanding unit fully adjustable. This is to use 'bookshelf strip' – metal strips with continuous rows of slots, into which you clip small metal lugs; the shelves rest on these. The strips (of which you'll need two each side) can be simply screwed to the insides of the uprights, or fitted into vertical grooves if you've got the power tools to cut them.

A home-made version of this system uses removable dowels in regular vertical rows of drilled holes.

Installing dividers

For the distances you can safely span with various thicknesses of various materials, see page 53. Really wide shelves may need extra support in the middle. Vertical dividers will provide this, and can also add to looks and usefulness. They're usually housed or dowelled in at top and bottom, and halved over intermediate shelves.

Alternatively, a square- or rectangular-sectioned timber upright, fixed to the front edges of the shelves, will help matters. It can be glued and pinned to the shelves, dowelled in or notched over them.

Frame shelving

If you only think in terms of box construction, you limit the scope of your projects. A shelf unit's sides can just as well be open frames as single slabs. This gives a lighter look, and also avoids the problems of using man-made boards. But you do need to pay even more attention to making the structure rigid. You'll certainly need extra strengthening pieces running from side to side.

Shelves can be supported in most of the ways already mentioned – with the additional possibility of placing them on the cross pieces in the frames themselves. These cross pieces can even be pieces of broomstick – in other words, each upright is in effect a ladder, with the shelves resting on the rungs.

Box modules

In fact, as far as freestanding shelves are concerned, the possibilities are limitless. One more example may help to demonstrate this. There's no reason why you shouldn't make your 'shelving' up as a stack of completely separate open-fronted boxes. They needn't even be the same depth from front to back. Such a system lets you rearrange its shape completely at will. Its main disadvantage is that most of the panels are duplicated, so the cost of materials goes up. But moving house is easy: each box doesn't even need packing!

As long as you make the structure rigid, the choice of design is yours.

FITTING DRAWERS TO CABINETS

Drawers are the classic way to get easy access to your storage space. Making and fitting them needn't be complicated: it's just a matter of knowing the best methods; and there's plenty of choice.

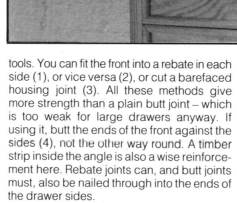

The word 'handy' could have been invented for drawers. They're indispensable in sideboards, in kitchen units, in desks, in bedside and dressing tables (and of course in chests of drawers!). You can install them in shelf units and even under beds.

If you're thinking of making and fitting drawers to your furniture, the important thing is to be familiar with the options available. There's a method for every purpose, and most are well within the beginner's capacity.

Drawer construction

A drawer, of course, is simply a box without a top. But, because it's constantly pulled out, its front corners are subject to particular stress. That's why traditional dovetail joints are best for the job – you can't pull them apart. However, it would be foolish to pretend they're easy to cut unless you've had a bit of experience. And other methods will do quite well for all practical purposes.

The easiest option of all is to buy a drawer kit. These consist of specially shaped plastic moulding to form the four sides of the drawer (three, if you're using your own front panel – see below) plus corner pieces which form a permanent connection.

The only piece you may need to provide yourself is the bottom panel, which fits into grooves already made in the sides. For a smaller drawer this can be hardboard; but thin plywood is much stiffer, and should be used for larger drawers and any which will be heavily loaded.

The only secret with drawer kits is to follow the instructions closely. So why bother with any other method? Mainly because the sides come only in standard heights, and these may be too shallow. Making your own drawers gets over this problem. The best material for the four sides is undoubtedly solid timber, though multi-ply is an alternative. The minimum thickness you need is about 10mm (3/8in), so you could use 12mm (1/2in) thick timber which has been planed. Choose the width that makes the best use of the space inside the cabinet. But don't make drawers deeper than their likely contents, or you'll waste space.

For the crucial corner joints, you have several choices – even without using power tools. You can fit the front into a rebate in each side (1), or vice versa (2), or cut a barefaced housing joint (3). All these methods give more strength than a plain butt joint – which is too weak for large drawers anyway. If using it, butt the ends of the front against the sides (4), not the other way round. A timber strip inside the angle is also a wise reinforcement here. Rebate joints can, and butt joints must, also be nailed through into the ends of the drawer sides.

The other possibility is dowels (5). They too are stronger if placed sideways.

Rear corners come under less strain, so making them is even simpler. The drawer sides often run past the back, to support the drawer when fully extended. You can either house the back into them (6) – stopping the housing near the top for neatness if you prefer (7) – or butt-joint it (8).

Just glueing and pinning the bottom panel to the bottoms of the sides isn't strong enough for most purposes. It can be grooved in all round instead; but the most convenient way of fitting it is in a grooved *drawer slip* moulding (9), which you can buy ready-machined from timber merchants. Mitre this and glue and pin it inside the drawer front and sides round the base. If you make the back narrower than the sides, you can slide in the bottom panel underneath it from behind as the last step in assembling the drawer, and just pin it up at the back.

Alternatively, you can make the back the same height as the sides, and simply glue and pin a mitred timber strip, square in section, all round the inside of the box. Lay the bottom panel on that. If you want it to be removable for cleaning, just leave it loose. If not, either glue and pin it in place, or (for a more professional result) mitre a quadrant beading and fix it above the panel in the same way (10).

Whatever you do, cut the bottom panel accurately to size and shape, so it will help to keep the whole structure rigid.

One more type of drawer is ready-made from plastic in its entirety. It's strong and easily cleaned. But, although there's a range of sizes, you naturally cannot arrange or alter any of its dimensions to suit your own requirements. You need to design your furniture to accept it – and you'll need to take special care to make the cabinet accurately to size so the drawer fits into it properly.

WAYS OF MAKING AND HANGING DRAWERS

Choose from these methods when you're putting drawers together from timber or plywood – and when you're fitting them.

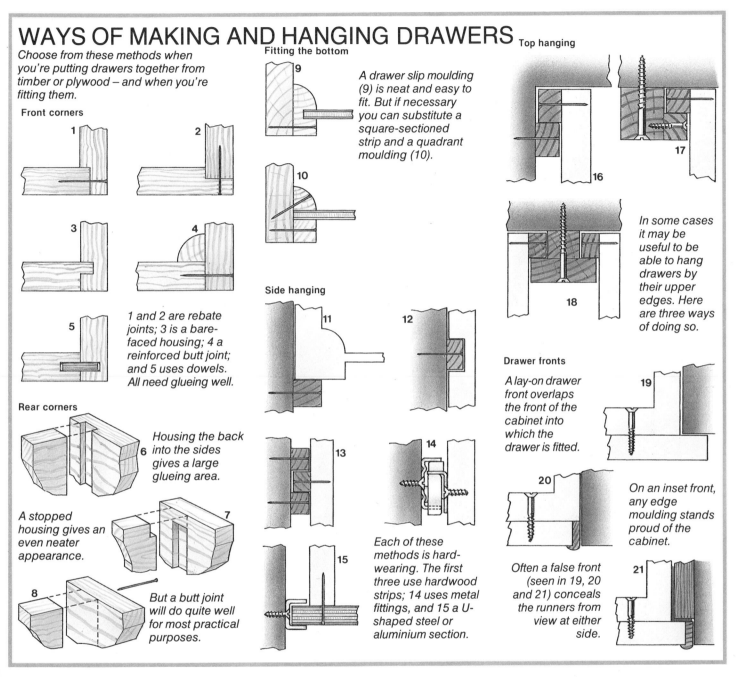

Front corners

1 and 2 are rebate joints; 3 is a barefaced housing; 4 a reinforced butt joint; and 5 uses dowels. All need glueing well.

Rear corners

Housing the back into the sides gives a large glueing area.

A stopped housing gives an even neater appearance.

But a butt joint will do quite well for most practical purposes.

Fitting the bottom

A drawer slip moulding (9) is neat and easy to fit. But if necessary you can substitute a square-sectioned strip and a quadrant moulding (10).

Side hanging

Each of these methods is hard-wearing. The first three use hardwood strips; 14 uses metal fittings; and 15 a U-shaped steel or aluminium section.

Top hanging

In some cases it may be useful to be able to hang drawers by their upper edges. Here are three ways of doing so.

Drawer fronts

A lay-on drawer front overlaps the front of the cabinet into which the drawer is fitted.

On an inset front, any edge moulding stands proud of the cabinet.

Often a false front (seen in 19, 20 and 21) conceals the runners from view at either side.

Installing drawers

Fitting drawers, too, embraces a number of possibilities. In the traditional method the drawer is the full width of the cabinet interior, and its sides simply rest on the cabinet bottom, or more usually on *runners* fixed to the cabinet sides (11). This system is not only simple but hardwearing. It also demands something above the drawer to stop it tipping forward as you pull it out. In modern box construction, this is usually the top of the cabinet itself, or the runners of the drawer above.

Nowadays, however, drawers are often *side hung:* in other words, the runners are halfway up the drawer sides. Often a strip of timber (12) or plastic, fixed to the side of the cabinet, fits into a groove along the side of the drawer. This takes up no extra space, so that the drawer still fills the whole width of the cabinet.

The sides in plastic drawer kits have grooves already made to mate with such strips. In timber or plywood, however, you'll have to cut them yourself. A simpler way to get a similar result is to glue and pin two parallel strips of timber to the cabinet side – leaving space for a third strip, glued and pinned to the drawer side, to slide between them (13).

Alternatively you can use metal runners (14). These come in two parts, one screwed to the cabinet and one to the drawer. Their rollers ensure a really smooth action – especially useful if you expect heavy loads.

You can even hang drawers with a timber strip fixed near the top of each side, instead of halfway up. This rests on a timber runner fixed to the cabinet (16). The arrangement can be adapted so that the drawer is hung from the underside of the top (17) – useful if you can't use one or both of the drawer or cabinet sides.

There's yet another option. This is to hang the drawer by means of its bottom panel – running it out past the sides, so that its edges can slide in metal or plastic U-sections (15),

MAKING AND FITTING DRAWERS

1 After deciding on the drawer heights, measure where each set of runners will come. Mark the positions on both cabinet sides at once.

2 Square each mark across, and glue and pin a hardwood strip against it. Use the square again to ensure accurate nailing.

3 Glue and pin on the second strip of each pair in the same way. Use a third strip, plus a piece of thin card, for clearance.

6 Make each box just less than the cabinet depth (front to back); on an inset drawer, allow for the false front, if any.

7 Pin joints after glueing. The sides fit into rebates in the front; the back is housed into the sides (see pages 40-43 for more details).

8 Cut three mitred lengths of drawer slip moulding, and glue and pin them inside the drawer front and sides, flush with the bottom edge.

11 Set a marking gauge to the distance from the bottom of each drawer side to the top of its lower runner; mark the drawer sides.

12 Pin and glue the third strip with its lower edge against this mark. Chiselling off its rear corners makes drawer insertion easier.

13 Cut out the false drawer front, allowing for any mouldings pinned round the edges. When finished, the front's width just fits the cabinet.

4 *Glue and pin pieces of thin plywood or solid timber to the cabinet, between the runners at the back, to make drawer stops.*

5 *Assemble the cabinet, then measure for the width of the drawer box. Hold two runners in the opening, and deduct their thickness.*

9 *Cut the bottom panel, insert it into the grooves in the moulding, and slide it home. The back is narrower to allow this.*

10 *Fix the bottom panel by pinning it into the bottom edge of the drawer back. If cut accurately to fit, it keeps the drawer rigid.*

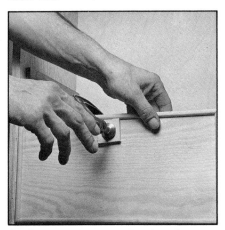

14 *Insert each drawer box into the cabinet, position the front, and adjust it till there's equal clearance all round. Then cramp it on.*

15 *Screw the front on from inside the box, fit a handle, and replace the drawer in the cabinet. The front conceals the runners.*

or between parallel strips of timber, on the cabinet sides. Provided you use thicker-than-usual plywood for the bottom – say 12mm (1/2in) thick – this is a robust construction. And, since the bottom panel supports the drawer rather than vice versa, this is one occasion when you can pin and glue it to the bottom edges of the sides.

Positioning drawers side-by-side creates problems. Obviously, you can only fix the outermost runners to the cabinet sides. For the rest you need intermediate supports. Traditional cabinet-making uses internal framing, but for the handyman the practical choices are to use a variation of the top-hanging method (18), or to fit upright dividers and fix the runners to them.

Drawer fronts

Drawer fronts, like doors, can be either lay-on (19) or inset (20). In other words, they either overlap the front of the cabinet or fit within it.

Commonly, the drawer front is a completely separate panel, screwed to the front of an already made-up timber drawer – even the inset type (20). For one thing, this enables the front to match the rest of the cabinet (including its other drawers, if any), whatever the drawer boxes themselves are made of.

Secondly, such a 'false front' conceals the drawer's front corner joints if they show, as they usually do. And thirdly, all methods of side-hanging drawers display unsightly runners. These too almost always call for a false front, because it can be extended at both sides to hide them (21).

Lastly, if you're using the traditional system (11) with runners underneath, you can likewise cover the resulting gap (customarily filled by a *drawer rail* running from side to side) by extending false drawer fronts downwards or upwards instead.

With a plastic drawer kit, you have the additional option of including your own front as an integral part of the drawer, fixing it to the other three sides with special connectors.

Other details

The final requirement is something to stop the drawer sliding too far in, hitting the back of the cabinet and eventually loosening it.

All you need is a small block of timber or plywood, fixed inside the cabinet at the back. Make sure its size and position, plus the drawer and runner dimensions, allow it to stop the drawer effectively. Don't rely on a lay-on front to do this, because the joints will suffer.

That's one reason why drawers demand thought. It's always wise to sketch what you're planning, so there's no doubt about how each drawer fits in relation to everything else.

Last of all, choose handles that are in keeping with the piece you're building – and position them elegantly. That usually means directly above one another.

MAKING KITCHEN BASE UNITS

Kitchen units are really nothing more than simple boxes with a few frills added. Here's how to design and build them – and how to arrange them for maximum convenience.

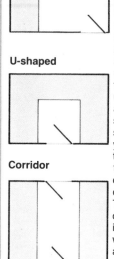

Nowadays even fancy-looking kitchen fitments don't mean complicated joinery and laborious cabinet-making. When you get beneath their patterned worktops and behind their solid timber doors and drawer-fronts, they simply consist of a series of boxes.

These are almost always made from plastic-laminated chipboard, and you can soon build similar ones yourself by the straightforward box-construction methods described in detail on pages 60-63. What's more, you can easily add the refinements which give a really distinctive result.

However, there's no point in just knocking up kitchen units without giving the job a good deal of thought first. That goes for all types of furniture, of course; but the average kitchen is such a busy place that any faults in design will make themselves felt especially sharply.

Kitchen planning

You have to remember that four distinct activities take place in your kitchen: the storage of food, its preparation, the actual cooking, and the serving.

Food storage space includes the larder, the refrigerator and the vegetable racks. Food preparation centres around the sink, and neighbouring worktops. For ease of plumbing, the washing machine usually has to go near the sink. Cutlery needs to be stored in this area too.

When it comes to cooking, the cooker is obviously the most important element; but pans and other utensils should also be stored nearby.

Serving is done from a worktop. If the kitchen is big enough for a breakfast bar, that should be in this area too.

A kitchen's efficiency depends on how easily it allows you to move within and between these activities. For a smooth work-flow, a kitchen should really be circular. That's impossible unless you live in a light-

house, so this ideal pattern has to be modified according to the shape of your kitchen and the position of its door. Despite the enormous range of room plans and sizes, there are only three basic kitchen layouts: the L-shaped, the U-shaped and the corridor – and you can't choose which you want.

So how are all the activities to be fitted in? the best item to start with is the sink. In most homes this has to go on an outside wall, in order to get access to the drains, and many people like to site it in front of the window so that they can look outside as they work.

Next, take the cooker. This is often used in conjunction with the sink. Furthermore, it's a good idea to have a worktop on each side of the hob, and between the hob and sink, because things often need to be laid down there. In a corridor kitchen, sink and cooker should be against the same wall, so that you don't have to carry containers of boiling water across the room.

With these two main elements in position, you can surround them with your units. Always keep the workflow in mind. Tall cupboards should be in a corner or at the end of a run, so as not to interrupt the worktop surface. This even applies when you have split-level cooking, with separate hob and oven, and the oven is housed in a tall unit because the oven doesn't need such constant attention as the hob.

Ready Reference

KITCHEN SHAPES

L-shaped

U-shaped

Corridor

The ideal workflow pattern is a continuous circle. But you'll have to adapt that to your own kitchen, according to the shape of the room and the position of its door. An L-shaped or U-shaped arrangement of units comes closest to the ideal. If you have to use the corridor arrangement, put the sink and hob on the same side, to save yourself from having to carry boiling water from one side to the other with the consequent risk of spillage. The oven can be on the opposite side if you prefer. The sink will probably go against an outside wall.

ADDING A DRAWER AND DOOR

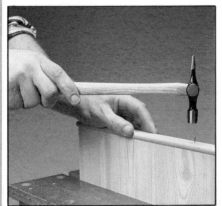

1 *Cut out the drawer-front, and if necessary glue and pin on a strip of moulding (eg, hockey stick), to conceal its top edge.*

2 *Cut and assemble the drawer, following the makers' instructions if using a kit; then attach the drawer-front, with its handle.*

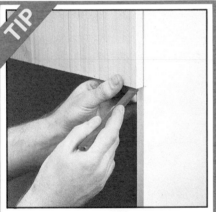

3 *Insert the drawer into the unit, and mark the position of the bottom edge of the drawer-front. This will give the exact height for the door.*

4 *Cut the door to size, mark the hinge positions, and fix the hinges to the door and the completed box. Put the drawer back on its runners.*

Similarly, it doesn't matter if, in a corridor kitchen, the oven is against the opposite wall to the sink, because you don't carry boiling water to and from the oven.

But if for some reason you have to include units of different heights in your scheme, try to make sure you don't change height next to the hob; it's important to be able to slide pans easily on and off it.

What dimensions?

Another vital consideration is how high your units should be. A height of 900mm (3ft) is usual for the sink, hob, worktops and any other surface on which you work while standing up. Of course, this isn't perfect for everyone, but on the whole it's a good compromise. Why not conduct a few tests to discover the height which is exactly (rather than just approximately) right for you?

The standard depth (from front to back) for all kitchen units is 600mm (2ft). This matches the depth of most kitchen appliances; it provides ample space on the worktop and in the cupboards underneath; and it means you can still install a 300mm (1ft) deep unit on the wall above without banging your head on it.

Lastly, you'll probably want to make work-tops as long as you can. Unless you have a really enormous kitchen, it's most unlikely you'll find yourself with too much working space!

In the corner, of course, you'll have cup-board space which is inaccessible. The two commonest solutions to this are to include extra frontage at an angle, and to install a special proprietary revolving corner unit which means you don't have to reach inside.

As for materials, timber-veneered chip-

board is an alternative to the plastic-laminated variety, but you'll have to varnish (if not paint) it to keep out moisture.

What width?

It's usually impractical to make a single box which runs right along the wall. Instead, make a series of smaller ones. You can choose any width you like for these units, and the sensible plan is to follow that of the cupboard doors you're going to put on. Among the widths available in veneered and plastic-faced chipboard are 300, 375, 450, 525 and 600mm (12, 15, 18, 21 and 24in) – so just select one of these. The long edges are already covered with matching edging strip, so it would be silly to lose them by cutting the board lengthwise to a non-standard width.

You can also buy very stylish ready-made louvred and panelled doors, which will give a sophisticated look with no extra trouble.

In all probability, you'll find that the total length of your units doesn't divide exactly by any standard width of board. But that doesn't matter, because you have a certain amount of leeway. For a start, there are two different ways of hanging the doors. Instead of insetting each door between the sides, top and bottom of the box, you can have lay-on doors, which overlap the front edges – and that means you can vary the amount of overlap. (Special hinges are needed for this – see *Ready Reference*).

Alternatively you can leave the odd amount as a gap between units (eg, for storing trays). The minimum width for this is about 100mm (4in), and 150mm (6in) is ideal.

Building the box

The only major difference between a kitchen unit and any other piece of box furniture is that its top doesn't form part of the basic structure. Instead, you fit two cross-bearers between the sides – one at the front, one at the back – with plastic jointing blocks.

The front cross-bearer can be of 50x25mm (2x1in) planed timber, but if you make the back one 50x50mm (2x2in) it's thick enough for you to screw through it later, when you come to fix the unit to the wall for stability. At that stage you may need to remove at least part of the skirting board for a close fit.

Add a back to the unit by pinning a piece of hardboard or thin plywood to the edges of the box (see pages 60-63 for details). This will help to keep it rigid. Fix units together side-by-side with screws, or preferably with special plastic fittings called cabinet connecting screws (see *Ready Reference*). And lastly, add a worktop which extends along the whole run of units – fastening it by screwing up through the cross-bearers.

You can buy worktops ready-made to a

DESIGNING THE UNIT

Here's a standard design of kitchen unit which isn't hard to make. It's really just a box – two sides, a bottom, a back, and two cross-bearers at the top to complete the structure and help support the worktop.

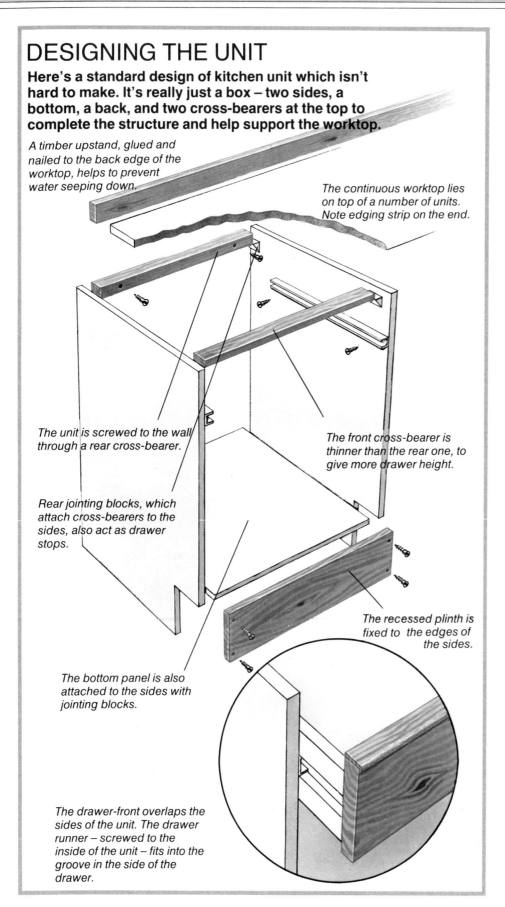

A timber upstand, glued and nailed to the back edge of the worktop, helps to prevent water seeping down.

The continuous worktop lies on top of a number of units. Note edging strip on the end.

The unit is screwed to the wall through a rear cross-bearer.

The front cross-bearer is thinner than the rear one, to give more drawer height.

Rear jointing blocks, which attach cross-bearers to the sides, also act as drawer stops.

The recessed plinth is fixed to the edges of the sides.

The bottom panel is also attached to the sides with jointing blocks.

The drawer-front overlaps the sides of the unit. The drawer runner – screwed to the inside of the unit – fits into the groove in the side of the drawer.

BUILDING THE BOX

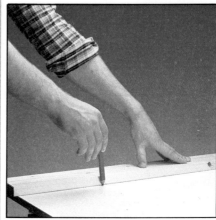

1 *Cut the bottom and side panels of the unit to size, and use the plinth to mark out its own height from the bottom edge of each panel.*

5 *Screw plastic jointing blocks up against these marks, at the front and back edges of the side panel, to take the cross-bearers.*

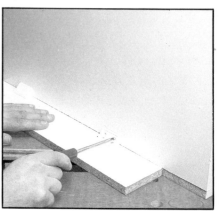

9 *Screw the bottom panel to the jointing blocks near the bottom edge. Then screw the other side panel to the bottom panel and cross-bearers.*

2 Square a line up to meet this one, at whatever depth you want for the plinth recess. Cut out the notch you've marked.

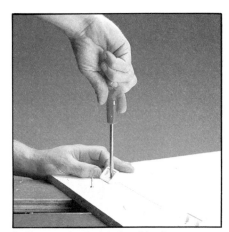

3 Screw plastic jointing blocks against the first line, to take the bottom panel. Make pilot holes with a drill or bradawl first.

4 Align each of the two cross-bearers with the top edge of the side panel, and mark out its thickness on the face of the panel.

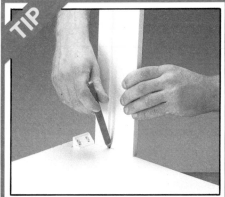

6 Mark the drawer runner's position, allowing for cross-bearers and jointing blocks. Use the drawer side for marking.

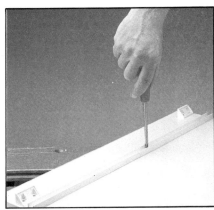

7 After measuring the same height further across the side panel, and joining the two marks, screw the runner against the resulting line.

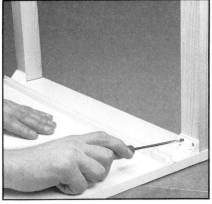

8 Screw the end of each cross-bearer to the appropriate plastic jointing block near the top edge of the side panel.

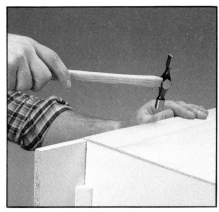

10 Cut out a back panel from hardboard or thin plywood – 4mm (³/16in) is enough – and nail it to the back edges of the box with panel pins.

11 Screw the plinth into the front edges of the side panels, underneath the bottom panel. Plastic tops will conceal the screw heads.

12 Fix the worktop to the cross-bearers by screwing through them. You can screw the unit to the wall through the rear cross-bearer first.

standard width of 600mm (2ft), and covered with an extra-tough plastic laminate which is curved ('postformed') round the front edge so it can't chip. If using a laminate, be sure you get a worktop grade, and not a 'vertical' grade (used on vertical surfaces only), which is thinner and less durable.

Even with the right grade, there are limits to its heat-resistance (you can't put pans onto it straight from the hob), and you can't chop on it. A still tougher material is ceramic tiles, which you could lay on a chipboard base; but these are more expensive, and noisy in use.

Whatever its surface, the worktop should overhang the front of the units – including any protruding doors and drawer fronts – by about 25mm (1in). This makes it more convenient to work on. A recessed plinth at the bottom (see pages 60-63) will keep your feet well clear of the base of the unit while you work.

It's important to make sure no water seeps down behind the worktop, otherwise it will get into the edge of the chipboard and damage it. You can get special plastic mouldings to fit in this gap. Otherwise, silicon sealant along the junction with the wall may do the trick; but a strip of timber – say 50x25mm (2x1in) planed, glued, and nailed or screwed, into the back edge of the worktop to form an upstand – will provide extra protection. It will also help to bring the worktop forward a bit, which is necessary if it's to overhang a unit of the same depth.

You may well find that an uneven floor makes it hard to line units up properly. The answer is to pack them up where necessary, eg, with wedges. Serious discrepancies call for either levelling the floor or adjusting the height of the units' sides.

Doors and drawers
When you come to fit the doors, there are quite a number of varieties of hinge. Your best bet is to go to a good hardware store, see what's in stock and ask for advice. The basic choice is between traditional butt hinges, and modern types which enable you to use a lay-on arrangement without obstructing the doors of neighbouring units when open.

If you're using an inset door, you'll need something for it to close against: either a strip of wood, or perhaps a metal or plastic catch.

You may want a shelf inside the unit. The way to fit this is either on top of wooden battens screwed to the sides, or with proprietary shelf fittings – of which, again, there's quite a range.

You can either run the doors all the way up to the top, or fit drawers as well. Drawers can be made yourself out of solid timber and plywood, or bought in the form of plastic kits

whose components you snap together. They can run either on strips of hardwood or plastic, or on metal fittings with built-in rollers. Both types of runner have to be screwed to the sides of the box. So if you want two or more drawers side-by-side (eg, on a double unit) you'll usually need to install dividers between them, to which you can screw the runners.

The trick when fitting a drawer is to make its front overlap the edges of the box sides – like a lay-on door. That way you cover up any discrepancies in the alignment. And you can add the drawer-front as an ornamental extra, perhaps of solid timber, screwing it to the existing front panel of a drawer that's already made up. When measuring and marking up the front, be careful to get it square – and the right height, so that it extends up to the bottom of the worktop and down to the top of the door.

But don't rely on an overlapping front to prevent the drawer sliding too far in. This will place too much strain on its fixings. Instead, screw a block of wood or something else (eg, a piece of what you're using for the runners) to each side of the unit in the appropriate position near the back. Alternatively, make use of the rear cross-bearer, or its plastic jointing blocks, for the same purpose.

Wire trays are another form of sliding storage that many people find convenient. They can be fitted instead of shelves, or indeed, in addition to them.

You'll find a lot of information about how to fit drawers and doors on pages 110-113 and 132-135.

Doubling up
The basic unit can also be doubled in width and fitted with a pair of doors. If you do this, it's best to add a divider in the middle to give the worktop extra support; notch the divider at the top corners to fit the cross-bearers.

A double unit will take a sink, let into a hole specially cut in the worktop. In this case you'll probably want to put a shelf below the sink so as to make some self-contained cupboards, and then run the divider up to the shelf.

Other fittings
If you go to a good stockist, you can enhance your kitchen units with a tremendous range of proprietary accessories. These include extending tabletops; pull-out ironing boards; telescopic towel rails; plastic and ceramic scoops for liquids and dried foods such as rice and sugar; foot-operated door openers, useful if your hands are full; built-in waste bins which pull out or fit on the inside of cupboard doors; fitted chopping boards; fitted bread boxes; and so on.

Ready Reference

TYPES OF HINGE
The traditional butt hinge is very useful for doors which are inset between the panels of the unit. But the pivot or 'knuckle' protrudes at the front.

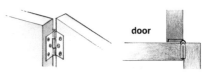

The concealed hinge, with its special mechanism, allows you to fit a lay-on door so that it won't obstruct the neighbouring door when open.

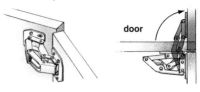

CABINET CONNECTING SCREWS
The cabinet connecting screws fasten completed units together.

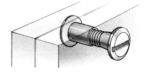

FIXING TO WALLS
Screw each unit to the wall through the rear cross-bearer. To stop water getting into the back edge of the worktop, use a plastic strip, silicone sealant, or a timber upstand.

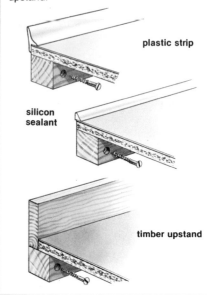

FITTING A KITCHEN:1

Ready-made cabinets are the classic way of providing kitchen storage. Some come factory-assembled, others in kit form. Installing them is straightforward when you know the tricks of the trade.

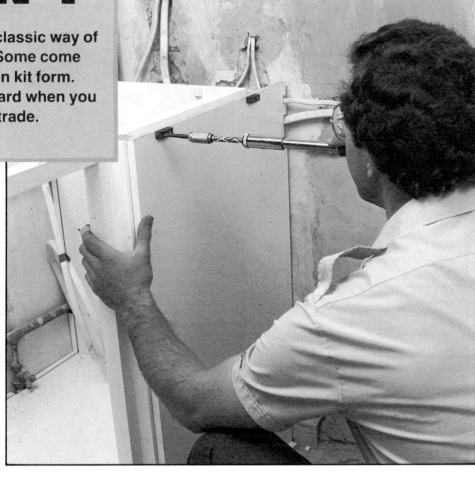

Nowadays, fitting out a kitchen almost always means installing a series of floor-standing and wall-hung cabinets – usually called 'units'.

These are highly standardised. Floor-standing or 'base' units consist of two side panels, a base panel, a thin back panel, and a recessed plinth at the front. There's usually a stiffening rail at the back as well, and there are often shelves inside.

There's no top panel, because the idea is to fill all the available space in the room simply by installing units side-by-side (using ones whose widths most nearly achieve this), and then to cover the whole lot with single lengths of worktop.

To allow this, widths vary considerably; 300, 500 or 600mm (12, 20 or 24in) makes a 'single' unit, 1000 or 1200mm (39 or 47in) a double, and 1500mm (59in) a triple. As for other dimensions, base units are almost always about 870mm (34in) high and 600mm (2ft) deep from front to back. Wall units come in several heights, but most are only 300mm (1ft) deep.

Variants include corner units, tall larder and oven-housing units, tray spaces, open shelf units, and a number of others.

Melamine-faced chipboard is pretty well the universal material for side and base panels, plinths, shelves and even stiffening rails. The back panel is usually melamine-faced hardboard. Most worktops are of chipboard too, but faced with a thicker and tougher laminate. The standard worktop thickness is 30mm (1³⁄₁₆in); the width is usually 600mm (2ft), and many lengths are available. Special double-edged worktops (and special units) are available for 'islands' in the centre of large kitchens.

The real variety comes in doors and drawer-fronts, which are made in any number of materials and finishes, and provide most visual impact in the average fitted kitchen.

Why units?

It's still possible, of course, to fit out a kitchen without units. You can fix softwood battens to the walls, floor and/or ceiling, and use them for mounting shelves, dividers, end panels, extra front rails and uprights, doors, and so on (see pages 105-109 and 155-159 for further information about this method).

However, any professional woodworker will tell you that chipboard is cheaper than time. It always makes more sense for him to install square, uniform cabinets – built in his workshop or factory with the aid of time-saving machines – than to spend long hours on site cutting everything to fit individually.

The do-it-yourselfer's time is free, so the equation is rather different. But there's no doubt that units do simplify things, and the extra cost of duplicated side panels in a row of cabinets is probably balanced by that of all the softwood you need to do it the other way. Besides, battens need lots of wall-fixings, whereas base units require only a couple of screws each. Under the added weight of the worktop, they won't shift.

Working with units

While planning for your basic kitchen requirements you can also be choosing the units you want. Its up to you to sort out your personal priorities from the vast selection on the market. The main differences lie in price, in finish, and in the number of variants and accessories available.

Once you've managed to settle on a short list of likely purchases, you can take the design a stage further by working out which combination of sizes will best fill the space at your disposal. Expensive ranges make this job easier because they generally come in a greater number of different widths.

Provided your measurements are accurate, most small irregularities such as uneven floors and walls can be overcome during installation. One thing that's worth a specific check, however, is whether the walls are square to one another. If any meet at much more or less than 90°, you may have to cope with the discrepancy by setting one or more rows of units away from the wall – and this may mean a slightly wider worktop to cover the resulting gap.

There are three types of unit: ready-assembled, flat-pack, and home-made (see pages 136-140 and 145-149).

The carcases, doors and drawers of flat-pack units (plus the worktops) all come in separate cartons. Your first task is to check that everything you've ordered is actually present. But don't put the cabinets together until you need them, or they'll take up an enormous amount of living space.

PREPARING TO FIT BASE UNITS

1 With a level and if necessary a long straight batten, find the floor's highest point along a line about 300mm (1ft) from the walls to be fitted.

2 Stand the side panel of a base unit on the floor at this point, and mark its height on the wall. For accuracy, make sure that it's vertical.

3 Rule a line at this level across all the appropriate walls. Check – with a panel – that it's nowhere less than a panel's height from the floor.

4 Start with a corner unit. Measure where it will stand along the wall, pack its side panels up if necessary, and cut them round any obstacles.

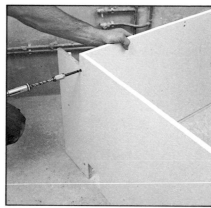

5 Begin assembling the corner unit by fixing the sides to the base. Some models use screws, some use dowels too, and others use special fittings.

6 Most units incorporate a stiffening rail at the rear. This one, as is usual with sink bases, omits the back panel to accommodate pipes.

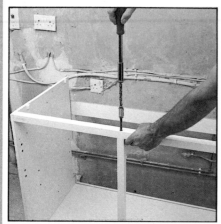

7 Double and triple units (ie, those wider than 600mm/2ft) generally have a pre-cut and pre-jointed front frame as well, for the necessary rigidity.

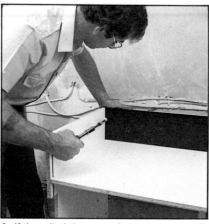

8 If the plinth is a rear-fixing type, you'll need to fasten it to the side panels at this stage – often with special jointing blocks. Other types are fixed later.

9 When positioning the corner unit (see also 4 above), remember that it must usually stand 100mm (4in) from the side wall so its door will be free to open.

INSTALLING BASE UNITS

1 Pack the unit's sides to your marked line if necessary, splitting hardboard for very small adjustments. The same packing can support an adjoining unit.

2 Check that the cabinet is level along its width. You may need a 1200mm (4ft) level, or a short one and a long straight timber batten again.

3 Don't forget to check that the unit is level in its depth as well. If it's necessary, you can vary the amount of packing under the front or back.

4 Two screws in wallplugs are usually enough to secure a base unit to the wall – but position each row of cabinets before fixing. See also 1, page 153.

5 When moving to the next row (in this case, the next unit) check the level from the cabinet(s) which you've already fixed in place.

6 Each corner unit will need a panel at the front too (even if another unit will meet it there). Here, a special support post is attached to the frame first.

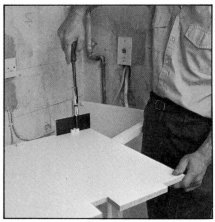

7 The front panel (here cut away to fit round pipes) needs a small section of plinth fixed on to cover the gap which would otherwise occur there.

8 Position the panel, pack it up in the usual way, and fasten it to the cabinet by whatever means the manufacturers recommend – eg, plastic joint blocks.

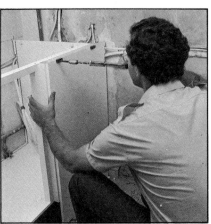

9 Fasten plastic blocks to the base unit's side and front panels, flush with the top, to secure the worktops when they're positioned later.

Even when you start the job, there's a definite sequence to follow which will minimise the snags. You should:
● find the highest point on the floor and mark your worktop height from that
● assemble a corner base unit, pack it up to that line if necessary and screw it to the wall
● assemble and install the other base units one by one, then fix the lot together
● assemble and install any tall units
● cut and position the worktop(s)
● mark the height for the wall units, assemble them and fix them, again starting in a corner
● fit shelves, doors and drawers.

Starting the job

The secret of success lies in the crucial first step of all: using a spirit level to find the highest point on the floor. Work near its perimeter – say 300mm (1ft) out, where the centre lines of the side panels will end up; it's on these that the base units rest. If two alternative likely spots are further apart than your level is long, span them with a straight batten and place your level on that to find which is the higher.

Then level the unit height all round the walls, working up from the height of this reference point. When the base units are assembled and positioned, their tops should all meet the resulting line or come below it. In the latter case, you just raise them – either with packing (usually scraps of hardboard), or with adjustable feet if these are provided. If you found the highest point to start with, there should be no problems.

Level units mean a level base for worktops, and provide a reference line from which to mark wall-unit heights later.

It's also vital to get all the fronts flush, so the doors and drawers will line up neatly. However, base units needn't fit snugly against the wall (just as well, for it may not be flat) – as long as they won't project further than the front edge of the worktop.

If this looks like happening and you can't get them further back, you'll either have to set the worktop out from the wall, covering the gap at the rear with tiles or an 'upstand', or buy a wider worktop.

Pipes, skirting-boards and the like require you to cut matching sections out of the base units' side panels with a coping saw or jigsaw. If the obstacle won't fit under the base or behind the back panel, you'll have to cut away either or both of these as well – and sometimes remove the back panel altogether.

Assembly itself is generally easy, but the exact details vary so much that there's no substitute for close study of manufacturers' instructions.

These photographs and those on pages 150-153 show in full detail the installation of a set of typical off-the-shelf flat-pack kitchen units.

INSTALLING THE OVEN

1 Assemble the oven housing (and any other tall units). Here you start by finding the shelf heights for your particular oven, and tapping in fittings.

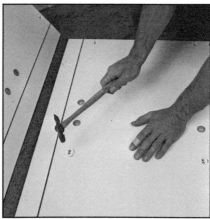

2 Connect the long side panels by fastening the shelves to them both. Here you just tighten the screw in each cam fitting to secure the panels.

3 Slide the back panel sections into their ready-cut grooves, and pin them to the shelves. For ventilation, omit the section behind the oven.

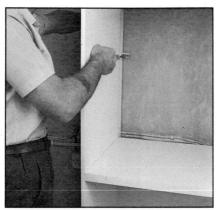

4 Position the unit in the room, make sure it's level, and fix it to the wall. Two simple brackets at oven level will probably suffice.

5 If you've spaced the shelves correctly, you should be able simply to push the oven into the housing so that it rests in place on the lower one.

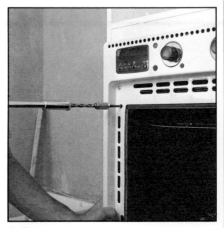

6 This particular oven is secured in the housing by turning a screw which makes a prong stick out and bite into each of the cabinet's side panels.

MAKING KITCHEN WALL UNITS

To make the best use of your kitchen space, and to keep everything handy, you need wall units. There are lots of ways of making them, and you can work to the dimensions which suit you.

A kitchen is basically a workplace. It can be bright, airy, colourful – but these qualities are wasted if it's not highly functional and convenient. That means (among other things) planning it so that everything you need can be reached and stored as quickly, easily and safely as possible.

So kitchen walls – at least up to waist height – are usually lined with appliances and storage facilities. Nowadays the latter often take the form of standard kitchen base units (see pages 136-140), covered by worktops. But, still on the principle that usefulness comes first, you might as well extend your storage space right up as far as you can reach, if not beyond. You're bound to need it. And that's where wall units come in.

There are several considerations to bear in mind from the beginning. Firstly, wall units mustn't start too low. Leave room below them for small appliances (eg, mixers and toasters) to stand on the worktop. You should also be able to see objects at the back of the worktop without stooping, and to pick them up without banging your head on the wall unit as you lean forward.

The exact gap needed depends on the worktop height and its depth from front to back, as well as the depth of the wall unit – plus, of course, the stature of whoever will be using the kitchen. So improvised tests are probably your best guide. If you also want to put a strip light on the wall, allow for it in addition to the space for appliances.

To take care of all these requirements, a gap of 450mm (18in) will usually suffice.

Secondly, wall units mustn't stick out too far. You'll need a depth of 300mm (1ft) for storing large plates, though less will otherwise. But don't make them any bigger than that, or you run an unnecessarily high risk of a crack on the head from a cupboard door carelessly left open.

Cupboards or shelves?

A wall unit needn't necessarily have doors at all. Open shelves have many good points. You can see most of their contents at a glance, and retrieve things instantly. Moreover, they cost less in materials – and they obviate the risk just mentioned.

Shelves can be fixed directly to the wall, as detailed on pages 52-55 (Shelving: the basics), using either permanent brackets or an adjustable system. Alternatively, you can make them up into self-contained units which are then hung in place. In fact, that's how you build wall cupboards – simply adding doors as the final step.

The point about cupboards is their clean lines: once the doors are closed, the clutter is hidden inside, and all you can see are the finish and external details you've chosen. Besides, many people would say that doors play an important role in excluding steam, grease and dust.

Designing for convenience

Whether you decide on cupboards or open shelves, you've got to think about making their contents visible and accessible.

Clearly the main idea is to keep everything within reach. That usually means that nothing must be more than 1800mm (6ft) from the floor at most. This dictates the maximum height for the topmost shelf in a wall unit – or for its top panel, if you're planning to store things on top of the cupboard.

However, there's no reason why you shouldn't build units that extend right to the ceiling – provided you only use the space above 1800mm, which is out of reach, for

Ready Reference

FITTING WALL UNITS

Traditionally, kitchen wall units are about 600mm (2ft) high. But the modern trend is to run them right up to the ceiling, combining clean lines with the maximum space for long-term storage.

If the ceiling isn't flat, you can fit a strip of wood into the gap, scribed to match the ceiling contours.

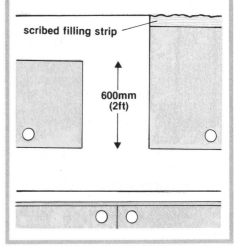

scribed filling strip

600mm (2ft)

PREPARING THE PANELS

1 *Cut all the panels to size, then groove them to take the back panel. Inset the grooves from the edge by the thickness of the hanging batten.*

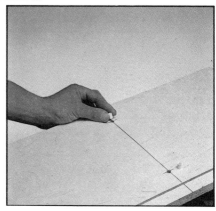

2 *Insert shelf-support bushes, if any, in holes drilled in the side panels, just below the height you've chosen for the intermediate shelf.*

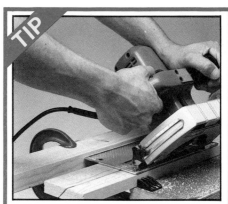

3 *Cut a piece of 100x25mm (4x1in) timber in half at an angle to make matching battens. Alternatively, plane two pieces of 50x25mm (2x1in).*

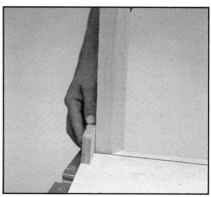

5 *Use the pins to mark out the corresponding holes in the two side panels. Inset the batten by the thickness of the top.*

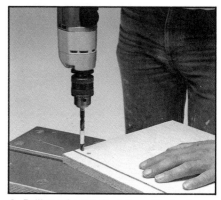

6 *Drill out the marked dowel holes in each of the side panels. Use tape round the bit to make sure you don't drill too deep.*

7 *Place the panels accurately in position together, and drill pilot holes for the screws through both pieces at each corner.*

storing things that you hardly ever need.

Conversely, articles you need all the time should be stored on the unit's bottom shelf. It's sensible to keep all heavy and bulky objects there, too (especially those which need two hands to retrieve them), so you don't have to stretch for them; unless, of course, they're stored in floor-mounted units.

Consider, too, the depth (from front to back) of the wall unit and its internal shelf or shelves. The deeper they are, the more you can store; it's also easier to reach the things stored at the front, particularly when leaning over a deep worktop below. But it'll be harder to see and reach items stored at the back — unless, that is, the shelf is below eye level.

Construction details

The techniques of making self-contained wall-hung shelving units are pretty much the same as those for floor-standing types, described in detail on pages 128-131.

These are usually straightforward box-construction methods involving the use of reinforced butt joints, dowels and so on. Intermediate shelves can be built into the structure permanently, or added with shelf supports of various kinds. Making these adjustable will give you freedom when it comes to deciding shelf heights.

The possible shelf-fixing methods are shown in *Ready Reference*, page 129. The only one of them that is fully adjustable is metal bookcase strip.

You'll need to pay special attention to making the cabinet rigid, since you don't want it to sag or fall apart. If the material is thin enough and the cabinet wide enough to warrant it, an upright halfway along the front can be a help. Fit it between the top and bottom panels, and secure it to the front edges of any intermediate shelves. Adhesive and nails, screws, dowels and plastic jointing blocks are all appropriate fixings.

Hanging the cabinet

There's also the question of fastening the unit in position on the wall. Obviously, you must do this properly if you're to avoid serious mishaps. One possibility is just to use screws (No 10 or bigger) driven into wall plugs. A second is to use proprietary fittings which are readily obtainable. Some are adjustable, and several come in two parts, one of which is screwed to the cabinet and the other separately to the wall before they're fitted together. This means they're a lot simpler to install than screws alone, and they make it easier to get the cabinet level.

But perhaps the neatest method of all is to use two battens with matching bevels. These battens can be cut from a single piece of timber with a circular saw whose blade is set at an angle; or you can use two separate pieces, each with one edge planed to the same angle. You screw one batten to the wall and fix one at the back of the cabinet,

4 *Sand the sharp edge off each batten, drill holes at both ends for dowels, and fit dowel marking pins into one pair of holes.*

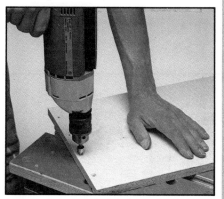

8 *Drill clearance holes through the outer panel in each case, then countersink them so that the screws will lie beneath the surface.*

ehind the back panel. Then, when you lace the cabinet in position, the bevelled dges will fit together and hold the cabinet ecurely in place.

Whichever method you use, don't hang he unit just by its back panel. Because this s usually of hardboard or thin plywood, and s probably only lightly fixed to the cabinet, ou'd run the risk of tearing or splitting it, or aving it come away altogether.

Instead, if you're screwing directly into the vall or using metal fittings, make sure the crews pass through a rail or rails securely xed to the cabinet structure. Such rails can e horizontal (positioned at the top of the nit, and perhaps the bottom as well) or ertical (screwed to the sides). They can ven run all the way round.

The important thing is not to expect the nain corner joints to take the whole weight of ne unit and its contents. So even a rail fixed o the top panel (as when you're using

ASSEMBLING THE UNIT

This kitchen wall unit is a simple box. The hanging batten at the rear – glued, dowelled and pinned – also helps to keep it rigid.

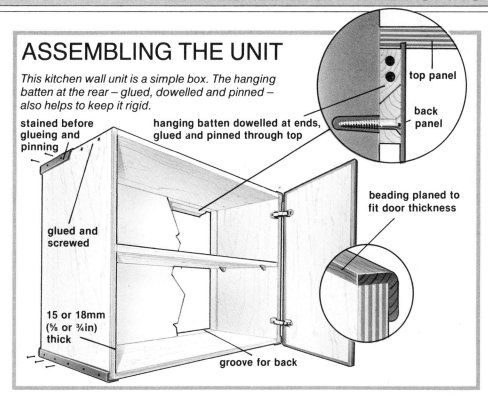

- top panel
- back panel
- stained before glueing and pinning
- hanging batten dowelled at ends, glued and pinned through top
- beading planed to fit door thickness
- glued and screwed
- 15 or 18mm (⅝ or ¾in) thick
- groove for back

HANGING A CABINET

Possible methods are: battens in various arrangements (1), mirror plates (2), keyhole plates (3), flush mounts (4), taper connectors (5) and cabinet hangers (6 to 8).

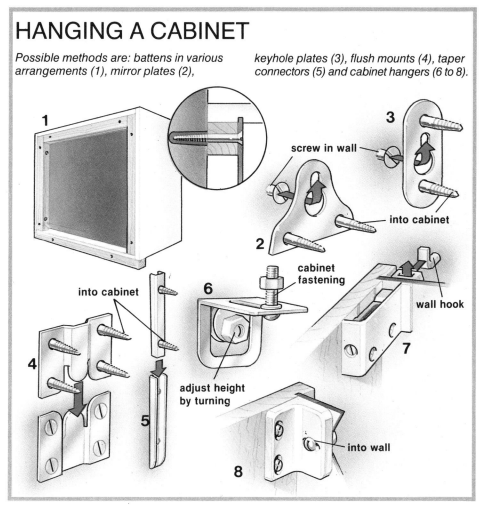

- screw in wall
- into cabinet
- cabinet fastening
- wall hook
- into cabinet
- adjust height by turning
- into wall

MAKING UP THE UNIT

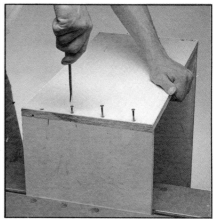

1 Assemble the top, the bottom and one side, and glue and screw the joints together. In chipboard, use plastic plugs or chipboard screws.

2 Cut the back panel to size and carefully slide it home into the groove which runs round the insides of the three panels.

3 Dowel and glue one end of the hanging batten into the cabinet side. Spread adhesive along the batten's upper edge, too.

5 Nail through the rear edge of the top panel and also into the hanging batten. This will give the cabinet some extra rigidity.

6 Cover each corner joint with a length of right-angled beading, stained for decoration before it is glued and pinned into position.

7 Cover the door edges with the same beading, mitred to fit. You may need to plane one edge down to get it flush with the inner face.

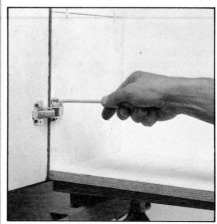

9 Place the doors in position and fix the hinges to the inside of the cabinet. Adjust them until both doors hang evenly and meet squarely.

10 Insert the shelf supports into the bushes (if any) in the cabinet sides, then cut the shelf to size and fit it into position.

11 Plug and screw to the wall the hanging batten that matches the one at the rear of the cabinet. Make sure that it's absolutely level.

4 *Glue dowels into the batten's other end, then fit the other side panel into position, glueing and screwing the joint like the others.*

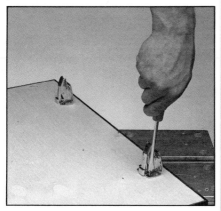

8 *Fix concealed hinges to the doors, after ensuring they suit the thickness. Inset them by the side panel thickness including any beading.*

12 *Lift the unit up against the wall and lower it so the two battens engage. You'll probably need someone to help support the unit's weight.*

matching bevelled battens), should be firmly jointed to the sides as well (eg, with dowels). This combination will also help to stiffen the cabinet.

What material?

Your choice of materials is bound to be from amongst the man-made boards every time. Chipboard will do just as well as blockboard or plywood, provided you protect its edges from moisture with timber lipping or at least a thorough paint system.

Timber-veneered boards are best varnished, after initial staining if you want a different colour or tint. But ordinary birch-faced plywood, widely available, is naturally a very pale colour well suited to kitchens. You can even bleach it to a creamy white.

Plastic-faced boards, of course, need no finishing and are easily washable. When buying them, there's a point worth noting. Although those usually stocked in DIY and hardware stores are handy because they come ready-edged in convenient widths, they are not particularly durable, scratch-resistant or smooth. You can buy much better quality plastic-faced boards – covered with superior, thicker laminate, like worktops – from good builder's merchants, who sell them as wallboards. Their only drawback is that they come in large sheets, and aren't edged.

For the back panel, a very suitable material is hardboard with a white melamine facing on the smooth side.

Fitting doors

Doors can, of course, be fitted in a lay-on or inset arrangement (see pages 110-113 for details). As for hinges, the natural choice is a modern concealed type, preferably with a sprung closing action so you don't need a separate catch. Most models fit into shallow holes drilled in the cabinet sides, and for these you'll require a special power drill bit called an end mill. However, there's at least one screw-on pattern.

Other perfectly workable alternatives are ordinary butt hinges, cranked hinges and cranked pivot hinges. Whichever hinge type you choose, remember two points. Firstly, plain steel hinges will soon discolour with rust in the moisture and steam of even a well-ventilated kitchen. Secondly, make sure before you buy that you know exactly how the hinges work, and that they're suitable for the design you have in mind – and for the thickness of the wood you're using. Try them out on scraps of timber or board if possible.

Lastly, a good way to make doors earn their keep is to fix wire racks on the inside. Available in various shapes and sizes, these neatly avoid the perennial problem of small containers – such as spice jars – which get lost at the back of the cupboard. To accommodate racks, you'll need to inset any shelves.

FITTING A KITCHEN : 2

Provided you've accurately positioned and levelled your base units, it should be no problem to install the worktops, wall units, doors, drawers, shelves and accessories which will complete your fitted kitchen. Here's how to ensure a trouble-free job.

Kitchen fitting is a classic example of a job you can tackle the right way or the wrong way.

The right way is very definitely to start as shown and described on pages 141-144. That is, by levelling and fixing the assembled base-unit carcases at a height determined by the highest floor point around the walls, ensuring the fronts are flush as well.

At the same time, you'll probably find yourself adding an extra panel to blank off the interior of each straight corner unit – that is, the half which has no door because it disappears under the adjacent worktop. Another little detail requiring attention may be the fixing of small sections of board to blank off the plinth recess where two straight units join at a corner. Look at the step-by-step photographs on page 143 for a clear view of these operations.

Any tall units, such as oven housings and larders, need to be assembled and fixed in position at this stage too (though they can't, of course, be made level with the other base units): see page 144. In addition, you can fit their 'top boxes' now.

Adding worktops

Your other preliminary task is to provide adequate support and fixings for the worktops.

As a rule the support simply comes from the base units themselves, plastic joint blocks being screwed to their side panels to hold the top in place. However, overhanging ends will need different arrangements – usually just a batten or a strip of board fixed to the wall, or to the side of a tall unit if the worktop butts against that.

In the particular kitchen shown here, the worktop runs through a floor-to-ceiling opening, making a serving counter with a hatch above. The space below it, which would otherwise offer from outside an unsightly view of the fridge, is closed by a transverse panel fixed to the walls.

Worktops must be cut to length, marked, and then shaped to fit round obstacles and hug the contours of the walls – though tiles or an upstand (of wood or plastic) will conceal smallish gaps. A jigsaw and Surform are useful tools here. With the former, remember

that positioning the panel upside-down will prevent chipping the laminate as you cut.

Once each section of top fits to your satisfaction, you'll be able to mark cut-outs for the hob and sink. Don't make them over-large.

When all is ready, lower and fix each section of worktop in place. Butt joins are usually covered with strips of purpose-made aluminium profile – cut to length by you and often screwed to the end of the appropriate piece before it's positioned.

Installing wall units

Now you're ready to put up the wall units. Start by deciding on a suitable gap between their undersides and the worktop – at least 450mm (18in), so you can easily see to the back of the worktop and store appliances there.

Add to that gap the height of the wall units, but subtract the distance by which their fixings are set down from their tops. Subtract, too, any clearance needed above them to drop them into place.

Mark the resulting fixing height along the wall or walls, using a spirit level, and screw the fixings on there. If the walls are out of square, packing behind the fixings may be needed first, so the cabinet fronts will be at right-angles in each corner.

Wall-unit fixings vary a lot, from simple timber battens to clever two-part brackets. The latter let you adjust the units' heights after you've hung them.

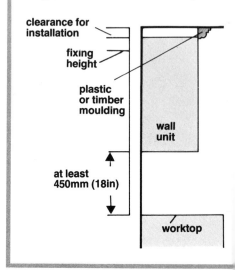

Ready Reference

DECIDING HEIGHTS

When choosing and installing wall units, bear in mind that you'll need certain minimum clearances:
● between worktop and units
● between units and ceiling.
If the latter gap is too small to allow storage, hide it with a cornice moulding.

clearance for installation

fixing height

plastic or timber moulding

wall unit

at least 450mm (18in)

worktop

INSTALLING WORKTOPS

Most worktops nowadays have a rounded ('postformed') front edge, though some have timber lipping.

All are expensive, so take special care when marking and cutting them. It's easy to ruin one with even a small mistake. In particular, don't forget to reverse everything as appropriate when working with the board face-down.

See Ready Reference for more details of how to go about shaping tops to fit, and to accommodate inset fitments.

Very often, worktops rest entirely on base units, simply bridging the gaps which house appliances. But sometimes – as in this kitchen – there are overhanging ends which also need support. Battens are used here, but many ranges offer special legs for the purpose; sometimes, too, you can use panels.

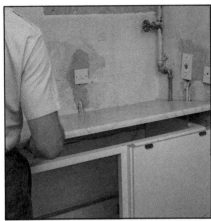

1 Where the end of a worktop meets a vertical surface, such as the side of an oven housing, a screwed-on batten is often the best way to support it.

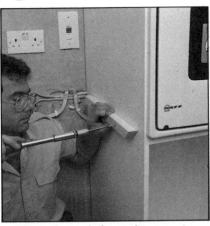

2 Scribe and cut the first section of worktop (in this case the left-hand one) to fit round obstacles such as pipes, and lower it into position.

3 If the hob goes over a unit, mark the unit's internal size on the underside of the worktop before setting out on it the complete cutout you'll need.

4 Cut out the hob opening and replace the section of worktop. Tiles or an 'upstand' will conceal any small gaps caused by uneven walls.

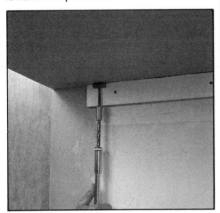

5 Where the worktop passes through the opening to form a hatch, a piece of board (or a timber batten) is screwed to the wall for support.

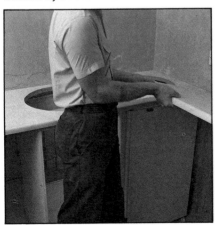

6 Below the worktop in the hatch, a panel fixed with plastic joint blocks closes the opening and conceals the fridge which will go inside.

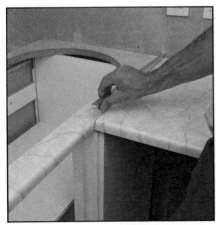

7 Cut out the sink hole with a jigsaw, just like the opening for the hob. Subsequent worktop sections are fitted like the first one.

8 Worktop joins are often finished with a metal strip. Screw it on before the worktop goes in, or push it in later for easy removal when cleaning.

INSTALLING WALL UNITS

1 *Measuring up from the worktop, rule a level line across the wall at the exact height where you'll be screwing on the wall-unit fixings.*

2 *Drill and plug the wall, and screw the fixings on. To avoid problems, make sure they're firm and correctly aligned. The screws should be at least No 10s.*

3 *Start with a corner unit, lifting it up onto its fixings. You may have to cut carcase panels round obstacles first, just as with base units.*

4 *As you fit subsequent units, check them for level at top or bottom. Proprietary fixings generally allow adjustment with a screwdriver.*

5 *A corner wall unit, like a corner base unit, usually needs a front panel to close off half its interior. You may need to take it down first.*

6 *Start the next row in a corner too. Out-of-square walls may mean considerable packing if the cabinets are to meet each other at right-angles.*

With all these systems, there's no need to hold the cabinet in position while fixing into the wall. However, it's still a very good idea to cut battens which will support each cabinet on the worktops as you offer it up, eg when marking for cutouts round obstacles.

Wall units are never tight up against the ceiling. This is not only because they must usually be lowered slightly onto their fixings, but also because they tend to sag very slightly afterwards – and, more importantly, because a sagging ceiling might otherwise prevent their doors from opening properly.

The resulting gap can easily be filled with a suitable timber or plastic moulding to avoid a dirt trap on the cupboard tops.

The units are assembled in a very similar way to base units. Here too, installation always starts in a corner, where a blanking-off panel may again be needed.

Check that they're level and that the fronts are flush. Then cramp each pair carefully together in order to fix them to each other. You can do this either with special plastic 'cabinet connector screws' or else with ordinary metal screws – best driven in where they'll be hidden, for example by the hinges. You can fasten the base units together in the same way at the same time.

Now is also the time to add any narrow panels or short shelves to fill odd gaps beside units. If they're to butt against walls, scribe them to fit over any irregularities.

Moreover, some types of plinth, screwed on from the front, are added at this stage – as are specialised accessories like built-in waste bins, pull-out fittings, carousels, wire racks and so on.

Finishing off

Provided all the units are square (check by measuring the diagonals of each to see if they're equal), the doors can now go on.

All mass-produced kitchen units these days have concealed hinges – complex-looking devices which in fact make life a lot easier on this particular job. They press-fit into ready-drilled circular recesses in the unit doors, where two screws secure them.

Then you just offer up each door to the cabinet and screw the other end of each hinge to it, using the pilot holes already there. Backward, forward, upward and downward adjustments are made by means of integral screws, so you should have few difficulties in ensuring rows of perfectly aligned doors.

Drawers, if any, come in kit form and are simply slid into the units. Shelves will most likely rest on plastic supports which you push into pre-drilled holes.

And that's about it. Unless you've installed home-made units with separate timber or wood-veneered doors, the cabinets won't even need any finishing treatment . . . so your fitted kitchen is complete.

COMPLETING THE JOB

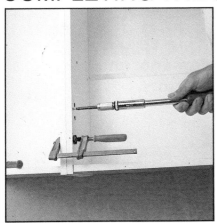

1 *Cramp each pair of units together, and secure them – either with screws (to be hidden by hinges) or with special connectors. Then fit the shelves.*

2 *Now is a good time to fit a cooker hood. Here again, what matters is accurate drilling, and plugging the wall securely to avoid disasters.*

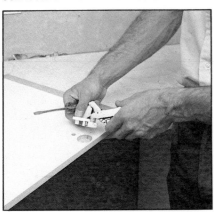

3 *To fit the doors, first decide which side you want them to open. Then press the hinges into their recesses and drive in the retaining screws.*

4 *As most doors are pre-drilled for hinges down both sides, you'll have to hide unused recesses by pushing in special plastic stoppers.*

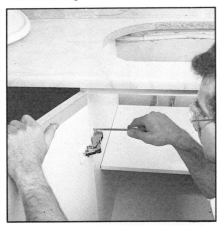

5 *Position each door in its unit and tighten the hinges there with the fittings provided. When all are on, make any adjustments needed.*

6 *The result should be perfectly aligned doors (and cabinets) with flush, level worktops. Now you're ready to complete the wall finishes.*

Ready Reference

PACKING OUT WALL UNITS

If your kitchen is out of square, both wall and base units will probably need packing out. The packing's thickness depends on the amount of the discrepancy, and on whether the angle between the walls is greater than or less than 90°.

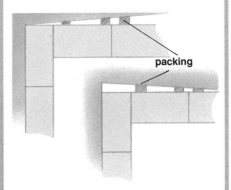

packing

PLINTH POSSIBILITIES

Some plinths are fixed from behind, others from in front after the units are installed. The latter sometimes have adjustable fixings so you can vary the height.

Either way, however, a floor whose level varies a lot – so that units need a lot of packing – means that plinths won't always fill the gap between floor and base panel.

A small gap can go at the bottom, where floor tiles will conceal it (A). A bigger one can go at the top (B), where it won't be seen from eye level. If the discrepancy is very large, you may need a wider plinth (C) – perhaps cut from solid timber.

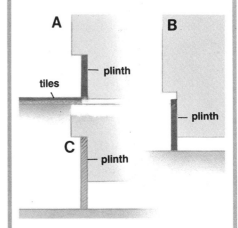

TIP: USE CORRECTION FLUID

If you do chip melamine-faced panels while cutting them, typewriter correction fluid makes an excellent job of touching up the finish.

CHAPTER 6

ADVANCED PROJECTS

For the really skilled woodworker, complicated framing-up jobs
and even structural work such as fitting a complete new door and
door frame or laying a new timber floor hold no terrors.

BUILT-IN WARDROBES

Fitted cupboards are not only cheaper than ready-made furniture; they're neater, too. And you can choose from any number of different details to suit your own needs and tastes.

The traditional wardrobe is, of course, a completely freestanding unit with a bottom, a top and four sides. Many people possess one as a hand-me-down, and there are plenty of handsome, well-crafted examples.

However, if you're thinking about providing storage facilities from scratch, movable furniture has at least four important disadvantages when you compare it with built-in pieces.

The first is its cost. Except perhaps for the very cheapest (and shoddiest) off-the-shelf wardrobes, you'll find it cheaper to buy the materials and fit your own units – simply because the walls, floor and ceiling of the room replace (instead of duplicating) some of the panels of the cupboard. This saves space, too; and it means you don't have to devote much thought to the often tricky question of making the cabinet rigid.

The second point is that factory-made furniture won't necessarily fit neatly into the room. A freestanding wardrobe that's too big for an alcove can be a real nuisance, obstructing free movement and even light. This problem, of course, doesn't arise at all when you design your own scheme to fit the room.

And when it comes to style, you needn't simply accept a manufacturer's idea of what constitutes elegance. There's a vast range of alternatives.

Lastly, all ready-made wardrobes create a natural dust-trap above and below. A fitted unit scores here, too, provided you run it right up to the ceiling.

Thoughtful design

So think positively. Aim to build a wardrobe – or a whole set of cupboards – which meets all your requirements.

The first consideration, naturally, is what you're going to store, and how much space it will take up. Look at pages 52-55, 136-140 and 145-149 for details where crockery, cutlery and other objects are concerned. When it comes to clothing, your best guide is a close look – tape measure in hand – at all the items likely to be involved. Coats, trousers, and so on must hang clear of the floor; and you need to be sure you provide enough depth from front to back if you're

planning to hang your garments sideways.

At the same time, consider the room itself, including existing furnishings (beds, for example), in relation to where you're going to site the cupboard. One obvious place, of course, is in an alcove (see pages 105-109 for more details), where it will be completely unobtrusive, and construction will be easiest of all. But it can just as well run right across one end of the room. Alternatively, it can start or stop (or both) part of the way along a wall, with the addition of side panels at one or both ends.

Visual effect, as well as convenience, plays a big part here. Even before you think about the details of materials, trim and finish, you know that full-width and full-height fitments will have cleaner (or, if you prefer the word, starker) lines than smaller ones.

They may provide other bonuses, too. Suppose, for example, that you have an unused and unsightly fireplace. There's no reason why you shouldn't build cupboards which run in a continuous line not only across the alcoves on either side, but also in front of the chimney breast, thereby concealing the whole thing. You could fit a fixed panel over the fireplace, but install shallow shelves behind doors in the cupboard area above the mantelpiece. Other items – pipework, perhaps, or even a washbasin or shower cubicle – can be hidden in the same way.

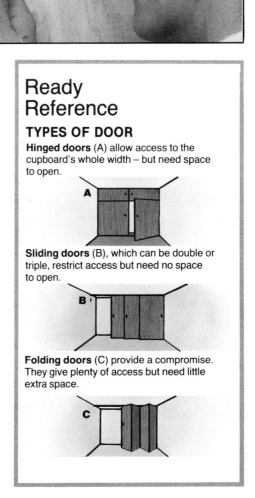

DESIGNING CUPBOARDS

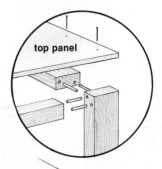

top panel

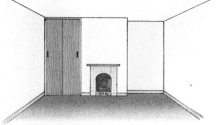

Above: One very natural location is in an alcove. A cupboard here makes use of what can be an awkward corner, while taking up no actual living space.

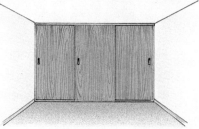

Above: You can also run cupboards right across the room. If appropriate, you can use both alcoves and hide the chimney breast too.

You can choose from many ways to construct fitted cupboards.

Above: Not only can you build the whole frame out from the wall behind, you can also add a panel overhead (top). This is often handy for long-term storage of objects too bulky to fit inside, such as suitcases.

Frame members which aren't fixed to the floor, wall or ceiling will require at least simple jointing.

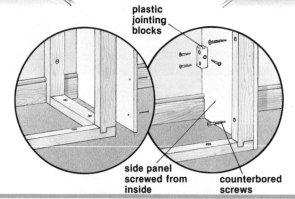

plastic jointing blocks

side panel screwed from inside

counterbored screws

Above: Cupboards needn't run all the way from wall to wall. Stop them short if necessary. Side panels can be fixed from outside (far left) – being either cut from thick board, as shown, or cut from thin plywood and pinned on. More neatly, they can be attached from inside (left), for example with counterbored screws.

PREPARING FOR WARDROBE DOORS

1 Your first job is to locate the joists and decide where to make your fixings. Then check whether the ceiling is level along that line.

TIP

2 If the ceiling isn't flat, you'll need a batten to take up the unevenness. Hold it in position and scribe the ceiling's contours onto it.

3 Plane the upper face of the batten down to the scribed line, so that it will fit snugly into place across the ceiling without any gaps.

Basic construction

One way to approach fitted-cupboard design is to think of a frame, screwed to the walls, floor and ceiling, on which doors are hung.

If you're using timber for this frame, it needs to be wide enough for wall fixing, and also thick enough to take hinges if any. Timber measuring 50x50mm (2x2in) or 75x38mm (3x1½in) is likely to be suitable; for various possible fixing details, see pages 105-109 for additional information. Remember that you'll almost certainly have to scribe the uprights to match the exact shape of the wall for a true fit.

If the cupboard runs from wall to wall and from floor to ceiling, you can get away without cutting corner joints, because all the pieces are fixed in position. If it stops short in either direction, at least one upright or crosspiece will need jointing in carefully. Mortise and tenon, bridle, halving and dowel joints are all possibilities. Top panels can be nailed to the frame from above; they can be of any board thick and strong enough to bear what's likely to be stored on them. Side panels – of blockboard, chipboard (plain, veneered or plastic-faced) or plywood – are best screwed from inside for strength and neatness, though you could economise by using 6mm (¼in) plywood, pinned from outside.

Fitting doors

Doors can be hinged, sliding or folding. Hinged doors can of course be lay-on or inset – see pages 110-113 for details. Lay-on doors are less trouble to fit, because they're unaffected by frames that are out of square; in fact, the doors will cover up any misalignment of the frame. Moreover, the frame makes separate doorstops unnecessary. See

You have a wide choice of possible hinge types, but make sure you take both the cupboard and hinge design fully into account before deciding which hinges to use.

Sliding and folding doors are very popular alternatives. You buy the track and sliding gear as a kit; it will come complete with fixing instructions. On a floor-to-ceiling cupboard, you need a secure ceiling fixing in order to mount the track safely. Cavity fixings into plasterboard (often secure enough in other situations) won't do. If you can't fix through into ceiling joists – and can't take up the floorboards upstairs in order to fit noggins between the joists and fix into those – go for hinged doors instead.

Sliding or folding doors which are fitted on a full-height cupboard can enable you to do without a frame altogether. You simply fasten their track directly onto the ceiling, and allow the doors to slide right from wall to wall. This is probably the easiest system of all to install. If a wall is uneven, fix a strip of timber down it to cover the gaps down the edge of the closed door. If, on the other hand, you're incorporating a side panel, fix that to wall, floor and ceiling via battens or even plastic jointing blocks. (You could hinge a door to it instead.)

Even sliding doors' obvious drawback – that they allow access to only part of the cupboard at any one time – can sometimes be overcome. If you run the unit across a chimney breast as suggested above, the doors from each alcove can slide into the middle and thus out of the way.

Look at pages 123-127 for further details on choosing and fitting various types of sliding doors. The principles are just the same whether you're installing them in a doorway or in a cupboard.

see pages 110-113 for details.

4 Re-position the batten, and use the spirit level again to check whether its lower face is now true. If not, plane it down a bit further.

5 When you've got the alignment right, drill and countersink the batten, drill the ceiling, and finally, screw the batten into position.

Ready Reference

STORAGE OPTIONS

You'll need hanging space for both long and short garments. This can either run lengthwise (A), or transversely (B) if necessary – though the latter is less convenient. The arrangement at A also includes drawer space.

Allow for shoes at the bottom. Any space at the top, for long-term storage, can be either inside the cupboard (A) – or outside (B) for really bulky items.

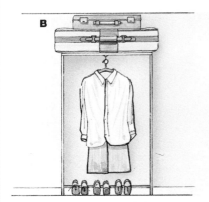

CHOOSING DRAWERS

Drawers for cupboards don't need fronts. You can buy ready-made plastic types, which slide in plastic runners as shown (A). Or you can make up your own, as detailed on pages 132-135 but with a low front (B). Timber runners could go underneath, as shown.

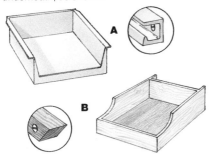

COMPLETING THE CUPBOARD FRONT

1 For sliding doors, screw the track onto the batten. Remember to allow for the depth of any beading to be fitted down the sides – see 9.

2 Cut each side upright to length (to fit under the ceiling batten) and mark on it the height of the skirting-board. Square the mark across the piece.

3 A good way to gauge the skirting-board's thickness is with a combination square; loosen the screw and adjust the square accordingly.

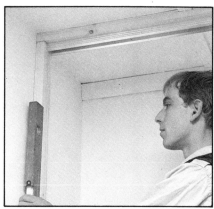

5 Fit the upright against the wall and check it for plumb in both directions. Then, if necessary, scribe and cut it, or else pack out any gaps.

6 Screw both uprights into position. With hinged doors, and often with sliding doors, you'll want to fix a similar batten to the floor as well.

7 Cut the doors to size, allowing for clearance and any overlap. For sliding doors, add wheels or sliders as instructed by the manufacturers.

9 Make adjustments so the doors hang properly. For sliding doors, fit floor guides, and pin beading down each side to hide gaps and exclude dust.

10 Often a pelmet strip (say 12mm/½in thick), nailed in position, is useful to hide the track and any ceiling batten when sliding doors have been hung.

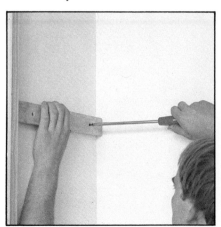

11 If you want an interior shelf, just screw battens to all three walls, ensuring they're level, and place a board on top of them.

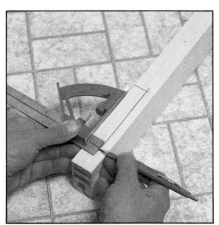

4 *Then you can hold a pencil against the square, run both down the side of the upright, and cut away the waste area you've marked out.*

8 *Hang the doors. Wheels or sliders just hook onto the track; hinges usually require screws. Either way, you'll probably need a helper.*

12 *Lastly, add door handles, plus whatever finishing treatment you think is appropriate, in order to make your fitted wardrobe complete.*

Making doors

The doors' appearance, of course, makes or mars the whole thing. But there's no limit to your choices here. For a start, they can be either full-height, or split at a certain level (available sizes may well decide this particular question for you).

As for materials and finishes, you can use plywood or blockboard, suitably edged, varnished or painted (chipboard is less than ideal because of its weight). You can decorate it with slim timber mouldings. You can paper it, or paste some fabric onto it, to match the rest of your decorations. You can use decorative wallboards, ready-made louvred doors, or even mirrored glass. And, in addition to sliding and folding tracks and gear, some firms supply aluminium edging which forms part of the hanging system, and turns sheets of board into handsome doors.

You can even buy complete 'cupboard fronts' – sets of hinged doors already hung in over-large frames, which can be cut down to the height you want. Scribed panels will hide any gaps at floor and ceiling level.

Internal details

Inside the unit, the first necessity is a rail for hanging clothes. Chrome- and brass-plated tubing is readily available; you can fix it either with the special brackets made for the purpose, or in notches cut in the upper edges of wall battens at either end.

At least one shelf, often at high level, is very useful. Use whichever fixing is most appropriate – see pages 52-55, and in particular *Ready Reference*, page 129. Choose the material and thickness according to what it will have to carry.

The occasional drawer, too, is invaluable for storing underclothes, socks and so on. Consult pages 95-98 and also pages 132-140 for constructional details and fitting methods. Since the drawer will be behind doors anyway, dustproofing isn't vital, and the front is often cut lower than the sides for easy access. You could also consider sliding wire or plastic trays – more commonly found in kitchen units, but also available in versions suitable for wardrobes.

Whatever details you choose, a properly designed fitted unit may well enable you to do away with other storage furniture altogether in a particular room. And of course, there's nothing to prevent you from combining it with open shelving to make a complete 'wall system'. This can provide space for books, ornaments, plants and whatever else you like – as long as the structure is strong enough to support it.

However you design the system, the crucial point is convenience. Try to ensure that each run of shelving gives the space you require at a height that's appropriate for the items concerned.

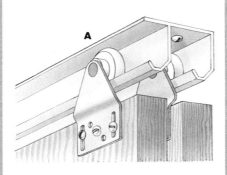
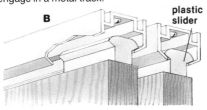
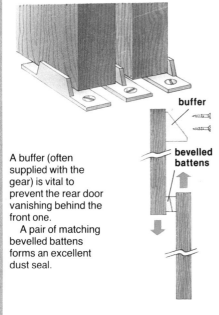

REPAIRING HANDRAILS & BALUSTERS

Replacing old spindles, or even installing a completely new balustrade, requires great care and attention, but it can add a really impressive feature to your home.

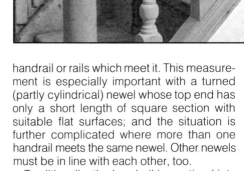

The staircase is probably the most complicated piece of joinery in the average home, so don't tamper with it unnecessarily.

However, maintenance work is sometimes essential for safety. This could involve simple jobs such as securing and repairing the 'guts' of the staircase: the treads you walk on, the risers (if any) between them, and the strings which support them.

But that's only half the story. The balustrade which stops you falling off the side is equally important. If broken or shaky, it should be attended to quickly. What's more, renovating it can make a big difference in terms of looks as well. Ranges of attractive components for it are available in both softwood and hardwood from many suppliers.

Newels and handrails

The basic items are the newel posts. These are fixed very firmly to the joists, often with coach screws or bolts. Any new fixings should be to the same standard: rock-solid.

You can't be too thorough here, because the newels not only carry the handrail between them – and thus the balustrade as a whole, which comes under great stress – but also at least partly support the outer string. This is usually either housed into them, or fitted via a large double haunched tenon, pegged with dowels which run through it sideways.

In addition, at least one tread and riser are usually housed into the newel where it meets the ends of the steps. You'll need to re-cut these grooves in any new post.

A newel post is either a single piece, or made up in sections – a square base, plus a more ornamental upper part which has a projecting peg to fit a hole in the base.

Even before fixing a newel, you must get all your measurements sorted out. Regulations dictate the heights of handrails – see *Ready Reference*. A rail must also be at exactly the same slope as the stairs: on a closed-string staircase, that means parallel to the string. Quite apart from considerations of safety and looks, a handrail that's out of true will give you problems when you come to fit the balusters.

So your first job is to cut the newel post, or its base, to exactly the right height for the handrail or rails which meet it. This measurement is especially important with a turned (partly cylindrical) newel whose top end has only a short length of square section with suitable flat surfaces; and the situation is further complicated where more than one handrail meets the same newel. Other newels must be in line with each other, too.

Traditionally, the handrail is mortised into the newel – either bodily, or via a tenon pegged with a dowel. Dowels on their own form a strong enough alternative. Nailing is another possibility: crude, but often adequate, provided you punch the heads and fill the resulting holes.

Lastly, you can screw through the rail at an angle. At the lower end, screw from underneath. If using screws at the upper end, you'll need to counterbore them and plug the holes with wooden pellets, finished flush.

At the bottom of a staircase, the handrail may start with an 'opening rise' instead. This is a graceful curve, made up separately, which terminates in a 'newel cap' fitting over a peg in the top of the newel post. It requires extra length in the newel – another thing to allow for when cutting.

An opening rise is joined to the main handrail with a 'handrail screw'. This is easy to fit (see illustrations) as long as you work carefully and use the right spanners and drill bits. It makes a secure joint between any two lengths of handrail; dowels are the only effective alternative.

Where a handrail meets a landing wall, it may be mortared into the brickwork, or sometimes fixed to a 'half newel' – like a newel cut in half lengthwise – lying flat against the wall.

Fitting balusters

In theory, fitting the balusters (or spindles, as the turned variety are called) should be a simple, repetitive job. But you must still work carefully if they're all to be tight and vertical.

First of all, check that the handrail doesn't sag in the middle. If it does, it will throw your measurements out, so fit a temporary support. Then, as you cut the balusters, measure for each one individually, in case there are variations. Position a sliding bevel in the angle between the newel and the handrail or string capping (see below) to gauge the exact slope for angled cuts.

When marking the balusters, double-check that angled cuts at both ends slope the same way. And, unless the balusters are absolutely plain, make sure you leave the same amount of the plain section at the bottom of every baluster which is cut to the same length; likewise at the top. If you're using an opening rise,

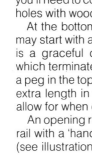

PREPARING THE NEWELS AND STRING

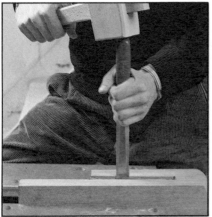

1 Each newel post must be the right height for the handrail, and securely fixed to a joist. Here the upper newel base has been cut away for a snug fit.

2 Position the newel base accurately, checking it for plumb in both directions, and carefully mark on it the housing or mortise for each string.

3 Cut out the stopped housing as precisely as you can. First work along the sides of the groove with a tenon saw or broad-bladed chisel.

4 Then work along the housing, if possible with a chisel the same width as the groove. Use it with the bevel downwards if necessary.

5 Lastly, make a cut that slopes inwards at the end to house the projecting end of the string, if any. This adds some extra strength.

6 Fit the housing over the string, and screw or bolt the newel base very firmly to the nearest joist or joists. Pack it out if necessary.

7 House the lower newel over the string and secure it to a floor joist like the upper one. Make sure the posts are exactly in line with each other.

8 With a two-part newel, you simply tap the upper part into the lower – being very careful that you don't force it and thus split the timber.

9 Before fixing a new capping to take the balusters, you may have to pack out the string with planed timber of a suitable thickness.

FITTING A HANDRAIL SCREW

1 *This is the usual way of joining lengths of handrail. Drill an access hole in one piece, and mark the endgrain centre with a template.*

2 *At your marked centre, drill a clearance hole for the bolt-threaded end of the fitting, through to the access hole. Make sure it's perpendicular to the wood.*

3 *Using a slightly smaller bit, drill a pilot hole in the other piece for the screw-threaded end of the fitting. Make it the same length as the screw.*

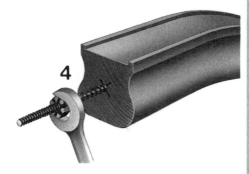

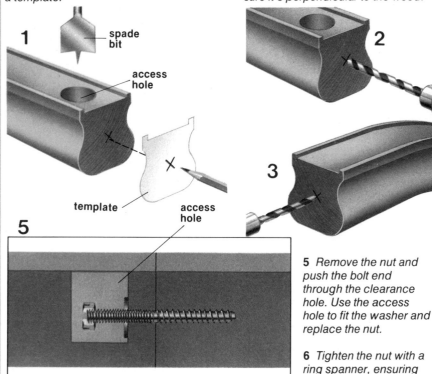

4 *Thread the special nut temporarily onto the bolt end so that you can use a spanner to drive the screw firmly into the second piece of wood.*

5 *Remove the nut and push the bolt end through the clearance hole. Use the access hole to fit the washer and replace the nut.*

6 *Tighten the nut with a ring spanner, ensuring the pieces are aligned.*

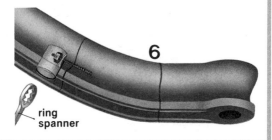

don't forget that any balusters below it must be longer than the rest.

There's also a rule that the spacing of balusters must be close enough to prevent a sphere 100mm (4in) in diameter from passing between them. Before you buy a set of new balusters, you'll have to measure the total distance between newels and divide it by that spacing (minus the baluster thickness) to find how many balusters you need. On a closed-string staircase, mark all their positions before fitting them.

There are several different ways of fixing balusters – see *Ready Reference*.

A common arrangement nowadays, and a very neat one, uses a factory-cut channel in the underside of the handrail. A corresponding 'capping', channelled in its upper surface, fits on top of the string – which may need to be packed out in thickness to receive it. The square or rectangular ends of the balusters fit into these channels, and are held in place by nailed 'spacer fillets' – cut off at an angle from timber supplied with the capping and rail, and ready-planed to fit the channels.

Cut strings present a different picture. The baluster at the front of each tread is a different length from the one at the back (though you'll still want to leave the same length of plain section at the top all the way up the stairs). The balusters fit into notches, sometimes dovetail-shaped, in the end of each tread, and are held there by lengths of pinned moulding.

Staircase shapes

There are quite a few variations in the way staircases rise from one level to the next.

The simplest shape is the straight flight. However, stairs can also turn a corner – and very often they double back on themselves completely, making either a 'dog-leg' or an 'open-well' staircase.

In a dog-leg staircase, the newel post at the turn supports both the upper and the lower flights, because it's mortised to receive the outer strings of both. The handrail and balusters of the lower flight terminate against the underside of the upper string.

In an open well (or 'open-newel') staircase, the flights are separate. There's a gap between them, and each one has its own newel at the level where the stairs turn. A short length of balustrade joins these two posts.

The turns in the steps may take the form of a half-landing – in effect, a platform made of joists (supported against the walls) covered with floorboards. The joist called the 'trimmer' along the edge of the landing has the newel or newels fixed to and often notched over it. The floorboard immediately on top of it has a rounded edge so it can act as the uppermost tread of the lower flight.

Instead of pausing at a half-landing, the stairs may continue to rise round the turn. On a dog-leg staircase, that means a half-turn of 'winders' – tapered steps. An open-newel staircase may have two quarter-turns of winders, one in each corner, separated by either a small landing or another short flight.

The balustrade in an open-well staircase may not always run between newels as described. The handrail may curl right round, with a continuous row of balusters beneath.

Apart from the opening rise, other handrail components are available for special situations. These include horizontal turns on landings, and places where the handrail has to change levels. In the latter case, a 'goose neck' made with a 'vertical turn' will meet the discrepancy.

BALUSTRADE FIXINGS

All sorts of details make up a balustrade. They vary a lot, but it's worth knowing the probabilities if you're considering renovation. The main drawing shows an **open-well** or open-newel staircase – so called because of the gap between flights.

Below: The lower newel is fixed to a joist, and supports the string and handrail. It's also housed for steps.

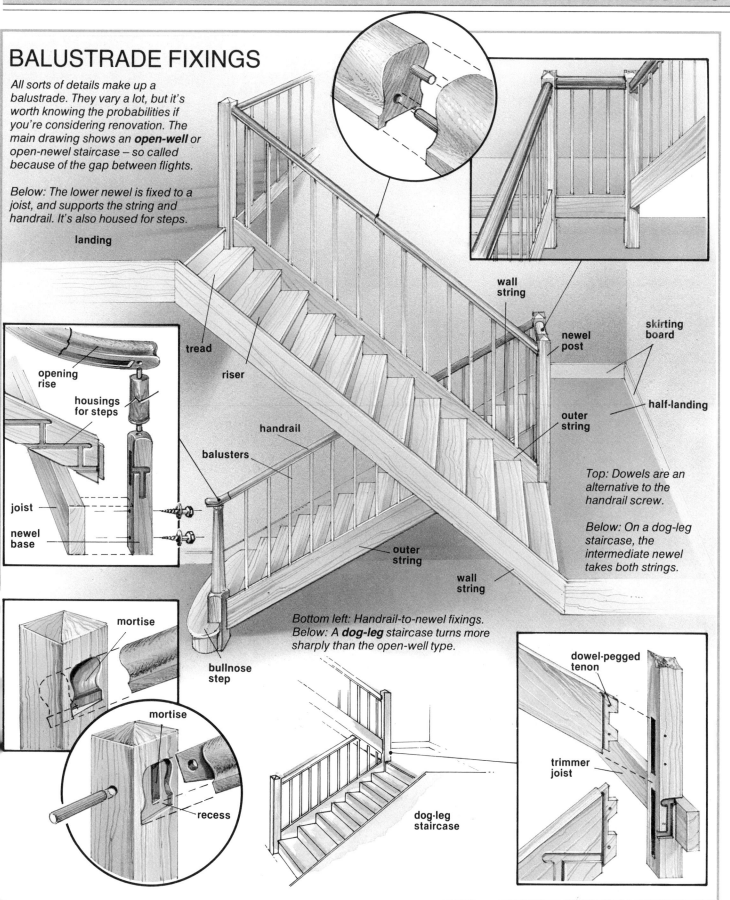

landing

tread

riser

opening rise

housings for steps

joist

newel base

handrail

balusters

wall string

newel post

skirting board

half-landing

outer string

outer string

wall string

Top: Dowels are an alternative to the handrail screw.

Below: On a dog-leg staircase, the intermediate newel takes both strings.

mortise

bullnose step

mortise

recess

Bottom left: Handrail-to-newel fixings. Below: A **dog-leg** staircase turns more sharply than the open-well type.

dog-leg staircase

dowel-pegged tenon

trimmer joist

FITTING THE HANDRAIL AND SPINDLES

1 If you're using an opening rise, fit it to the rail with a handrail screw (see illustrations) and then to the newel post as shown here.

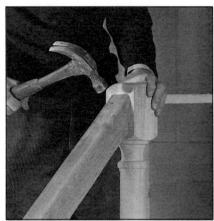

2 Nails form the easiest handrail fixing. Punch them in and fill the holes with wood stopping. Alternatively, use tenons or dowels or both.

3 Cut the capping and nail it to the string. It's vital that this should be exactly parallel to the handrail, so the spindles will all be the same length.

4 Provided the newel is plumb, a sliding bevel will give the exact slope of the handrail and string. Use it to mark the cuts on the spindles.

5 Cut the spindles at your marked angles. In theory they should all be the same length when vertical – but check before cutting each one.

6 Fit each spindle against the handrail and capping. If you're using spacer fillets, cut them to length at an angle and nail them in place.

Ready Reference

SAFETY RULES

A run of stairs more than 600mm (2ft) long must have a handrail on at least one side (though not necessarily beside the bottom two steps). This rail must normally be no

On a landing, the minimum height is 900mm (35in). The space between the balusters should be less than 100mm (4in).

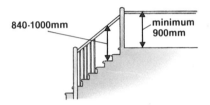

840-1000mm   minimum 900mm

FIXING BALUSTERS

There are several ways of fixing balusters in place – although, if you're only replacing old ones, you'll probably want to keep the existing arrangements.

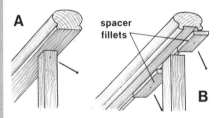

A   spacer fillets   B

Balusters may be just nailed to the handrail (A), or held by spacers (B).

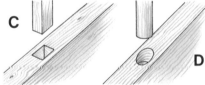

C   D

Fixing to a closed string may be via nails, mortises (C), or bored holes (D).

Spacer fillets are also used in a capping (E), fitted over the string. This may or may not have a channel cut in its underside.

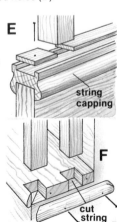

E

string capping

With a cut string (F), each tread will have its own notches for the balusters. Lengths of moulding hold them in position.

F

cut string

MAKING FRAMES IN TIMBER

Making strong, square frames has always been an essential skill in woodwork. Here are the joints to use, and a host of craftsman's tips on efficient design and assembly.

A frame, of course, is simply a structure made from narrow, thin pieces rather than wide, flat ones.

Over the centuries, craftsmen have used framing to solve all sorts of woodworking problems in their struggle to produce tough, attractive and profitable work quickly from the materials available to them. And all the answers they've come up with are now at your disposal.

For example, the earliest storage items – and even chairs and benches – were made in the simplest way: from wide slabs or planks of solid wood, pegged or nailed together. They were simple and strong. But, apart from being enormously heavy, they had another enemy. All timber, whether felled yesterday or a thousand years ago, shrinks and swells according to the amount of moisture in the air around it.

Any woodworker who forgets or ignores this is in for trouble. In the ordinary way, nothing can stop it happening. If a wide piece of wood is fastened at both sides so it can't move bodily (eg, when built into furniture) and then dries out a lot, it will simply split. Similarly, plank doors tend to jam shut in winter and – what is just as annoying – grow too loose in summer.

This meant, also, that only plain timber could be used, because highly 'figured' pieces – those with complex grain patterns – warp more. The trouble is, they're also the most attractive.

Greater wealth and sophistication brought a demand for higher standards than this, so the furniture makers of Tudor England had to think of new techniques. That's when frame construction came into its own.

Beating shrinkage and swelling

The amount of moisture movement you can expect in wood is greatest across the grain – lengthwise, it's usually negligible. But it's always proportional to the size of the piece. If a 200mm (8in) wide piece of pine shrinks by 3mm (⅛in), a 100mm (4in) wide piece will only shrink by half that – ie, 1.5mm (¹⁄₁₆in) – under the same conditions. Therefore the average frame won't move much, even on large items.

What's more, if you run a groove all round a frame's inner edge, and insert a solid panel into that (but don't glue it), it will be free to shrink and swell as it likes without causing trouble – while still filling the space. It can be quite thin, too, so relatively little material is used.

This clever technique is still very common today – especially in doors, both for buildings and for cupboards: proof that the technique is a sound one.

But the story doesn't end there. Cabinet-makers later found they sometimes needed large slabs, after all, on which to lay the exotic veneers that became available. However, like framed panels, these were still connected with much thinner members. The sides of an eighteenth-century chest of drawers, for example, are generally linked only by rails – dovetailed at the top and stub-tenoned lower down. And these are often themselves part of horizontal frames, which can be used just for stiffness but usually double as drawer mountings. (For more information on this subject, see pages 132-135 for details.)

This mixed construction can be extremely complex. The main rule is to design so that assembly breaks down into separate stages, at each of which you're only cramping one frame in one direction to prevent distortion.

More recently still, man-made boards have changed the situation again. Since they hardly shrink or swell at all, they enable true 'box construction'(see pages 60-63 for details) – like the plank designs of medieval times, but without their snags. Simplicity has made this method enormously widespread in storage furniture. However, it can seem a bit primitive even there. This is why, for the most part, the frame still dominates when making stools, chairs and table bases, for example, where spaces don't have to be enclosed.

Framing joints

To a great extent, framing means mortise-and-tenon joints (see pages 65-69 for details). If well cut, they're stronger than any other type. Even if not, their large glueing area provides strength in reserve.

MAKING PANELLED FRAMES

Grooved frames

Plan your groove to coincide with mortises. If stopped (1 and 2), it's best cut after them, so their ends form buffers for the plane. If it runs through to the end of the piece, fill its end with a square haunch (3).

The groove should not be deeper or wider than the mortises (1). It can be narrower (2) if shallower than the tenon's inner shoulder.

1

mortise

groove

2

inner shoulder

3

haunch

Rebated frames

If cutting a rebate before assembly, run it right along the piece, or at least to the end of the mortise. Give each tenon one 'long' shoulder to fill the rebate, and one 'short' one (4).

Whether rebating before or after assembly, either include the mortise width (ie, the tenon thickness) in the rebate depth (4), or plan the rebate so it misses the joint altogether (5 and 6).

4

long shoulder

short shoulder

5

6

Moulded frames

If cutting a decorative moulding on the frame itself (9 and 10), mitre it at the corners (11 and 12), using a mitre template. Plan joints, rebates (9 and 11) and grooves (10 and 12) to avoid it.

9

10

Panelling techniques

7

flush panel

fielded panel

planted moulding

raised panel

Using beading

8

bolection moulding

mitre template

11

12

These joints come in dozens of varieties. The tenon can have shoulders on one, two, three or four sides, or even none. It can either pass through the mortise piece or not. It can come in pairs (side-by-side or one above the other) or threes. It can be wedged from the far end, dovetailed and wedged from the near end, pegged from the side, or even pegged as well as wedged.

Another good option to use in this case is the bridle joint – like a mortise-and-tenon joint in reverse. Choosing this will save you the bother of cutting a proper mortise. Bridles too can be pegged.

Dowels offer stiff competition, being invisible, and strong when used in frames. But it's debatable whether they're any easier to fit accurately than tenons.

The section on pages 32-35 outlines further alternatives. Leaving aside nailed butt joints, one of the simplest is the halving. However, even if well cut and thoroughly glued, this doesn't have the strength of a mortise and tenon or even a bridle, except perhaps when it's pegged or dovetailed or both. For many purposes, too, its appearance is a problem.

The best-looking of all corner joints is the mitre. Unfortunately, it has three disadvantages. Firstly, it needs very accurate cutting, and even then it may open up if the wood shrinks at all. Secondly, it's not easy to cramp; you can't use sash-cramps, with their crushing force – although a good alternative is shown in *Ready Reference*. Thirdly, it's relatively weak, even if strengthened in one way or another. Of course, as with most framing joints, you can always screw through the mitre and then plug the hole with matching timber.

The mitre halving joint makes a good compromise between the halving's somewhat greater strength and the mitre's better looks. Stronger still is the corner bridle/open mortise joint with a mitred front, which gives the same effect.

All these types of joint are described and illustrated in detail on pages 24-26. At the other extreme, certain self-assembly fittings are very efficient.

Fitting panels

The framing of panels, eg for cabinet doors, represents frame construction at its most sophisticated.

For one thing, grooving the frame is only one way of supporting the panel. It has the advantage that all the assembly is done in one go; the snag is that both groove and panel need to be cut carefully before that.

An accurate rebate, on the other hand, can be as easily cut after the frame is glued as before – and the panel can be marked up from it. You'll need lengths of beading to hold the panel in place – but these let you make it

removable if they're screwed in. Cut them slightly over-length and, if pinning them, work from the ends inwards. This will give a snug fit.

If you haven't got a power router or a suitable plane, a third alternative is to use two sets of beading – fixing one before inserting the panel, and the other afterwards.

Types of panel

But the real beauty of the frame-and-panel system lies in its immensely varied possibilities.

Solid timber, the traditional infill material, can be used in the form of finely figured hardwoods without the risk that warping will cause problems. However, it should be left to shrink a bit before being cut into panels; and even then it must never be glued into the groove or rebate – at least, not along more than one edge – in case further shrinkage splits it. In fact, if it's grooved in, its corners should be waxed first, so that excess glue from the framing joints doesn't grip them. It's also wise (and usually easier) to apply the finish to the panel before assembly; this means that shrinkage can't expose bare timber around its edges.

Man-made boards, on the other hand, can be glued in, thereby making the structure a lot more rigid. If the panel is veneered, the grain usually looks better if it runs vertically.

Glass panels should ideally be inserted with a thin strip of leather or suede around the edges, the excess being trimmed off after the retaining beading has been fixed. This will stop any rattling.

Fabric is another option. Either wrap it round the edges of a board and staple it there from behind (allowing for twice the fabric's thickness in the groove or rebate which receives the panel), or stretch it over its own light softwood frame and screw that in place.

With paper, you can use similar methods. Instead of stapling, you could paste it to a board – on both faces of thin boards, to prevent any warping. Otherwise, pin it directly into a rebate as in the photographs.

What's more, you can add ornament to a frame-and-panel structure by cutting a decorative profile along the edges of the frame, glueing on lengths of moulding, using moulded retaining beads, or combining these methods. If the panel is of timber or board, you can glue mouldings to that; in the case of timber, you can cut a profile in the solid wood. The illustrations on page 1469 give examples of all these techniques.

Table and chair framing

It's in structural frames for tables and chairs that the mortise-and-tenon joint is most important of all. Although dowels will sometimes do, halvings and mitres are generally out because they're not strong enough, and

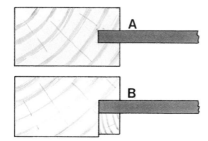
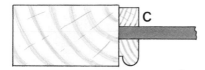
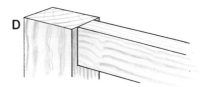
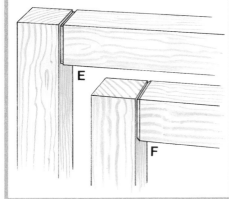

CUTTING FRAME COMPONENTS

1 When making a frame, eg, for a folding screen, start by squaring the width of each tenon piece (usually a rail) across the mortise pieces (usually stiles).

2 Cut the rails (over length if using through tenons) and mark the longer of the two 'shoulder lengths' – the frame's internal width plus two rebate widths.

3 Make a second mark further in along the piece, distancing it from the first by the width of your planned rebate. Mark both rails at once.

6 Cut the rebates with a power router or suitable type of hand plane. Make sure you position them correctly in relation to the tenon cuts.

7 Make the tenon shoulder cuts – again double-checking that the long shoulder will be on the rebated face of the rail at each end of the piece.

8 Cut identical rebates in the stiles after mortising. Unless they run right along, stop them short of each mortise and begin to chisel from its far end.

---

the mitre's visual qualities aren't usually needed anyway.

However, corners where rails meet legs – especially at the backs of chair seats – may still need reinforcement. This can take the form of a glued and screwed block in the internal angle; on tables, the hanger bolt is a good alternative.

Such joints are subject to great stress from more than one direction. As soon as the pieces begin to move in relation to one another, the strength of the joint will decrease very quickly.

To combat this, it goes without saying that your cutting must be very accurate. An additional point is that ordinary PVA wood-working adhesive isn't ideal in such situations, because it retains a certain elasticity when it sets. Urea-formaldehyde adhesive (also readily available) is better here, since it sets very hard and also helps to fill any slight

gaps in the fit – as PVA does not.

Beds present a special problem in design and construction, because they usually have to be capable of being dismantled so you can get them through doors, up and down stairs and so on. This restricts the number of glued joints you can include, and often means using screws, bolts and assembly fittings instead.

Some specific tips on table design are given in *Ready Reference*.

Setting out frames

Success in framing begins with sensible design. First of all, any tenon should be one-third the thickness of the piece in which it's cut (let's say the rail). If it's less, it may break. If more, it may burst the other piece (let's say the stile) if it's a bit tight in the mortise. This assumes, of course, that the pieces are the same size.

Secondly, make blind mortises about 3mm (⅛in) too deep, to accommodate excess glue. Otherwise, if the stile is very narrow it may balloon out as the rail is fitted.

Thirdly, don't position a corner mortise too close to the end of a piece, or you may split the wood – either when cutting the mortise or when inserting the tenon. If you can't avoid this, you can always leave extra length on the stiles (forming 'horns'), and cut them down to size only after the joints are glued – see pages 68-69.

It's worth noting that a 'haunch' (see pages 65-67) is often recommended as a way to stop the pieces twisting in relation to each other. But it's very doubtful if this is worth the trouble involved – except where the rail is as wide as 200mm (8in) or so, as is sometimes the case on a full-sized door.

Fourthly, bear in mind that you may not be able to get the faces of the pieces exactly

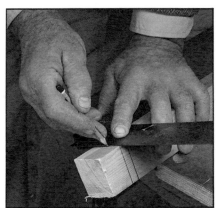

4 *Square both these marks right round each end of each rail. Then mark out the thickness of your tenons (ideally using a mortise gauge).*

5 *Make the lengthwise cuts for the tenons. Be careful to get them different depths, each stopping on one of the two shoulder lines.*

9 *After making a vertical cut, turn the chisel bevel-downwards and finish the rebate so it neatly includes the mortise in its length and width.*

10 *To profile the ends of the stiles, use a hardboard or thin plywood template. Shape it and the stiles with a jig- or coping saw, plus sandpaper.*

Ready Reference

TIP: CRAMPING MITRED FRAMES

If you haven't got a web cramp, you can improvise very effectively. Tie some string round the frame (A), not too tightly. Then insert eight blocks of wood between string and frame, near the middle of each side (B), and push them towards the corners to exert high pressure.

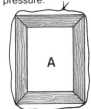
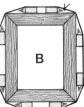

DESIGNING TABLE FRAMES

For comfort and convenience, you need to bear several things in mind when you're building a table.

First, the top rails mustn't be wide enough to obstruct people's knees. Standard dimensions are shown below.

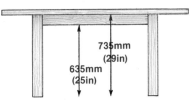

735mm (29in)
635mm (25in)

Secondly, try to keep the space at ankle level clear, so people can move their feet freely. A central stretcher rail will help to stiffen the structure.

central stretcher rail

Thirdly, allow for people sitting at the ends of the table as well as along its sides.

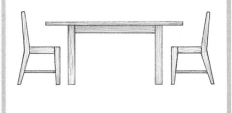

flush when the joints are fitted, especially if you're cutting several. The way round this is either to inset the rail so that the joint isn't meant to be flush anyway, or to deceive the eye by making a narrow groove all round the end of the rail (see *Ready Reference*).

If you're framing a panel (see illustrations on page 166), don't just cut the frame joints and then think about how the panel will be fitted. Instead, plan the size and position of the groove or rebate to correspond with those of the mortises and tenons – and, if necessary, vice versa.

Even if a groove is meant to be central, work it from the same face of each framing member, so that any inaccuracy won't stop the panel entering smoothly. For the same reason, make it a comfortable 1mm too deep for the panel all round – but, if the panel is solid, not much more, or it may shrink right out of the groove on one side.

Assembly techniques are shown in the photographs. When you're doing it yourself, follow three rules. Make a dry run; glue sparingly; and check for accuracy before it's too late. Accurate cramping is essential for good results.

The various combinations of joints, grooves, rebates, mouldings and mitres may start to make your head spin when you think how to build a particular item. At first you may find it hard even to draw them or mark them out. Moreover, even when you get them right, they may look pretty bizarre – making you think you've got things wrong, or that there must be a simpler way to do the job, or both!

Often there is a simpler way: you can cut halvings instead of mortises and tenons, and use lengths of moulding instead of cutting grooves. But even complex ways have nothing odd about them – they're just sets of answers to particular problems.

ASSEMBLING A FRAME

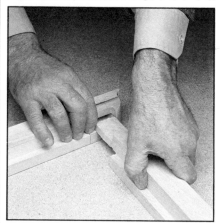

1 Fit the components together on a flat surface, without using adhesive. The intermediate rails are the same as the top and bottom ones, but are rebated twice.

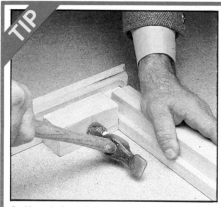

2 Knock the joints apart at right-angles, using a hammer and block of wood. 'Wiggling' the rails out can very easily damage the mortises.

3 Apply adhesive sparingly and tighten your cramps, still on a flat surface to reveal any twisting. Have a damp, clean rag ready to remove excess adhesive.

4 Immediately check the frame for squareness. A try-square is no good here: use a 'squaring stick' instead. This can have a nail through one end.

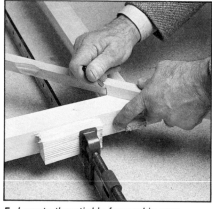

5 Locate the stick's far end in one corner and mark the frame's diagonal size at its near end. Then check that the other diagonal is the same length.

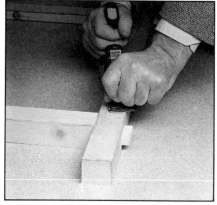

6 Plane the faces of the joints where necessary so that the pieces are flush – if that's what you intend. Trim the ends of the tenons likewise.

7 Paper panels can be neatly fixed into the rebates with drawing-pins – which also, of course, allow easy removal if the paper gets dirty or torn.

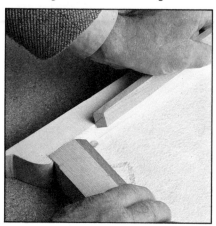

8 Mitre lengths of beading to fit tightly round the inside of the frame and to conceal the drawing-pins. Drill and countersink them for screws first.

9 Screw (but don't glue) the beading into position. Complete the folding screen with similar frames, linking the stiles with ordinary butt hinges.

FITTING DOORS AND FRAMES

The finest external door is only as good as its frame. A sound and sturdy frame is vital to keep out intruders and the weather; what's more, it needs to match the door in size and style.

Not all doors have frames. Internal doors are generally fitted into 'linings', also known as 'casings'. A lining differs from a frame in being made from wider pieces of timber. These are usually flat, cut at the time of installation to the lengths required, and fitted together in the opening with simple housing or rebate joints.

A frame, on the other hand, is a fairly sophisticated piece of joinery, often in hardwood, which comes ready-made. It's heavier and stronger than a lining, and it's always used for external doorways; as a result, it's specially designed to keep out the weather. Lighter frames are sometimes also found in internal doorways – especially those in thin walls, because the pieces in a frame are narrow and squarish in section, not flat. Rebates are moulded in them to receive the door, and they're usually machined in other ways as well.

Joints, usually mortise-and-tenon, are already cut in the frame components, so that you can't choose your own length and width. In other words, the opening in the wall has to fit the frame you've bought, because you can't make the frame fit the opening. So you need to make sure you buy the right size of frame for the door in the first place.

A door frame may consist of only three pieces – the head, which goes at the top, and the two jambs which go on either side. In that case, for an external doorway you'll have to buy a separate threshold or sill (the part you step on). However, four-piece door frames, which include thresholds, are also available.

Why install a frame?

Strong though it is, an existing door frame isn't invulnerable. Often fully exposed to the elements, it may eventually rot, usually in the bottoms of the jambs. Hard knocks (and even an attack by vandals or burglars) may necessitate replacement, too.

Alternative reasons for installing a new frame may be to improve security, fire protection, weather resistance or appearance. Ask your timber merchant or other joinery supplier about frames with the particular characteristics you're looking for. Yet another reason for fitting a new frame

may be because you want a new door, and the old frame is the wrong size or is otherwise unsuitable.

Lastly, you might want to make a new doorway where none existed before (eg, for access to a back yard). This might mean enlarging an existing window opening by removing the brickwork beneath the sill. But if you're making a completely new opening, remember you'll need a lintel to support the wall above, and flashing to stop moisture from penetrating and causing rot and damp within the structure.

Removing an old frame

Before putting in your new frame, you may well have to take out an old one. It's worth knowing the quickest way of doing this (see *Ready Reference*).

First, saw through the head in two places, making the cuts slope upwards and inwards, towards the centre of the frame. The middle portion of the head will then come away easily.

Next, saw through the jambs – again at an angle – downwards and outwards. This enables you to pull the lower part of each jamb up and out. Then you have plenty of freedom to work the top corners of the frame away from the brickwork.

Lastly, clean up the opening, removing any loose timber plugs to which the frame

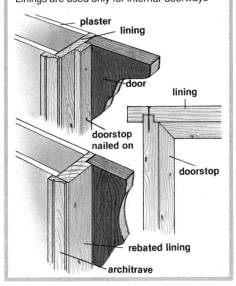

FITTING THE DOORS

1 Decide and mark the hinge positions along the inner edge of each door. Heavier doors need three hinges, but two usually suffice.

2 Mark the hinge recesses' depth with a marking gauge, and use a hammer and chisel to cut them. Begin by chopping round the edges.

3 Cut across the grain, then finish the recesses by carefully removing the waste. You need a sharp chisel; don't split the timber.

4 Position the hinge, making sure it's absolutely straight. Use a bradawl to make starting holes for the screws; then drive them home.

5 Position each door in the frame, and prop it up at the right height. Then use the loose leaf of each hinge to mark its recess in the frame.

6 Screw the hinges to the jambs, after chiselling out the recesses as in the door. Half the knuckle's thickness projects beyond the edge.

7 A neat way of fixing glass into a door is to start by laying putty or other suitable sealant in the rebates before you insert the glass.

8 Then lay the panes of glass (ready cut to size) into position, making sure that they are bedded carefully into the putty or sealant.

9 Finally, pin mitred lengths of glass bead all round. Don't glue them, in case you need to remove the glass (eg, after a breakage).

may have been fixed plus, of course, any rubble which may be lying at the bottom.

Removing a doorframe while keeping it intact for subsequent re-use is a trickier business, since at the top corners frames often have 'horns' (these are projections where the head overhangs the jambs at either side; they are built into the brickwork for maximum stability). You'll have to extract these by carefully cutting out the mortar joints from between the bricks around the horns.

To remove the fixings at either side of the frame, carefully cut away any plastering or rendering that conceals the frame edges and run a pad saw fitted with a hacksaw blade down between the jamb and the wall on either side; saw through any obstacles you meet. This will be easy enough if the fixings are nails or screws, but quite hard if they're metal anchors.

Occasionally, steel dowels are also used to fasten a door frame to the floor, projecting down into it from the ends of the jambs. They prevent the jambs from working loose with heavy use. Although they can often be omitted when fitting a new frame, their presence makes it very difficult to remove an old frame in one piece. But it may be possible to chip the floor away round them.

Lastly, place a large flat piece of timber against the edge of the frame, in various positions all round it in turn, and hit it so as to knock the frame out of the opening.

Fixing a new frame

There are three ways of fixing the jambs to the walls on either side. Firstly, you can screw them into plastic or fibre wallplugs; in external doorways, use screws which are rust-proof (eg, stainless steel) or rust-resistant (eg, zinc-plated), not plain steel ones.

Secondly, you can attach the jambs to metal anchors or fixing cramps, cemented into the brick joints. And thirdly, you can nail them to wooden plugs wedged between the bricks.

The first of these methods is probably the simplest, but the second is the strongest, and the last means you can get a secure fixing in brick or blockwork even if there are gaps between the frame and the wall, because you can cut the plugs off to exactly the length you need. The method works as follows.

Assemble the frame and see how it fits the opening. If it's too big, your best plan is to enlarge the opening slightly, by chopping away up to one third of a brick's length from either side of the opening. Then insert the timber plugs, opposite each other, firmly in the brickwork joints – at least three on each side. Drop a plumbline from the top of the opening on one side, and mark its position on each plug there.

Measure the width of the frame (from outside edge to outside edge) and, working from the mark you've already made on one of the plugs, mark that width on the plug opposite. Then drop the plumbline past this and mark its position on the other plugs that side. Lastly, cut off all the plugs at the marks. The plug ends should now give an opening which is exactly the right width for the frame, with its sides vertical and parallel, even if the wall itself has ragged edges.

After that you can insert the frame for final fixing. Although most frames are made of preservative-treated timber, the new frame should also be primed first – and ideally given a complete paint finish of undercoat and top coat on all surfaces which will adjoin brickwork or concrete, to keep out any damp which finds its way through and so prevent rot. However, few people bother with this.

Once the frame is in position, check that the head is level and that one jamb is more or less plumb (vertical). Nail through that jamb into the top plug. Adjust the jamb further till it's exactly plumb, and nail it into the bottom plug. Then repeat the procedure for the other jamb; in addition, before you nail through its bottom end, sight across both jambs to ensure that the frame isn't twisted.

Finish off by nailing into all the intermediate plugs, and punching all the nail heads below the surface of the timber.

This is also the time to mortar the horns, if any, into the brickwork.

Finishing the job

The final stage is to pack timber into any remaining gaps between the frame and the wall. On an internal door frame, you'll need to finish the whole thing with architrave mouldings, which may need to be fixed to timber grounds (see page 174). In an external doorway, a mastic seal between frame and wall on the outside is also essential to keep out the damp.

For protection against driving rain, the threshold of an external door frame will either be rebated (ie, stepped), or will have a metal 'water bar', if not both. The latter rests in a groove along the top of the threshold, into which it needs to be set on a bed of non-setting mastic. The bottom of the door will have to be rebated to fit over it.

If you've bought wisely, the door should fit the frame exactly – but you can always saw and plane off small amounts from the top, bottom or sides if necessary.

Hanging the door is a straightforward matter of marking out and chiselling hinge recesses on the door, screwing the hinges into them, and repeating the procedure on the frame. For fuller details of what's involved, see pages 45-47.

Remember, however, that a door must hang quite vertically. The hinges should be exactly above one another; you may have to enlarge or pack out the recesses.

(see page 174)

Ready Reference

REMOVING A DOOR FRAME

This procedure is especially appropriate when you're removing a frame from a solid wall:

● start by sawing through the head at an angle in two places; the piece in the middle should then come away easily

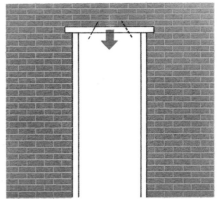

● next, saw through the jambs at an angle, and remove the lower part of each; you may have screws or nails to contend with here. And, if the jambs are fixed to the ground with metal dowels inserted into the end grain, you'll have to pull these free at the same time

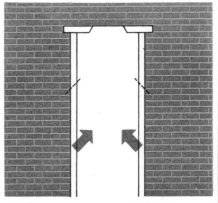

● lastly you can remove each of the top corners from the brickwork or blockwork. Having cut away the rest of the frame first means that you now have freedom to work any 'horns' (projecting ends of the head) loose from the wall. ·

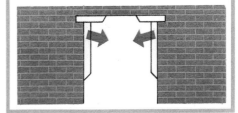

WAYS OF FITTING DOOR FRAMES

External doorways

Here are two ways of fitting a frame into an outside wall. Note that mastic and a dpc are both used to prevent moisture from penetrating.

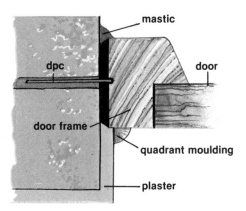

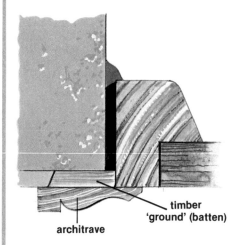

Internal doorways

A is a common arrangement, B a specially shaped frame, and C a frame narrower than the wall is thick: lengths of wood make up the width.

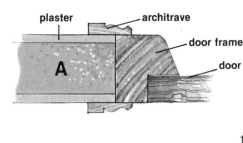

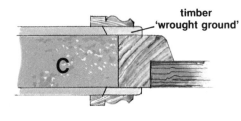

Fixing frames to walls

Apart from screwing into wall plugs, you can use metal anchors (A), or timber plugs (B), cut as shown and driven into the joints between bricks.

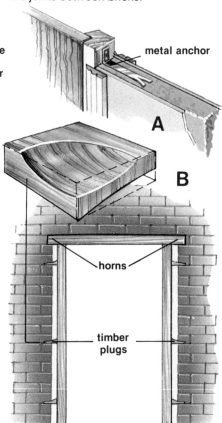

Joins between frame and skirting

Usually skirting (nailed to battens fixed to the wall) is butted against the back of the architrave (A).

If the skirting is too thick (B), add a 'plinth block' below the architrave. Chamfer its edges for neatness.

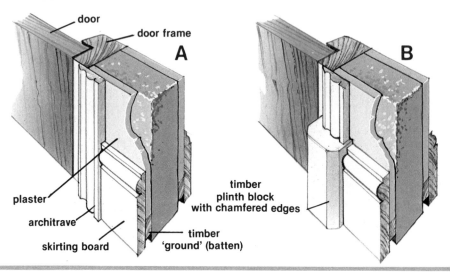

Threshold design

A ready-made hardwood threshold has either a metal water bar, which you bed in mastic as shown, or a rebate which does the same job.

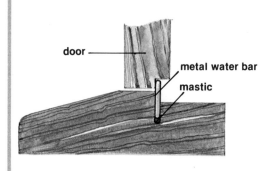

LAYING A NEW TIMBER FLOOR

Suspended timber floors, consisting of floorboards nailed to joists, can last for years without giving trouble. But there may eventually come a time when they need replacing.

Timber floors are durable and long-suffering. But eventually they can become loose, worn, damaged by woodworm and sometimes cracked. This means annoying creaks, an uneven surface (which in turn causes worn patches on your floor-coverings) and, in extreme cases, actual hazards. All these are signs that it's time to think about laying a new floor.

Even the joists on which the floorboards rest can become distorted, and may sag towards the middle of the room. A bonus of laying new floorboards is that you can compensate for this sagging into the bargain, so that you end up with a floor that's newly flat and level as well as sound.

Timber or chipboard

Before detailing how to use floorboards, it's worth pointing out that there is an alternative to them, namely chipboard. This will be dealt with more fully in another section. Special flooring grade chipboard is usually 18mm (¾in) thick, although it's also available in greater thicknesses for added rigidity where the joists are spaced more widely than usual. It can even be bought with tongued-and-grooved edges.

Chipboard is a fair bit cheaper than solid timber floorboards, and it doesn't shrink. Moreover, because it comes in bigger pieces you have to hammer in fewer nails when you're fixing it. But by the same token it takes more work to fit, because you may have to cut out large sections to accommodate chimney breasts and similar obstacles; and removing it, if that should ever become necessary, is harder, especially if you're trying to keep the pieces intact. Lastly, it should never be used where it's likely to get in the least bit wet – in bathrooms, for example – because if moisture penetrates the edges they'll soon swell and break up.

Buying floorboards

Floorboards are made of planed softwood, and come in two varieties: square-edged, and tongued-and-grooved (T & G). In the latter type each board has a tongue down one edge and a matching groove down the other. T & G boards take a little more effort to lay (the

tongues fit the grooves very tightly), but they repay that in being draughtproof, and in their greater strength: once laid, they form what is in effect a solid sheet.

The tongues and grooves aren't centred in their respective edges. Boards should be laid with the tongues towards the bottom, not the top; this allows more wear before the tongues become exposed. Standard widths for floorboards (ie, across the face, excluding the width of the tongue) are 100mm (4in) and 150mm (6in), though these vary slightly with the supplier. The standard nominal thickness is 25mm (1in), planed down from sawn timber to 20mm (¾in) or so.

Boards planed down from 32mm (1¼in) to a finished thickness of about 25mm (1in) are also available, and they make a fine substantial floor; but they cost more. Remember, too, that if they're thicker than the old boards they probably won't fit under the existing skirting. You'll either have to butt them up against it (which may create problems when it comes to supporting their ends,

since the last joist may be flush with the wall surface) or replace the skirting too.

Floorboards must, of course, be laid across the joists, not parallel to them. To work out how much timber you'll need, make careful calculations, dividing the length of the room by the width of board to find how many lengths to buy. A good tip is to visit your timber merchant even before this, to find out the exact width of the boards he stocks.

If possible, buy boards which will just span the width of the room with a little to spare. In any case, make sure you get enough to cover the total length you need (found by multiplying the number of board widths by the width of the room).

Buy the boards a week or two before doing the job, and stack them flat inside the house. This will give them time to dry out and therefore shrink a bit before you lay them. The precaution is important because, if they shrink appreciably afterwards, you'll be left with unsightly gaps, no matter how tightly you fit them during the job.

HOW THE JOISTS RUN

Right: The way the joists run in your house will depend on a number of structural factors. Where the joists meet a chimney breast at right angles, trimming and trimmer joists will surround the hearth as shown here.

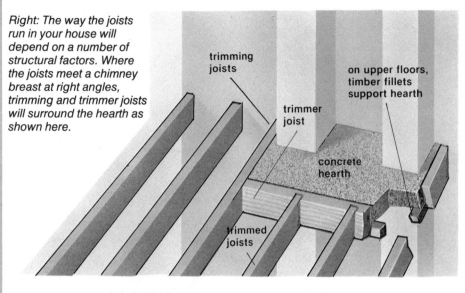

Right: Where the joists run across the face of the chimney breast, the arrangement will look like this. Again, the hearth will be supported on timber fillets, while a hardwood surround may frame the hearth itself.

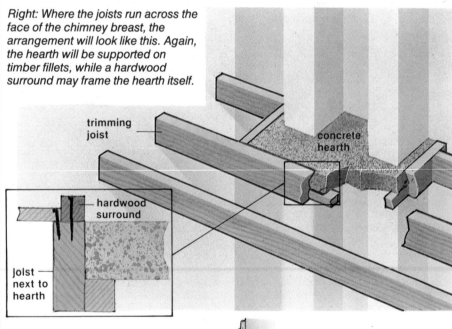

Skirting details
Normally, the floorboards are tucked in under the skirting board (top left), but if thicker boards are used you can conceal the gap with quadrant moulding (centre). Where a joist is right alongside the wall, add a strip of timber to it to support the board ends at the required height.

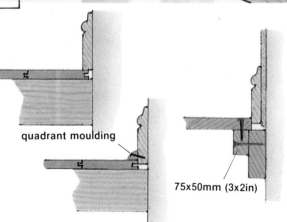

You may have to cut the boards to length straightaway in order to get them into a convenient indoor spot for stacking.

Removing old floorboards
Your first job is to take up the old boards. Decide where you're going to start (probably near a wall but not right up against it) and lever up the first board with a bolster and, if necessary, a claw-hammer. If it's tongued-and-grooved, you'll need to cut through its tongue first with a pad saw, a floorboard saw, a tenon saw, or a circular saw whose depth of cut is set to the floorboard thickness. Be very careful not to cut into the joists.

After you have lifted one end, by far the quickest way to continue (and to lift all the other boards) is to use a long piece of substantial timber – say 75x50mm (3x2in) – as a lever, and a shorter piece as a fulcrum. With stubborn boards, you can put your feet on the lever.

Make sure none of the boards are screwed down. If they are, don't try to lever them up before undoing the screws!

In a wide room, you'll probably be able to wiggle and release from under the skirting even those boards which span the room's full width. In a narrow room, you may have to saw across them first.

You'd do well to extract the nails from the old boards as you put them aside, to avoid injury if you tread on one – especially if you mean to keep some of the boards for re-use. And you'll need to extract any nails left in the joists. If they won't come out, drive them in flush.

Note that, if gaps between boards are the only problem with your old floor, you can give it a new lease of life by carefully lifting them up, removing the nails, scraping down the boards' edges to clean them up for a snug fit, and then re-laying them all tightly against one another in just the same way as you lay new boards (see below). The odd damaged board can be replaced by a new one of the same thickness. You'll need to add a strip of board along the wall after re-laying the last board, to make up for the gaps.

Laying new boards
Before starting to lay the floor, place a straight-edged piece of timber (a floorboard will do) across the joists to check whether their top edges are in line. If not, cut packing pieces (planing them to the right thickness or using hardboard) and pin them in position.

Then measure for the first four or five boards, and cut them to length. For economy aim to use up any short pieces that you may be left with. If making up a length from two or more of these, make sure they meet in the centre of a joist each time, so that it supports the ends of both. See that the ends are cut squarely and butt tightly against one another – and stagger such joints, so that they don't occur one after the other on the same joist.

Lay the first board in position with the groove facing out into the room, and scribe it to fit against the wall. Then cut it to shape, removing the waste from the tongue side, and nail it down to each joist through its face.

After that, the basic procedure is to lay the boards on the floor in sequences of four or five (inserting the tongues, if any, into the grooves); cramp them tight and nail them down.

There are two ways to cramp floorboards. You can use pairs of wedges, cut from 75x50mm (3x2in) planed softwood, tapped together between the last board and another piece of timber nailed across the joists. Or you can hire flooring cramps, which clamp themselves onto the joists while being tightened against the floorboards. They exert tremendous pressure, and you'll have to use offcuts of floorboard (including their tongues) as 'softening' to prevent the cramps from damaging the edges of the boards you're laying.

The right nails to use for fixing are cut floorbrads about two and a half times as long as the floorboards are thick. These are blunt and thus won't split the timber. Drive two through each board wherever it crosses a joist. Make quite sure at all times that you know where pipework and electrical wiring runs. A nail through a gas pipe or mains cable is no joke.

Remember, when laying a timber floor at ground level, it's vital not to leave any wood debris under the boards after laying them, since it can encourage the spread of rot.

Making boards fit

No room is without various irregularities in, and protrusions from, the walls at floor level, and you'll have to cut the boards to fit round them. The first and last boards must be scribed to fit along the walls, and you'll also need to cope with the chimney breast (if any) in a similar way. A combination square is ideal for scribing round small obstacles.

A fitted cupboard can create problems if the floorboards run into rather than parallel with it, but these aren't insurmountable (see *Ready Reference*). You can remove the bottom cross piece in its frame, and replace it after laying the floorboards. Or you can leave the cross piece there, saw through the old floorboards immediately in front of it, and butt the ends of the new ones up against them. In the latter case, the remaining old boards (those under the cupboard) may no longer be supported; if not, you'll have to screw down through the cross piece to hold them in position.

In places where you need access to pipes and wiring, you can include a trap-door in the form of a short board such as an off-cut (or a full-length board, cut into two), held down by countersunk screws instead of nails. In the case of T & G flooring, you'll have to plane or chisel the tongue off the adjacent board first.

PREPARING THE JOISTS

1 *Lever up the end of a convenient board with a bolster. If the board has a tongue, you'll have to saw through that beforehand.*

2 *Use a piece of timber as a lever to finish removing the first board and then to tackle the rest, taking one board at a time.*

3 *If necessary, saw the old boards in two so that you can get them out with ease from under the skirting at either side of the room.*

4 *Pull the old nails out of the joists with a claw hammer, using a piece of wood under its head to provide you with more leverage.*

5 *Lay a straight piece of timber across the joists, and measure the gaps below it to see how far the joists have sagged out of level.*

6 *Cut packing pieces, plane them to a thickness which will fill the various gaps, and nail them to the tops of the joists.*

LAYING THE FLOORBOARDS

1 Boards will have to be scribed to fit round obstacles. Cut out the waste portions with a coping saw, or use a tenon saw and chisel.

2 Scribe and cut the first board to fit along the wall if necessary, then use a chisel to wedge it in place as you nail it to the joists.

3 Where two boards make up a length, nail one down, then push the other against the far wall and square its length across from the first board.

5 With the cramps still tight, nail the nearest board down onto the joists. Always check for pipes and cables before nailing.

6 You can remove the cramps before nailing the other boards down. Note that pairs of boards should always meet in the centres of joists.

7 Pairs of wedges, tapped together, are an alternative to flooring cramps. Again you'll need 'softening' blocks between them and the boards.

9 At the end wall, plane the tongues off two boards and wedge one up against the last board which you have nailed in position.

10 Use the other board, or a piece the same width, to scribe a line on the first board so that you can cut it down to the right width.

11 Cut to the scribed line, swap the boards round, and press them both into position with a piece of wood before nailing them down.

4 *After nailing the first length, lay the next-three or four in position and cramp them together tightly. Flooring cramps are ideal for this.*

8 *When you come to a chimney breast, mark out on the floorboard how much you'll need to cut away from it for a snug fit around the obstacle.*

12 *Finish the job by systematically going over the whole floor and punching all the nail heads below its surface for safety's sake.*

Finishing the job

You can't, of course, use wedges or cramps to get the last couple of boards tight, because there's no room for them. An alternative procedure is as follows.

After cutting the last two boards to length and planing the tongues off both, place one of them next to the last board already nailed (see *Ready Reference*). Wedge it tightly against the board by using a chisel as a lever (see photograph 9, left). Then scribe the profile of the wall on it, using a block of wood the same width as the boards. Even if the wall were dead straight and parallel to the board edges, you'd still need to do this in order to find out the width to which you need to cut the last board down: it would be quite a coincidence if a full-width board fitted exactly into the final gap.

Then cut the board along the scribed line, lay the whole board next to the last board nailed, and place the cut board next to the wall.

Now you can spring them both into place at once – using a piece of timber to press them flat – and nail them down.

When you've laid all the boards, punch all the nail heads below the surface. Then look at how neatly the boards fit under or butt against the skirting. If the effect is ragged, you can improve it enormously by nailing quadrant moulding into the angle (fixing it to the skirting, not the floor).

The choice of finishing treatment is of course yours. You may be going to lay carpet; but brand-new floorboards do give you the opportunity to make a feature of them. They'll provide a pleasant texture if painted – but you might well want to give them a clear varnish finish, perhaps even staining them first in another timber colour. Whatever happens, you must treat them in some way, otherwise they'll soon become very grubby (in fact they'll probably need a lot of cleaning up after they're laid, because of the mess the job creates).

And do make sure the paint or varnish will stand up to the wear it receives. Use only full gloss paint, complete with appropriate primer and undercoat, or three coats of heavy-duty floor sealer (furniture varnish is not really hard-wearing enough).

Replacing skirtings

If your old timber floor was in bad enough condition to need replacement, it's possible that the skirting boards are in pretty poor shape too. If that is the case, now is the time to consider replacing them. The job will be dealt with in detail in another section, but briefly all you have to do is to prise off the old boards carefully with a bolster chisel or crowbar (they are usually nailed to the wall through wooden packing pieces with cut nails) and nail up new boards with new packing pieces when you have laid new floorboards.

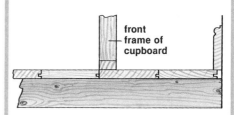
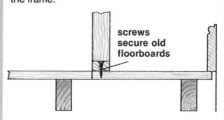
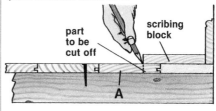

BUILDING CHAIRS 1: design

A chair is a personal thing. If you build it yourself you can make it to measure, as well as saving money. Here's what it takes to design and construct a good chair.

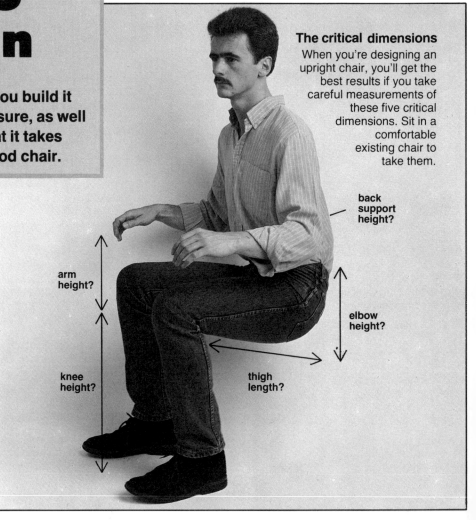

The critical dimensions
When you're designing an upright chair, you'll get the best results if you take careful measurements of these five critical dimensions. Sit in a comfortable existing chair to take them.

back support height?

arm height?

elbow height?

knee height?

thigh length?

When it comes to furniture, do-it-yourself carpenters often stop at storage units and shelving. Some may tackle the odd table or bed, but many fight shy of chairs.

Chairs, it's true, call for careful design and sometimes specialised techniques – chiefly those of shaping and nowadays laminating (see pages 99-103 for more detailed information on this technique), because they often have curved components. This is why chairmaking has always been considered a separate craft from general furniture-making. But the commonest types of upright chair are basically nothing more than simple frames (see pages 165-170 for details); as long as you proceed sensibly, their making can be an enjoyable way to save yourself money.

Besides, a chair – more than any other item of furniture – appeals to individual tastes, habits and physiques: so no mass-produced example can please or suit everyone. A home-made chair, on the other hand, can always be exactly right for you.

What chair do you need?
Your starting-point must always be the chair's intended place and purpose.

Easy chairs, which usually have extensive upholstery, pose questions which you may want to steer clear of. Upright chairs, however, fall into fairly well-defined groups – each with its own requirements.
● Dining chairs must go easily under the table, even when they're unoccupied, and should match its appearance. Their width must allow them all to fit; what's more, you may want them to stack
● Work chairs must also be compatible with the desk or table where they're to be used
● Garden chairs must be weather-resistant, and comfortable to relax in. Some are folding
● Children's chairs, of course, must be special sizes – and you may want to make them adjustable to cope with growth.

The 'comfort' of a chair isn't an absolute quality. It depends not only on personal factors but also on usage. It's not much fun trying to eat your dinner at a kitchen table from a deep, fluffy armchair. In any given situation, the body shouldn't have to labour

to sit comfortably. Padding and upholstery are far less important here than the relative sizes and angles of the components.

A personal project should, of course, be tailored to personal needs, but the following rules of thumb are well tried.
● Seat heights range from 400mm (16in) to 450mm (18in), depending on use. Most desk chairs are slightly higher than chairs for dining tables. Whatever the height, remember that the user must be able to sit fully back while keeping his or her feet flat on the floor – so the height should be considered in relation to the depth from front to back. If the chair has a straight back, a depth of up to 460mm (18½in) is usually acceptable, but with a curved back 420mm (16½in) is normally the maximum. These limits ensure the blood supply to the legs isn't impaired by the front edge of the seat.
● To hold the user correctly and stop him sliding forwards it's best if the seat also slopes gently – normally at 5-8° from the horizontal, which represents about 18mm (¾in) of height from front to back. This helps to support the lumbar curve of the spine and

the natural tilt of the pelvis, avoiding strain.
● A back rest is also vital for comfort, and normally a rail 200mm (8in) above the seat is considered correct. In a high-backed chair the support should extend to shoulder height, but at a rake of 20-25°.
● If arms are required, their fronts should ideally never protrude past the front legs, in case hands get caught between table and chair. Armrests are usually 200mm (8in) above the seat.

All these requirements of usage and comfort – not to mention any special ones for individual cases, plus personal preferences in terms of looks and 'feel' – may seem pretty daunting. However, if you list them you'll find you've actually made things much easier by giving yourself a thorough design brief. And if you take into account your own limits in skill and understanding, there's an excellent chance the idea will become a reality.

Finding a format
When you set about finding a 'solution' to the brief you're faced with, a useful step is to look at how others have tackled similar

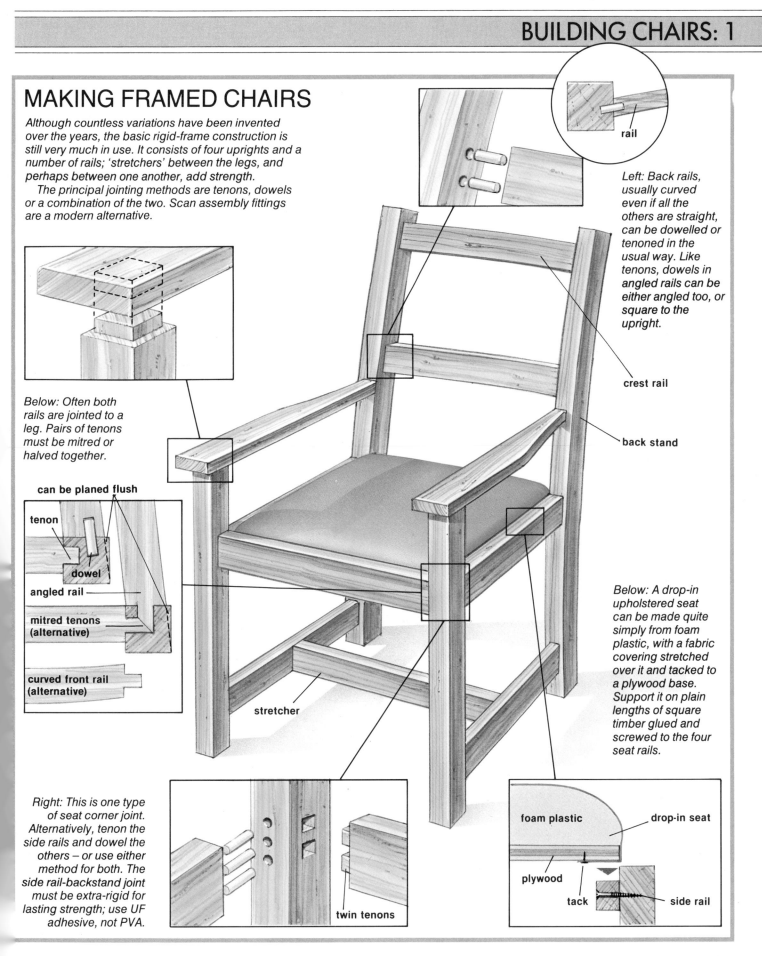

MAKING FRAMED CHAIRS

Although countless variations have been invented over the years, the basic rigid-frame construction is still very much in use. It consists of four uprights and a number of rails; 'stretchers' between the legs, and perhaps between one another, add strength.

The principal jointing methods are tenons, dowels or a combination of the two. Scan assembly fittings are a modern alternative.

rail

Left: Back rails, usually curved even if all the others are straight, can be dowelled or tenoned in the usual way. Like tenons, dowels in angled rails can be either angled too, or square to the upright.

crest rail

back stand

Below: Often both rails are jointed to a leg. Pairs of tenons must be mitred or halved together.

can be planed flush

tenon

dowel

angled rail

mitred tenons (alternative)

curved front rail (alternative)

stretcher

Below: A drop-in upholstered seat can be made quite simply from foam plastic, with a fabric covering stretched over it and tacked to a plywood base. Support it on plain lengths of square timber glued and screwed to the four seat rails.

Right: This is one type of seat corner joint. Alternatively, tenon the side rails and dowel the others – or use either method for both. The side rail-backstand joint must be extra-rigid for lasting strength; use UF adhesive, not PVA.

twin tenons

foam plastic

drop-in seat

plywood

tack

side rail

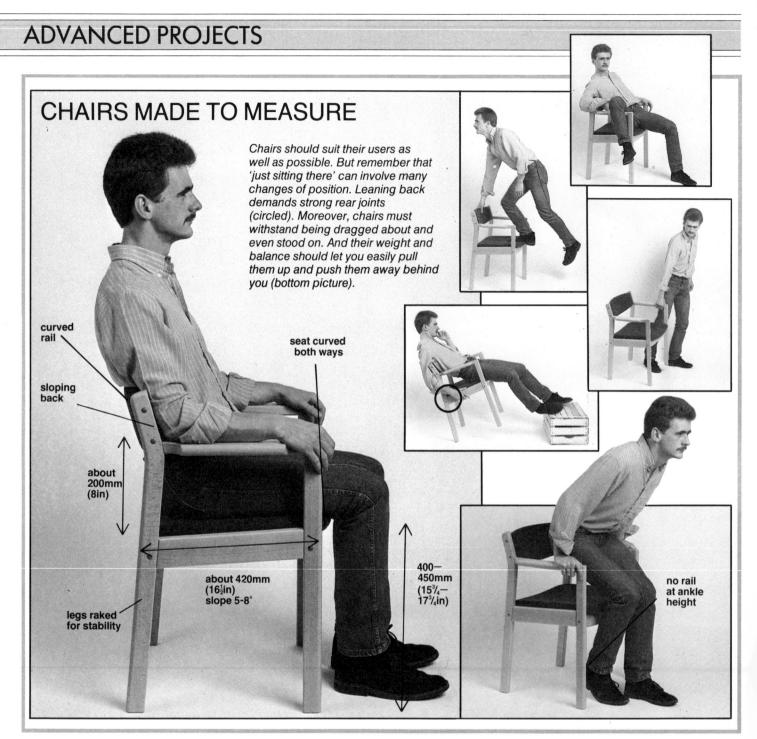

CHAIRS MADE TO MEASURE

Chairs should suit their users as well as possible. But remember that 'just sitting there' can involve many changes of position. Leaning back demands strong rear joints (circled). Moreover, chairs must withstand being dragged about and even stood on. And their weight and balance should let you easily pull them up and push them away behind you (bottom picture).

curved rail

sloping back

seat curved both ways

about 200mm (8in)

about 420mm (16½in) slope 5-8°

legs raked for stability

400—450mm (15¾—17¾in)

no rail at ankle height

problems. Visit exhibitions and shops, and glance through magazines.

You'll soon realise just what an amazing number of chair formats have come into being over the years – even without counting their major and minor variations. You're most unlikely to hit on one that's never been tried, so it's often wise to adopt a known and tested design, altering it to make it your own.

The commonest wooden chair format is the rigid open frame made from rectangular- or square-sectioned pieces, with a seat of cane or upholstery – the latter often fitting between the rails as a separate element with its own solid base.

Traditionally the squareness of this structure has been relieved by shaping, moulding and carving the components, which makes even a simple frame appear very sculptural. Today, however, technical, aesthetic and commercial pressures have made squareness acceptable – which is our good fortune, because all the curves and embellishments require special skills and equipment, plus a fair bit of experience.

In this format, evolved by cabinet-makers, the chair's rear legs provide its back by extending upwards past the seat (the trades-man's term for these components is 'back-stands'). But chairmakers have a dual

heritage – its other strand rooted in the Chiltern forests, where the familiar and much-loved 'Windsor' chairs have been produced for many generations. The local beech, ash and elm lend themselves well to turning (on a woodworker's lathe) and steam-bending; they go to make a chair – gracious in its simplicity and immensely practical – which is easily recognised because a solid seat intervenes between its legs and back. It's like a stool to which a back has been added. Although it uses framing, its components are generally cylindrical in section and fit into drilled holes.

Not many people can tackle steam-bending

or indeed turning at home. However, you shouldn't write off the intervening-seat format, because it's still a perfectly viable option when you're using everyday techniques.

Ensuring strength

Whatever its format, a chair must be strong and stable enough to give the user confidence. It will come under greater stress than most of your other furniture – but chairs that 'rack' (distort) or wobble are disturbing, and generally give way under casual use.

The most important factors here are the timber, the component sizes and the joints.

The timber must be tough, and well enough seasoned not to shrink after assembly, or the joints will quickly fail. Hardwood is traditional; beech, ash, elm, mahogany, oak, walnut and teak have all been popular. Beech is the favourite workaday wood for its dense, straight grain.

Today even cheap species of softwood are also in use. There's nothing wrong with this in principle, but it's imperative you pick your own pieces – free from splits, warping, and large knots and wandering grain which will detract from their strength. In addition, your design should allow for the tendency of softwood to split and compress, and you must be careful not to weaken the components too much by mortising.

Either way, let commonsense be your guide when deciding on sizes – but err on the side of caution.

Jointing methods

The standard chair format calls for legs and backstands joined by horizontal rails at seat level and usually elsewhere, plus sometimes stretcher rails lower down.

The best joint for any wooden structure where endgrain meets side grain is the mortise and tenon, which relies almost totally on a snug fit between the meeting surfaces. See also pages 24-26 and 165-170 for more details on joints.

There is, however, another factor which is vital in chairmaking though unusual elsewhere: the fact that it's rare for all components to meet at right angles to each other. The strength of the chair and its complexity of assembly will both be affected by how you deal with this situation

For example, the seat may taper from front to back. Here you'll have to decide whether the side rail tenons should follow the line of the rail, with angled shoulders and mortises, or should be angled to the rail and square to the shoulder and mortise. Take into account the size of the angle and how difficult angled mortises would be to cut. In general it's far simpler to keep the mortise at right angles to the surface, with an angled tenon, and suffer the loss of strength incurred by having marginally 'short-grained' tenons (see

Ready Reference). This also tends to simplify assembly because the cramping becomes a parallel pull between front and back frames. However, experienced chairmakers do argue strongly for the harder but perhaps more technically correct method.

The problems of short grain must also be borne in mind when dealing with any curved components that aren't laminated or bent, as grain should usually run straight along the main area of the piece to give the best compromise in terms of strength.

Another strength problem arises where two major horizontal members meet a single vertical member at the same level – eg, the seat rails and the top of a front leg. If the mortises are correctly proportioned they'll meet or connect, so the tenons must do so too. The answer is to mitre the ends of the tenons carefully or halve one into the other. However, depending on the proportions of the parts and the quality of the timber, this kind of junction remains suspect.

Where the design allows it to be done discreetly (eg, under a drop-in or fully upholstered seat) you can incorporate screwed wooden 'chair brackets' (see *Ready Reference*) fixed to the insides of the rails. These are often used too casually; to be really effective they must fit well and have a diagonal grain direction.

Commercially, most chairs today are assembled not with tenons but with dowels (see pages 36-39 for details). Rarely acceptable individually, these are used in twos or threes depending on the thicknesses and widths of the components. No rules govern their distribution other than common sense – but, unless they all fit exactly, you can encounter considerable difficulty. Industry has the advantage of sophisticated multiple boring machines. For the do-it-yourselfer a number of jigs and gadgets are on the market which work with varying degrees of success.

However, when aligned correctly dowels make a very satisfactory joint for chairs. One tip – provide an escape for air and glue by saw-'kerfing' them first, or by using proprietary dowels which are chamfered at each end and pre-fluted.

You can also mix mortise-and-tenon and dowel joints. In some situations one or more dowels can anchor a tenon firmly in position by passing through it or clipping its edge.

Getting under way

The section on pages 185-189 works through a chairmaking project in terms of the practical steps involved. You'll find that chairs are perhaps the most satisfactory of all items of furniture to make. That's because, once found to be useful and comfortable, they can inspire deep affection – plus great reluctance to give them up!

Ready
Reference

ANGLES AND CURVES

Chair parts often meet at odd angles. Tenons can either follow the angle of the component (A), which is stronger, or be cut square (B), which is easier to achieve.

canted tenon

flat for seat rails

Curved parts should be cut so the grain runs as straight as possible, again for strength. On each leg, include a flat portion to receive the end of the rail.

TIP: USE BRACKETS

'Chair brackets', glued and screwed into the angles between seat rails, are a traditional method of reinforcement. The grain should run diagonally as shown.

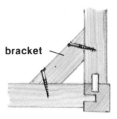

bracket

TYPES OF SEAT

There are four ways of making the seat for an upright chair.

Solid timber can take the form of
● wide boards, usually glued edge-to-edge. Allow for natural movement, eg with table shrinkage plates.
● slats, either laid side-by-side, or 'coopered' – shaped to a curve: see pages 185-189.

Plywood can be bought, or made in shapes by laminating (CARPENTRY TECHNIQUES 49).

Upholstery is a specialised craft, and even foam plastic can demand expertise in choosing the right grade, in creating shapes and so on. There are two main types of upholstered seat:
● stuff-over ('overstuffed') seats form an integral part of the chair
● drop-in seats, which are removable, have their own frame or base.

Woven seats, again calling for special skills, are in either cane or rushes. Rushwork is easier.

VARIETIES OF CHAIR

Though selected from thousands of wooden chair designs, these all do similar jobs. Most, too, are made in surprisingly similar ways – the odd ones out being the Windsor chair (3) with its bent components, and the laminated chair (9).

1 *Chair of the mid-17th century, only a step from the framed chest*
2 *Walnut chair of the Queen Anne period, with 'cabriole'-shaped front legs and a cane seat*
3 *Windsor chairs are country designs using bending and turning. This type is from the 1780s*
4 *Another country chair of the same period, but the straight legs and distinctive back show it's based on a Chippendale design*
5 *Again from the late 18th century, this is one of several patterns associated with Hepplewhite*
6 *Sabre legs and scrolled back-stands, among other things, denote a Regency chair. Rope ornament came in after the Battle of Trafalgar*
7 *This design was very popular in Victorian times*
8 *Modern chairs often follow the traditional format but leave out ornament and minimise curves*
9 *Laminations allow bold curves which are strong yet require no joints.*

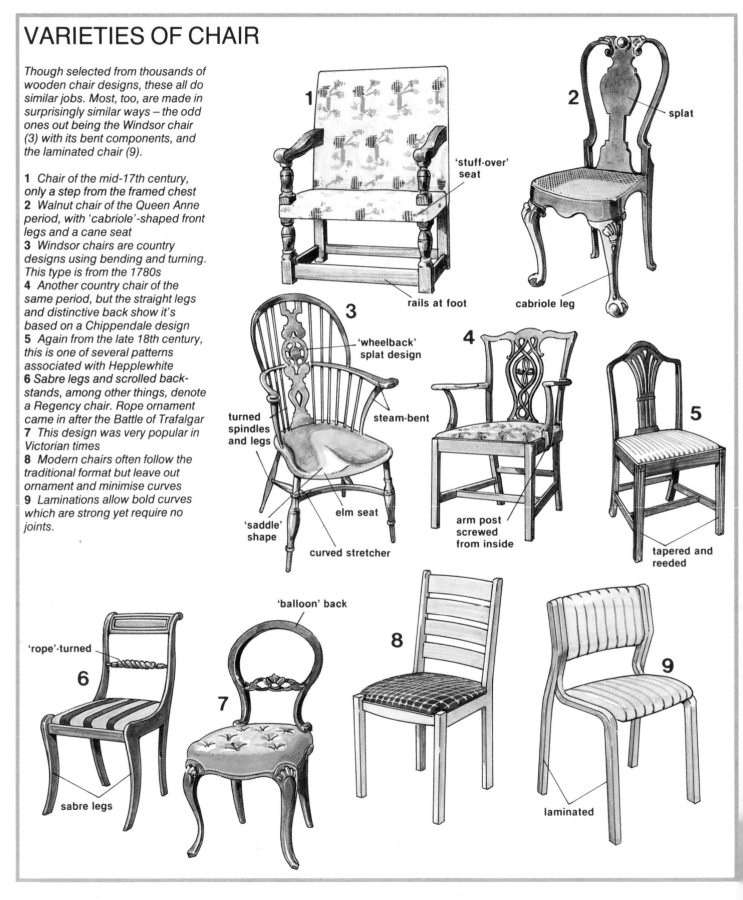

1

'stuff-over' seat

rails at foot

2

splat

cabriole leg

3

'wheelback' splat design

turned spindles and legs

steam-bent

'saddle' shape

elm seat

curved stretcher

4

arm post screwed from inside

5

tapered and reeded

'rope'-turned

'balloon' back

6

8

9

7

sabre legs

laminated

MAKING CHAIRS:2 construction

Making a chair, like designing one, holds no great difficulties if you go about it methodically. The secret is to plan for the tools and techniques you possess.

The thing to remember about any woodworking project is that you have the final say on what goes into the design.

This means, of course, that you decide exactly how the job is done – and thus, in many cases, whether it's done at all! If a particular detail looks difficult, there's generally a way round it.

If you don't like cutting mortises and tenons, use another jointing method: dowels, for example. If you have no jigsaw, avoid the type of curves for which it's needed, or use another tool such as a coping saw. If you have no router or rebate plane, make 'rebates' with two lengths of wood instead of one – and so on. In a way, ingenuity is more important than skill.

This point is especially vital in chairmaking, because of the awe which the task sometimes seems to provoke. This superstition is unnecessary because the procedure is under your control, so you can make it very nearly as easy as you like.

The first requirement, therefore, is to settle on the right design. The section on pages 180-184 gives more detailed advice.

But even a simple chair is often too complex to make out of your head or from a vague sketch. Before buying any materials, let alone cutting them, do make a formal drawing. This will prevent you from forgetting or confusing dimensions, and will probably pose a few unexpected questions.

Scale drawings are useful for general arrangement and proportion, but for the actual making it's sensible to prepare a 'rod' – that is, a full-sized drawing in elevation (side and/or front view) and plan (top view) on a suitable piece of board. You can then try the cut components against it.

Very likely (and very sensibly) you'll want to stick to right angles as far as possible, and cut down on the amount of shaping necessary. But you'll find it hard to make a really comfortable chair without any slopes or curves at all, so it's worth considering how best to approach these aspects when you only possess ordinary do-it-yourself tools.

Angled joints are tackled by accurate setting-out, perhaps with the help of a sliding bevel, and by referring to your rod.

Shaping is best done to marked lines. Chamfers and bevels are, of course, taken off with a plane. The curves found in modern chairs can usually be shaped with a jigsaw or curved Surform (professionals use a bandsaw). A spokeshave, however, leaves a finer finish, and will also clean up after you've used the other tools.

Remember that a jigsaw's depth of cut is usually too small to put a curve in the thickness of a piece.

Your actual working sequence is of course much affected by the details of the chair you're building. But it generally consists of
● cutting the components roughly to length
● reducing them in width and/or thickness
● making the joints
● doing any shaping required. Shaping usually takes place before assembly, though you might occasionally want to shape around a joint after it's been glued for the best results.

You'll probably be assembling either a back and front frame, connected by seat rails (and perhaps also 'stretchers' nearer the ground), or two side frames connected likewise. It's sensible and often necessary to assemble each of these two sub-frames first. That way you'll gain accuracy, avoid con-

fusion on final assembly, and almost certainly use fewer cramps.

Make sure that the surfaces of the wood are well protected when cramping, or annoying bruising can occur. And remember to do all your cleaning-up beforehand, as it's almost impossible to scrape or sand an assembled chair properly. A wise plan is to 'dry-assemble' first, flush any small discrepancies in the jointing, clean up and then finally glue and cramp the chair together.

Sash cramps will exert pressure only in straight lines; but you can adapt them, eg with a strong batten placed behind the back rail of a tapered seat. Longer than the rail, it projects at each side. The cramps can then lie parallel, each with one 'shoe' over a projection and one over the front rail.

If you make a chair accurately and assemble it in the appropriate order, the frame will generally pull itself into the correct alignment. However, you should check this throughout the assembly procedure. On shaped frames you can't use a square, but a measurement across each curve will generally do the job. Either way, watch for twisting – usually assessable by eye.

Take particular care over the way you cramp up the various assemblies.

A MULTI-PURPOSE UPRIGHT CHAIR IN OAK

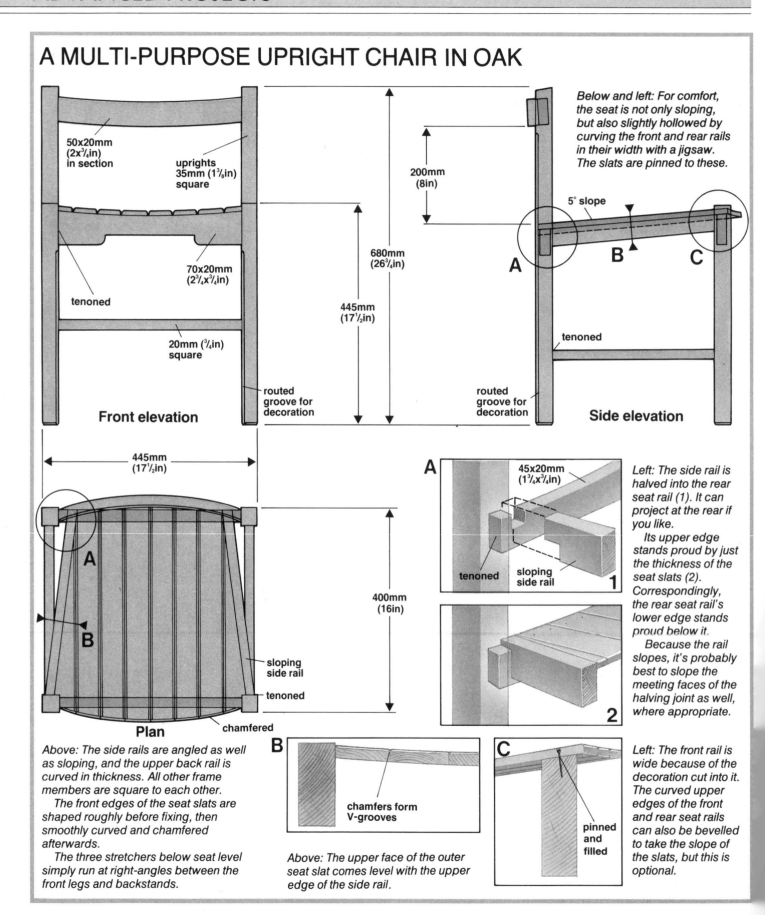

Front elevation

- 50x20mm (2x³/₄in) in section
- uprights 35mm (1³/₈in) square
- tenoned
- 70x20mm (2³/₄x³/₄in)
- 20mm (³/₄in) square
- routed groove for decoration

680mm (26³/₄in)

445mm (17¹/₂in)

Side elevation

Below and left: For comfort, the seat is not only sloping, but also slightly hollowed by curving the front and rear rails in their width with a jigsaw. The slats are pinned to these.

- 200mm (8in)
- 5° slope
- tenoned
- routed groove for decoration

Plan

- 445mm (17¹/₂in)
- 400mm (16in)
- sloping side rail
- tenoned
- chamfered

Above: The side rails are angled as well as sloping, and the upper back rail is curved in thickness. All other frame members are square to each other.

The front edges of the seat slats are shaped roughly before fixing, then smoothly curved and chamfered afterwards.

The three stretchers below seat level simply run at right-angles between the front legs and backstands.

A
- 45x20mm (1³/₄x³/₄in)
- tenoned
- sloping side rail
- 1
- 2

Left: The side rail is halved into the rear seat rail (1). It can project at the rear if you like.

Its upper edge stands proud by just the thickness of the seat slats (2). Correspondingly, the rear seat rail's lower edge stands proud below it.

Because the rail slopes, it's probably best to slope the meeting faces of the halving joint as well, where appropriate.

B
- chamfers form V-grooves

Above: The upper face of the outer seat slat comes level with the upper edge of the side rail.

C
- pinned and filled

Left: The front rail is wide because of the decoration cut into it. The curved upper edges of the front and rear seat rails can also be bevelled to take the slope of the slats, but this is optional.

MARKING UP THE SIDE RAILS

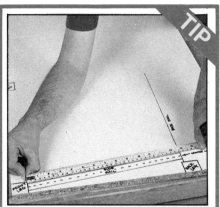

1 Draw a 'plan' (top view) of the chair's angled side rail plus the legs it connects, and measure its length (excluding joints).

2 Because the rail slopes, this isn't its true length. To find that, first rule a line elsewhere and mark out on it your measured length.

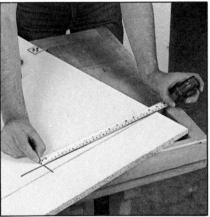

3 Then rule a line at 5° to this one, and measure along it to a line squared down from the point you've just marked. This is the true length of the rail.

4 Again from your plan, take the angle between side rail and leg. Ideally, use a second bevel, so you can keep the first one set to 5° for later use.

5 Mark this angle across the thickness of the side rail. Then, measuring from this line, mark on the rail its true length and repeat the angled mark.

6 Mark the 5° angle across the thickness of each piece at both ends – remembering that the left-hand rail is the reverse of the right.

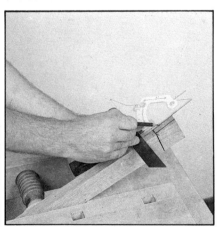

7 Reverting to the 'plan angle', use your bevel and a set square to mark one 12mm (½in) thick tenon on each rail, so it will be at right-angles to the leg.

8 With the same tools, mark a tenon shoulder on the upper edge. This will mask any gap when you come to fit the tenon into its mortise.

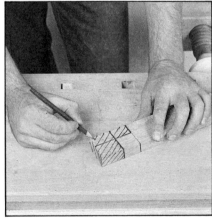

9 Lastly, mark out a halving in the lower part of the far end. Allow for the thickness of the seat slats at the top, and halve the remainder.

COMPLETING THE CHAIR

1 On each front leg, mark out the mortise for the side rail – setting the rail a little way down from the top, and also allowing for the shoulder.

2 Mark out the front rail mortise, allowing for the seat slat thickness. A haunched tenon (9, below) will pass under the side rail tenon.

3 Square the lower ends of all uprights, line them up flush, and mark on each backstand the height of the front rail (not the side rail).

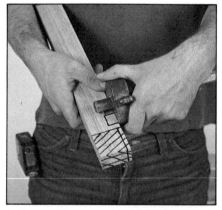

7 Using a square and mortise gauge (you don't need a bevel) mark out tenons on each end of the rear seat rail. Include a shoulder, again for neatness.

8 With your bevel set to the plan angle, mark out on the rear seat rail's upper edge the halvings where the side rails come in to meet it.

9 Square these marks across the faces of the piece, and – working from the top – gauge the halving's depth; this is the same as in photograph 9, page 187.

13 Cut all parts to length and make the joints, including the stretcher tenons. Then assemble the front frame without adhesive to check how it fits.

14 Assemble the back frame too. After making any adjustments, you can glue and sash-cramp each frame together and let it set before joining them both.

15 The way in which the side rails meet the rear seat rail dictates the sequence of work. They connect the pre-assembled back and front frames.

4 *Returning to your drawing, measure down from the horizontal to the rear end of the side rail. This will give you the height of the rear seat rail.*

5 *Transfer this measurement to the backstand, working down from your pencil mark (3). Then set out the mortise for the rear seat rail.*

6 *Turn the leg and backstand over in opposite directions to mark the stretcher mortises. Always check that you're working on the correct face.*

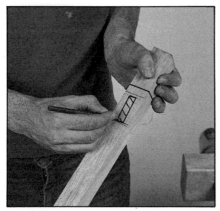

10 *Mark on each backstand its height, plus the back rail mortise (sloped 5°). Set it the right distance from the seat, and allow a shoulder.*

11 *Mark out tenons, square to the back rail, and use a flexible curve or template for the shape. A curved Surform will remove the waste well.*

12 *Make haunched tenons in the front rail. Use a template for its curve (and that on the rear seat rail) and mark its decorative shape at the front.*

16 *Alternatively, band cramps let you glue up all at once. But first see the joints are tight – band cramps won't 'pull them up'.*

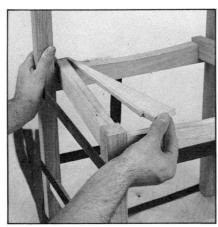

17 *Add the seat slats, working inwards from each side. Chamfer their long edges, and cut the outer slats to fit round the front legs.*

18 *If necessary, plane the middle two equally to fit; then press them in so all are tight. Pin them, and curve and chamfer the front edge.*

INDEX

Adhesives
  laminating, 101-2
  veneering, 90,91
Alcove cupboards, 105-9
  doors, 109
  shelves, 108-9
Angle irons, 31

Balusters, 160-4
Bed framing, 168
Beds, basic
  construction, 114-7
Bedside cabinet, 80
Bench hook, 28,29
Blockboard, 16
  box furniture, 60
  shelving, 52
Boards, man-made, 14-16
  edgings, 16
  shelving, 52
  sizes, 14,15,16
Box furniture, basic, 60-3
  doors, 110-13
Box guide (router), 80
Bunks, basic
  construction, 118-22
Button polish, 17

Cabinet, bedside, 80
Cabinet scraper, 13
Catches
  box furniture doors, 113
Chair
  construction, 185-9
  design, 180-4
  dowels, 183
  framing, 167-8,181,182
  joints, 183
  types, 184

woods, 183
Chipboard, 14
  box furniture, 60
  plugs, 30
  shelving, 52
Circular saws see Saws, circular
Cladding see Panelling
Cleaner, furniture see Restorer
      and cleaner
Cooker see Oven
Corrugated timber connectors,
  29
Cupboards, alcove, 105-9
  doors, 109
  shelves, 108-9

Danish oil, 17
Doors
  basic box furniture, 110-13
         framed, 113
         handles, 113
  casings, 171
  external, 171-4
      frames, 171-4
  folding, 110
  front
         bolts,49
         finger-plates, 49
         'furniture', 48-51
         handles, 49
         latches, 48,51
         letterplates, 48-9,51
         locks, 48-51
  kitchen base units, 140
  linings, 171
  room
         hinges, 45,46,47
         how to hang, 45-7
         types, 45

sliding, 110,111,123-7,155-9
Dovetail nailing, 28-9
Dovetailing
  using router, 81-2
Dowels, 36-9
Drawers
  built-in wardrobes, 157,159
  cabinet, 132-5
  kitchen base units, 140

Fibreboards, 14
Finger-plates
  front doors, 49
Finishes
  furniture, 17
Floorboards
  laying new, 176-9
  removing old, 176
  sizes, 175
  square-edged, 175
  T & G (tongued and grooved),
    175, 179
Floors (timber), laying 175-9
Frame construction, 165-70
  joints, 165,167
French polish, 17
Furniture finishes, 17

Glue see Adhesives

Handles
  box furniture doors, 113
  drawers, 135
  front doors, 49
Handrails (staircase), 160-4
Hardboards, 14
  packing for panelling
Hardwoods, 10-11
  choosing, 13

sizes, 10
Hinges
  basic box furniture, 110-11,
    112
  fitting, 22
  room doors, 45,46,47
  kitchen base unit doors, 140
  kitchen wall unit doors, 149
  types, 20-2

Insulating board, 14

Jigs
  jointing, 35
  router, 80,81
Joint cutting
  using circular saw, 88-9
Jointing blocks, 31
Jointing jig, 35
Joints
  board, 25
  box furniture, 60-3
  bridle, 167
  butt, 27-31
  chairs, 183
  dovetail, 95-8
        lap, 98
        types, 97
  dowel, 36-9
  framing, 24,25,26,165,167-8
  halving, 32-4,167
  housing, 40-3,89
  L-type, 24,25
  marking gauge, 32
  mitre, 34-5,88,167
  mortise-and-tenon, 65-9,82,
    83,84,165,167,183
  overlap, 28-9
  scarf, 25

T-type, 26,28-9
types, 24-6
using router, 77-9,80

Kitchen
  base units
    construction, 136-40
    doors, 140
    drawers, 140
    installing, 141-4
  planning, 136-7,145-6,149,
    150
  wall units
    construction, 145-9
    how to hang, 146-7,
    149
    installing, 150-3

Lacquer, synthetic, 17
Laminates, plastic
  trimming with router, 77-8
Laminating, 99-103
  adhesives, 101-2
  strap, 102
Laminboard, 16
Latches
  box furniture doors, 113
  front doors, 48,51
Letterplates
  front doors, 48-9, 51
Linseed oil, 17
Locks
  front doors, 48-51

MDF (medium-density
  fibreboard),14
Man-made boards, 14-16
  edgings, 16
  shelving, 52
  sizes, 14,15,16
Marquetry, 90
Mitre
  block, 35
  box, 35
  cramp, 35
Mortising
  using router, 82,83

Nailing
  dovetail, 28-9

skew, 31
Nails, 18-19

Oil finishes
  furniture, 17
Olive oil, 17
Oven
  installation in kitchen base
    units, 144

Panelboard, 14
Panelling, 56-9
  TGV (tongued, grooved and
    V-jointed),56
Panels
  frame construction, 166,167
Pegboard, 14
Pelmet
  sliding doors, 125,127
Planing, 9
Plastic coating, 17
Plinths
  kitchen wall units, 153
Plywood, 14,16
  box furniture, 60
  shelving, 52
Polishes, 17

Recess cutting
  using router, 80,81,84
Reinforcing blocks, 30
Restorer and cleaner
  furniture, 17
Reviver, 17
Router, 70-84
  bits, 70,71,75,76
  circle cutting, 78
  dovetailing, 81-2
  edge cutting, 75-7
  fixed-base, 70
  freehand use, 78-9
  groove cutting, 72-3
  guide pin, 84
  jig, 80,81
  joint cutting, 77-9,80
  lathe, 84
  mortising and tenoning, 82,83
    84
  overarm, 81,82,84
  plunging, 70-1,74

recess cutting, 80,81,84
safety precautions, 71-2,79
  82
spindle, 82
table, 81,84
template guide, 81
templates, 81,84
trimming plastic laminates,
  77-8

Saw table, 89
  laminate cutting, 101
Sawing, 8,28,29
Saws, circular, 85-9
  angled cuts, 89
  blades, 87
  drill attachments, 85,86
  guide batten, 88
  housing cutting, 89
  integral, 85,86
  joint cutting, 88-9
  mitre cutting, 88
  rebate cutting, 88,89
  rip fence, 87,88
  safety precautions, 85
Screws, 18-19
Shelves
  kitchen wall units, 145
Shelving, 52-5
  adjustable, 54
  alcove, 55
  edgings, 52,53
  fixing, 55
  movable, 55
  planning, 52,53
  types, 55
  types of support, 55
  units, 128-31
    dividers, 131
    supports, 128-9,
    131
Shiplap, 56
Skew nailing, 31
Skirting boards
  replacing, 179
Softboard, 14
Softwoods, 8-9
  sizes, 8,12
Spindles (staircase) see
  Balusters

Staircase
  repairing handrails and
    balusters, 160-4
  safety rules, 164
  shapes, 162
Synthetic lacquer, 17

Table framing, 167-8,169
Teak oil, 17
Tenoning
  using router, 82,83,84

Varnish, 17
Veneering, 90-4
  adhesives, 90,91
  caul, 93-4
  hot, 91,93
  lipping, 91
Veneers, constructional see
  Laminating

Wardrobes, built-in, 155-9
  drawers, 157,159
Wax polish, 17
White polish, 17
Wood
  bleach, 17
  bruising, 9
  chairs, 183
  faults, 9
  grains, 13,99
  laminating, 99-103
  panelling, 56-9
  planing, 9
  resin in, 9
  sawing, 8,28,29
  shelving, 52
  shrinkage and swelling, 156
  splitting in, 9
  types, 8-16
Worktops, kitchen
  installing, 150-151